English Syntax

Edinburgh Textbooks on the English Language – Advanced

General Editor
Heinz Giegerich, Professor of English Linguistics, University of Edinburgh

Editorial Board
Heinz Giegerich, University of Edinburgh – General Editor
Laurie Bauer (University of Wellington)
Olga Fischer (University of Amsterdam)
Willem Hollmann (Lancaster University)
Marianne Hundt (University of Zurich)
Rochelle Lieber (University of New Hampshire)
Bettelou Los (University of Edinburgh)
Robert McColl Millar (University of Aberdeen)
Donka Minkova (UCLA)
Edgar Schneider (University of Regensburg)
Graeme Trousdale (University of Edinburgh)

Visit the Edinburgh Textbooks in the English Language website at
https://edinburghuniversitypress.com/series-edinburgh-textbooks-on-the-english-language-advanced.html

English Syntax

*A Minimalist Account of
Structure and Variation*

Elspeth Edelstein

EDINBURGH
University Press

Edinburgh University Press is one of the leading university presses in the UK. We publish academic books and journals in our selected subject areas across the humanities and social sciences, combining cutting-edge scholarship with high editorial and production values to produce academic works of lasting importance. For more information visit our website: edinburghuniversitypress.com

Edinburgh University Press Ltd
The Tun – Holyrood Road, 12(2f) Jackson's Entry, Edinburgh EH8 8PJ

Typeset in Janson MT
by Servis Filmsetting Ltd, Stockport, Cheshire, and
printed and bound by CPI Group (UK) Ltd, Croydon, CR0 4YY

A CIP record for this book is available from the British Library

ISBN 978-1-4744-2551-3 (hardback)
ISBN 978-1-4744-2553-7 (webready PDF)
ISBN 978-1-4744-2552-0 (paperback)
ISBN 978-1-4744-2554-4 (epub)

Contents

Acknowledgements

All infelicities in this book are down to me alone, but I would like to thank the following people for helping to make this work possible.

Heinz Giegerich first suggested that I write this text for Edinburgh University Press, and commissioning editor Laura Williamson has guided me through this process. I am indebted to both of them for their immense patience and assistance during writing.

A number of anonymous reviewers gave feedback on the initial proposal and draft of this work. Their comments have been extremely helpful in shaping the final product.

My colleagues and students at the University of Aberdeen have also provided a great deal of support in various ways. Thanks go in particular to the 2019 cohort of Minimalism and Microvariation, who read the first few chapters of this text. I am also especially grateful to Robert McColl Millar, who offered encouragement and some much-needed relief from marking at a crucial juncture.

Fiona, Arthur and Jean Edelstein have, as always, cheered me on when I wasn't sure I would get there, and uncomplainingly given off-the-cuff grammaticality judgements.

Big thanks are also due to my children, who have provided (mostly) welcome distraction, and put up with my not always being as available as they or I would like. And most of all to Will, without whom this book simply wouldn't have got written.

This book is dedicated to the memory of William A. Edelstein.

Note on companion website

Also included at the end of each chapter, and in order to support
university-level teaching, there is an on-line companion website that
can be found here: edinburghuniversitypress.com/englishsyntax. On
this platform there are detailed answers to selected exercises from the
text which can be downloaded and used to support the book as a teaching resource.

Glossary

Accusative Case applied to non-subjects in English. Some coordinated subjects may also be morphologically accusative.

Accusativus cum Infinitivo (ACI) Latin for 'accusative with infinitive'. Syntactic configuration in which a predicate selects for an object which also serves as the subject of a finite complement, as in *I want him to leave*. See also **Object Control, Raising-to-Object**.

acquisition Gaining proficiency in a language without explicit instruction, typically in childhood.

adjunct An optional element Merged in a phrase that is not selected by the head of that phrase.

adjunction Merge of an element not selected by the head of a phrase.

Adverb Climbing (AC) A configuration in which an adverb preceding a verb which takes an infinitival complement modifies an embedded verb, as in *He intentionally seems to have insulted her.*

agent Theta role assigned to an argument that acts as a cause, and is typically sentient and capable of intention.

agent-oriented adverb Adverb that requires an argument with an agent theta role.

Agree Matching of feature values between a head and a constituent Merged within the phrase it projects.

alternative embedded passive (AEP) Embedded passive construction with *need/want/like* lacking *to be*, as in *The car needs washed.*

amn't gap Lack of *amn't* form in Standard English paradigms.

anaphor Lexical item that gets its reference from that of some other lexical item, such as *each other* or *himself.*

antecedent Element in the discourse which determines the reference of an anaphor or other element.

argument An entity, typically an NP, that completes the propositional meaning of a predicate.

aspect Grammatical information about the temporal structure of an event. Distinct from tense.

asterisk (*) Symbol marking a string as ungrammatical.

asymmetric c-command C-command relation between two elements in which one c-commands another, but not vice versa. An element will asymmetrically c-command nodes dominated by its sister (but will be in a symmetric c-command relationship with its sister).

atelic For verbs, having no grammatically marked endpoint, as in *She is running.* Not telic.

Attract Movement operation whereby a syntactic element motivates Remerge of another syntactic element to check its features.

attributive adjective Adjective, or phrase, that Merges in a nominal projection, as in *The happy boy*. See also **predicative adjective**.

auxiliary verb Verb which expresses grammatical information, used in conjunction with a lexical verb.

backshifting Matching of the tense on an embedded verb to the tense of a main verb, as in *He knew that she was happy.*

Bare Phrase Structure Minimalist approach to syntactic representation that eliminates apparently superfluous aspects of X-bar theory.

bare verb Verb lacking infinitival *to* or any other inflectional morphology.

base generation Merge of a syntactic constituent in its initial position.

binary branching Branching structure created by Merge of two constituents.

binding Syntactic relation in which one element determines the reference of another. Constrained by c-command.

binding domain Domain or section of the syntax in which binding applies.

bound One element is bound by another if they are co-referenced and are in a c-command relationship.

bracketing notation Representation of syntactic structure using brackets [ ] to group constituents.

branches Lines connecting nodes in representations of syntax trees.

case Overt morphological marking on a nominal of sentential function (e.g. as a subject or object). Typically only occurs on pronouns in English.

Case Abstract feature assigned to all nominals representing sentential function (e.g. as a subject or object).

categorial properties Properties of elements belonging to particular lexical categories (e.g. nouns, verbs, etc.).

categorial selection (c-selection) Selection of an element according to the syntactic requirements of a particular head, resulting in Merge.

c-command One element **c-commands** another if the first branching node that dominates that element also dominates the other element.

chain A series of the same syntactic element formed by Movement/ Remerge within a derivation.

checking Elimination of uninterpretable features in a derivation by matching with interpretable ones prior to Spell Out.

clitic A morpheme that cannot stand independently as a word but is not integrated into its host in the same manner as an affix.

cognate complement An object that shares the root of an otherwise intransitive verb, as in *She smiled a smile.*

collocation A string of words that typically occur together.

common noun A noun that does not pertain to a specific named entity. Not a **proper noun**.

competence The capacity of our internal syntax-specific cognitive systems.

complement An element Merged in a phrase that is (c-)selected by the head of that phrase.

complementary distribution Non-co-occurrence of syntactic elements, indicating that they fulfil the same syntactic function or occupy the same position.

complementiser An element that introduces an embedded clause, such as *if, that* or *whether.*

concealed passive A type of embedded passive with an *-ing* participle, as in *The car needs washing.*

constituency test A diagnostic used to determine whether a string functions as a constituent in a particular syntactic context.

constituent A piece or 'chunk' of syntax that is syntactically well-formed (adheres to a language's grammatical rules), and meaningful.

constituent negation Use of negation in which *not* applies to a particular lexical item or phrase, as in *He seemed to be not unhappy.*

Control A configuration in which an argument of a matrix predicate determines the reference of an argument, represented by the silent element PRO, of a non-finite embedded predicate.

Control Shift Control contexts in which the Controller may vary depending on context, as in *He asked her to leave early.*

copula A *be*-verb that connects a subject to a complement expressing equivalence or a property of that subject, as in *He is happy.*

corpus A collection of written and/or spoken language assembled for the purpose of linguistic investigation.

covert movement Remerge that applies at LF after Spell Out rather than during the syntactic derivation, so that it is invisible to PF.

crash Failure of a derivation to produce a grammatical utterance at Spell Out due to the presence of remaining uninterpretable features.

decomposition Splitting of a single lexical item so that it Merges more than once in the course of a derivation.

Deep-Structure (D-Structure) Pre-Minimalist concept of underlying syntactic structure.

degree of perfection adverb Adverb denoting how well something is done, such as *beautifully*, *poorly* or *terribly*.

deontic modal A modal denoting permission or obligation.

descriptive adequacy A descriptively adequate grammar is one that consists of a set of rules that lets us form grammatical sentences and excludes ungrammatical ones for a language, matching up with native speaker intuitions.

descriptive grammar Approach to grammar based on how language is actually used by native speakers.

determiner A lexical category consisting of functional elements that apply in nominal constructions, such as articles and pronouns.

deverbal noun A noun derived from a verbal root, such as *consumption* from *consume*.

direct object (DO) An object selected by a transitive verb.

ditransitive A verb that selects for two objects, or a construction using a verb of this type, such as *I'll give you it*.

domain The section of syntax over which a particular syntactic operation applies.

dominance One node **dominates** another if it is 'above' it in the tree, i.e. if it is its mother, grandmother, great-grandmother, etc.

do-**support** Insertion of a dummy *do* verb, typically in questions or negative contexts where no other auxiliary is available, as a Last Resort operation to prevent a derivation from crashing, as in *I do not like haggis*.

Double Negation (DN) Use of two negative forms together that cancel each other out semantically to form a positive, as in *He is not unhappy*. Also used colloquially by non-linguists to refer to **Negative Concord**.

double object A verb that takes a direct object and an indirect object in a PP, or a construction using such a verb, as in *I'll give it to you*.

Doubly-Filled COMP Filter A restriction in English that precludes co-occurrence of a *wh*-word with an overt complementiser, as in **I know what that he ate*.

dynamic verb A verb denoting an action, as in *drink*, *laugh* or *run*.

echo question A question that repeats the form of a declarative sentence with the *wh*-word marked intonationally, as in *You did what?*

Economy Underlying principle of Minimalist syntax, which seeks to represent linguistic systems in an optimal way, under the assumption that the system itself functions optimally.

E-language A speaker's externally produced utterance.

ellipsis Phonological omission of an element that can be understood from context.

embedded clause Clause that occurs within another clause, as in *I think [that he is happy]*.

empty category An unpronounced syntactic element.

endocentricity Property of syntactic phrases which means that their features come internally from their heads.

epistemic modal A modal denoting possibility or necessity.

escape hatch Phase edge to which an element must Move in order to Move out of a clause.

eventive reading Interpretation of a participle or adjective describing the process leading up to an endstate.

experiencer Theta role assigned to an argument, typically denoting a sentient entity, that receives emotional or sensory input.

explanatory adequacy An explanatorily adequate grammar is one that goes beyond the catalogue of rules for each language to the mechanisms by which Language works, regardless of the specific tongue, allowing evaluation of competing hypotheses.

expletive A 'dummy' element that is not semantically contentful, such as non-referential *it* in weather expressions. Expletives are not assigned theta roles.

Extended Projection Principle (EPP) Requirement in English that finite clauses have overt subjects.

external argument Argument Merged in the *v*P.

feature Formal property of a syntactic element encoded in lexical items.

floating quantifier Quantifier such as *all* which does not appear adjacent to the nominal it modifies, as in *The children have all left*.

focus 'New' or emphasised information in an utterance, which may be marked by syntactic position or intonation.

fronting Constituency test in which a potential constituent is Moved to the beginning of a sentence, as in *Those books, I like*.

function words Words which contribute grammatical information.

functional specifier approach Hypothesis that particular adverbs are Merged in the specifiers of a fixed set of functional projections that is present in every clause.

functional verbs Auxiliary verbs which express grammatical information such as tense and aspect.

garden path A grammatical sentence which is difficult or impossible to parse due to a misleading initial interpretation as the result of linear presentation.

generative grammar An approach to grammar which has as its underlying assumption the notion that syntactic derivations are built up piece by piece.

gerund A deverbal noun formed in English by affixation of -*ing*, as in *Knitting is my hobby.*

gloss An aligned word-by-word translation given under an example in another language.

goal A syntactic element that is Attracted by a probe to check the features of that attractor.

Government and Binding (GB) Precursor to Minimalist syntactic framework.

grammatical Conforming to the syntactic rules of a language.

grammaticality judgement Opinion sought from a native speaker regarding whether a string is grammatical.

Greed Attraction of a goal (attractee) by a probe (attractor) to meet the requirements of the probe, rather than those of the goal.

hash (#) Symbol used to mark a string as semantically anomalous.

head Syntactic element that selects dependents in a phrase and determines the properties of that phrase.

head-directionality Determination of whether a head precedes or follows its dependents.

head-final A phrase, or language more generally, in which a head follows its dependents.

head-initial A phrase, or language more generally, in which a head precedes its dependents.

Head(-to-Head) Movement Remerge of a head in another head position.

hypercorrection A form produced by a speaker following a (perceived) prescriptive norm that deviates from what we would otherwise predict from their grammar.

idiolect The language of an individual speaker.

I-language A speaker's internal linguistic system. See also **competence**.

immediate dominance One node immediately dominates another if it is 'above' it in the tree with no intervening nodes, i.e. if it is its mother.

immediate precedence One node immediately precedes another if it is 'before' it in the tree (left-to-right) with no other nodes intervening. A sister on a left branch will immediately precede a sister on a right branch.

implicit knowledge Knowledge that is not overt or explicit.

indirect object (IO) The first object in a Standard ditransitive construction, or the second, realised within a PP, in a double object construction.

information structure Presentation of information according to whether it is 'old'/known or 'new'/emphasised. See also **topic** and **focus**.

in situ Where an element has not been Moved overtly from its initial Merge position.

intensifier An adverb applied to another adverb or adjective that denotes particular emphasis, such as *really* or *very*.

intermediate projection A node that dominates the head of a phrase and is dominated by a maximal projection.

internal argument An argument Merged within the split Verb Phrase, within the VP or AgrOP. Not an external argument.

interpretable feature A feature that can be interpreted at the point of Spell Out. May check an uninterpretable feature to prevent a derivation crashing at Spell Out.

intersective adjective An adjective that identifies the noun that it modifies as belonging to a set of things with a property which overlaps with the set of things denoted by the noun, as in *a happy child*.

interspeaker variation Differences in language use among different speakers.

intonational break A small pause between constituents in speech, sometimes referred to as **comma intonation**.

intransitive verb A verb with no object.

intraspeaker variation Variation in language use for a single speaker.

introspection Use of a speaker's own judgements to determine grammaticality.

inverse scope Semantic interpretation of an element within the scope of another element which it precedes, as in *She may not leave*, meaning 'It is not the case that she may leave'.

Language The human capacity for acquiring and speaking languages.

language faculty The part(s) of the brain responsible for linguistic computation; the cognitive capacity for Language.

Last Resort An operation such as *do*-insertion which applies to rescue a derivation that would otherwise crash at Spell Out.

learning Gaining proficiency in a language (or other skill/knowledge) through explicit instruction.

lexical array A set of lexical items for a given sentence.

lexical category A group of words, traditionally called a word class, which behave in a similar way grammatically (e.g. nouns, verbs, etc.).

lexical item An element stored in the mental lexicon, such as a word or idiom.

lexical verb A semantically contentful verb.

lexicon A speaker's mental dictionary, containing information on lexical items.

licensed Where an element is permitted in a particular syntactic/ semantic context.

licensor An element that is required for another element to be licensed.

Linear Correspondence Axiom Hypothesis that c-command/m-command maps directly to linear precedence.

linearisation Mapping of hierarchical structure to linear order.

linking verb A verb that connects a subject to a complement expressing equivalence or a property of that subject, as in *He seems happy*.

little v (v) A causative head within the split VP that assigns a theta role to an external argument and Accusative Case to internal arguments.

locality Notion of closeness restricting the domain over which a syntactic operation, such as theta role assignment, may apply.

Logical Form (LF) Level of representation to which a syntactic derivation is sent at Spell Out for semantic interpretation.

logophoric Use of e.g. *-self* pronouns not subject to typical requirements for anaphors.

long-distance reflexive Co-reference of an anaphor with an antecedent outside its binding domain.

mass noun A noun denoting an uncountable or amorphous entity.

matrix verb The main verb in a clause.

maximal projection A node that dominates every other node projected by the head of a phrase.

m-command One element m-commands another if the first maximal projection that dominates that element also dominates the other element.

Merge An operation by which two syntactic elements are combined to form a constituent with the label of one of those elements.

middle A construction in which a typical object is used in subject position without passive morphosyntax, as in *This book reads well*.

Minimal Link Condition (MLC) A preference for the shortest possible Movement chains, based on notions of Economy.

Minimalism A programme of syntactic research with the goal of maximal Economy and simplicity, based on the notion that linguistic systems are themselves optimal.

modal concord Use of a modal verb in tandem with an adverb giving the same meaning, as in *I might possibly do that*.

modal verb A verb which expresses necessity, possibility, obligation or permission, such as *may* or *must*. In English, these lack tense morphology found on other verbs and select for bare infinitives.

mother A node that immediately dominates, i.e. is directly 'above', another node in a tree structure.

motivation The underlying reason for a syntactic operation, especially Movement.

Move Alpha A pre-Minimalist rule which broadly stated that a syntactic constituent could be Moved anywhere at any point in the derivation.

Movement Displacement of a constituent to another part of the structure. In Minimalist terms this is accomplished by Remerge; the 'displaced' constituent does not syntactically vacate previous Merge positions.

multiple modal construction A Non-Standard construction in which more than one modal verb is used in a single clause, as in *I might could do that.*

mutually intelligible Languages able to be understood by each other's speakers.

Negative Concord (NC) Use of two negative elements to denote a single negative semantically, as in *I don't have no money.* Colloquially referred to as 'double negation'.

Negative Polarity Item (NPI) An element that may appear only in a negative or interrogative context.

Negative Raising (NR) A construction in which a verb that takes a finite CP clause as a complement is negated, but the negation is interpreted as applying to the verb within the embedded complement, as in *I don't think he has any enemies.*

node The point on a tree at the end of a branch or branches.

Nominative Case applied to subjects in English. Some coordinated subjects may also be morphologically accusative.

non-finite A verb or clause without tense.

non-terminal node A node formed by Merge of constituents.

Not-Transportation Hypothesis that Neg-Raising results from Movement of *not* from the embedded to the matrix clause.

null complementiser An unpronounced complementiser, as in *I think Ø he likes haggis.*

Object Control An ACI construction in which the matrix verb assigns a theta role to its object, as in *I asked him to leave.*

observational adequacy An observationally adequate grammar is one that consists of a set of data that tells us what is possible or impossible in a given language.

optionality A situation where all speakers of a particular language or variety have multiple options for a particular structure.

parameters Aspects of grammar that differ by language, in the limited way circumscribed by UG.

parse To linguistically analyse and comprehend an utterance.

Partial Control A Control structure in which a singular Controller controls a plural subject for the non-finite clause, as in *She wanted to meet in the park.*

particle A discontinuous element that acts as part of a verb, such as *out* in *She threw it out.*

percentage (%) Symbol used to indicate that a particular construction is grammatical only for a subset of speakers.

percolation Copying of features up to higher nodes in a tree, sometimes beyond a maximal projection.

perfect Aspect denoting completion of an action, as in *I have gone.*

performance Actual production of language (as opposed to **competence**).

phase A section of a syntactic derivation sent to Spell Out as it is completed; a CP or vP.

phase edge The highest projection in a phase to which a constituent must first be Moved in order to Move out of that phase.

phi-feature A grammatical feature such as case, gender or number.

Phonological Form (PF) Level of representation to which a syntactic derivation is sent at Spell Out for the assignment of pronunciation.

phrase A word or group of words that makes up a constituent with a head that determines its overall category and behaviour.

Positive Polarity Item (PPI) Elements that resist appearing in negative contexts.

precedence One node precedes another if it is 'before' it in the tree (left-to-right).

predicate A semantic function that requires certain 'gaps' to be filled by arguments, entities that complete its propositional meaning.

predicative adjective Adjective, or phrase, that Merges as a complement of a copula or linking verb, as in *The boy looked happy.* See also **attributive adjective**.

prescriptive grammar Approach to grammar based on normative judgements about how language 'should' be used.

presupposition An underlying assumption about truth within a proposition. For example, *I know that he is happy* presupposes *he is happy.*

preterite A simple past tense form, as in *I looked in the mirror.*

Principle A A condition in binding theory which states that an anaphor must be bound in its binding domain.

Principle B A condition in Binding theory which states that a pronominal must be free [not bound] in its binding domain.

Principle C A condition in Binding theory which states that an R-expression must be free [not bound] everywhere.

Principles Properties that all languages have in common.

Principles and Parameters (P&P) Model that says that all languages have certain properties in common and others that vary in a limited way circumscribed by UG.

Principle of Structure Dependency Universal principle that syntactic operations apply to hierarchical syntactic structures rather than linear strings.

PRO A silent pronoun which functions as the subject of the lower nonfinite verb in Control constructions.

probe An element which Attracts a goal to check its features through Merge.

projection Transmission of the features of a head to the rest of a phrase.

pronoun A functional element that stands in for an NP/DP, such as *they* or *you*.

proper noun A nominal that is a specific named entity, such as *Billy* or *Glasgow*.

proposition A falsifiable idea or statement about the world.

question-answer A constituency test in which the potential constituent is the answer to a question, as in *What did you read? The book.*

Raising-to-Object An ACI construction in which the matrix verb does not assign a theta role to its object, as in *I expected him to leave.*

recipient A theta role assigned to an entity that receives something.

recursion Nesting of elements of the same type inside each other, or repeated application of a syntactic operation to elements created by previous applications of that operation.

Referring expression (R-expression) A lexical item that does not get its reference from an antecedent.

relative clause An embedded clause that modifies an NP.

relative pronoun A pronoun that introduces a relative clause, such as *that* in *There is the book [that I read].*

resultative reading Interpretation of a participle or adjective describing an endstate.

resumptive pronoun A pronoun within a relative clause that is co-referent with the relative pronoun, as in *There's the book that I read it yesterday.*

rules What is possible within the grammar of a given language.

scope Semantic interpretation of an element within the semantic interpretation of another.

semantic selection (s-selection) Selection of an element according to the semantic requirements of a particular head, as mediated by theta role assignment.

semantically anomalous An utterance that is grammatical but unacceptable based on real-world knowledge.

semelfactive A verb denoting an instantaneous event, such as a *sneeze* or *flash*.

sentential negation Use of negation which applies to an entire clause, as in *He does not like it.*

sister An element Merged directly with another element to form a constituent.

specifier A dependent immediately dominated by the maximal projection of a phrase (especially in X-bar theory).

Spell Out The point at which a syntactic derivation, or part of that derivation, is sent for interpretation at PF and LF.

Split Control A Control construction in which PRO has multiple Controllers, as in *I suggested to her to meet at the park.*

split VP A structure in which a single lexical verb is decomposed into multiple phrases.

static verb A verb that denotes a state rather than a process.

stranding Movement in which a quantifier remains or is 'left behind' in an intermediate Merge position, as in *The children have all read the book.* See also **floating quantifier**.

strength Property of a syntactic feature that varies according to whether it requires local Merge of another for feature-checking.

string A linear series of words which may or may not constitute a grammatical clause or constituent.

strong feature A feature that requires Remerge of another feature in a local configuration to be checked.

subcategorial properties Properties of lexical items that differ within a lexical category, such as transitivity for verbs.

subject-auxiliary inversion Reversal of usual SVO order in particular contexts, especially questions, as in *Have you eaten the cake?*

subject contact relative Non-Standard construction in which a subject relative pronoun is omitted, as in *There's the boy baked the cake.*

Subject Control A construction in which a predicate that selects a non-finite clause complement assigns a theta role to its subject, as in *I want to leave.* The subject of the embedded clause is PRO.

Subject(-to-Subject) Raising A construction in which a predicate that selects a non-finite clause complement does not assign a theta role to its subject, as in *She seemed to have left.* The subject of the embedded clause Moves to become the subject of the main clause.

subsective adjective An adjective that gives a property which denotes a smaller group of things within the set of things denoted by the noun, as in *a tall building.*

substitution Constituency test in which a potential constituent is replaced with a single word, as in *I saw [the boy] and she saw [him] too.*

surface scope Semantic interpretation of an element within the scope of another element which it follows, as in *She must not leave*, meaning 'It is required that she not leave'.

Surface Structure (S-Structure) Pre-Minimalist concept of syntactic structure derived from Deep Structure by transformations.

symmetric c-command Mutual c-command relation between two elements. Sisters symmetrically c-command each other.

syncretism Identical surface morphology representing different morphosyntactic properties.

syntax Putting words together in an ordered way; the study of this component of grammar.

syntax tree A representation of hierarchical syntactic structure using branching notation to group constituents. Shortcut for bracketing notation.

tag question A question appended at the end of a declarative clause, typically reversing its polarity, as in *She didn't read it, did she?*

telic For verbs, having a grammatically marked endpoint, as in *She jumped in.*

temporally independent infinitive A non-finite complement that can be interpreted on a different timescale from a matrix verb, as in *Today I expect to leave tomorrow.*

tense Grammatical expression of temporal information pertaining to the point when an event occurred.

terminal node A node in a syntax tree which dominates no other nodes.

theme Theta role assigned to an argument that is affected by the predicate.

theta-criterion Requirement that every argument occur in one, and only one, theta position.

theta role Semantic relation assigned by predicates to arguments within a syntactic derivation.

to-infinitive A non-finite verb or clause with a non-finite *to* marker, as in *I want to leave. To* is assumed to appear in T.

topic The entity that an utterance is 'about'; 'old' or 'known' information. See **information structure**.

transformation In pre-Minimalist frameworks, an operation applied to D-Structure to produce S-Structure.

transitive verb A verb that selects for a single object.

unacceptable Characterisation of a sentence or construction as not something a speaker would produce, not necessarily for reasons of ungrammaticality.

unaccusative An intransitive verb that does not assign an agent theta role to its subject, such as *arrive* or *disappear*.

Unaccusative Hypothesis Proposal that assignment of Accusative Case is tied to assignment of an external (agent/cause) theta role.

unergative An intransitive verb that assigns an agent theta role to its subject, such as *clap* or *jump*.

ungrammatical Not conforming to the syntactic rules of a language.

uninterpretable feature A feature that cannot be interpreted at the point of Spell Out. Must be checked by an interpretable feature to prevent a derivation crashing at Spell Out.

Universal Grammar (UG) A set of syntactic structures and/or operations shared by all languages.

variety A form of a language used by a subset of speakers of that language.

Visibility Condition A requirement that an argument have Case, or be in a Case position, in order to be 'visible' for assignment of a theta role.

VP-internal Subject Hypothesis Proposal that subjects are initially Merged within the split VP before moving to their final subject position within TP.

VP shell Phrase within the split VP.

weak feature A feature that does not require Remerge/Movement of another feature in a local configuration to be checked but may be checked by selection or other means.

***wh*-in-situ** A question in which a *wh*-word is not fronted, as in *She did what?*

***wh*-question** A question with a *wh*-word such as *who* or *what*, as in *What did she do?*

***yes-no* question** A question with subject-auxiliary inversion that requires a *yes* or *no* answer, as in *Did she see him?*

Y-model Minimalist representation of syntactic derivations in which lexical items input into the syntax are subject to Merge and Move operations, followed by Spell Out to PF and LF.

1 Got grammar?

1.1 Introduction

A well-known nursery rhyme in English begins:

> Baa, baa, black sheep,
> Have you any wool?

Yet many people who learned this song in childhood, and thus accept it as wholly unremarkable (conversations with sheep notwithstanding), would not be able to use a sentence with this form in their own speech. There are a number of alternative ways to pose the question in the second line.

(1) a. Have you any wool?
    b. Do you have any wool?
    c. Have you got any wool?
    d. Do you got any wool?

You will likely find that at least one of the versions in (1) is what you would use; which one of them will depend on a host of factors, such as where you are from, your age and level of formality. The others may sound odd or plain wrong. The form from the nursery rhyme (1)a has an old-fashioned ring for a lot of modern speakers, myself included. One or more of these sentences might well set your teeth on edge (as (1)d would for the advertising executive who described 'Got Milk?' as 'not even English'), but each of them is nevertheless acceptable for a significant portion of native English speakers.

Most of us have a sense that certain modes of speaking are incorrect or uneducated or downright lazy. We imbue the way other people and we ourselves string words together with all sorts of ideas about character and propriety. These judgements often come from the idea that the 'Standard' form of a language, whether that be English or another tongue, represents some communicatory ideal. But actual data

1

gives lie to the notion that 'Standard' forms are linguistically superior. All of the questions in (1) are entirely comprehensible, and as such equally effective in conveying the same message, an enquiry regarding whether the addressee is in possession of the fleece off a sheep. From this perspective, each form can be said to fulfil its linguistic purpose. There is thus no reason to deem any one of them better than the others, except according to whether they adhere to an arbitrarily chosen norm. In essence, the forms of a language that are considered 'Standard' are selected according to social and psychological factors rather than linguistic ones. While these judgements about language are interesting in themselves, they are tangential to the study of the structure of language.

The term 'Standard' implies uniformity: a standardised language is one in which there are agreed, typically quite narrow, norms of use. Standardisation has potential advantages in creating a shared linguistic understanding among speakers from different backgrounds. That said, 'Standard' has become a loaded term, carrying a whiff of judgement regarding validity or correctness, with the implication that 'Non-Standard' forms must be intrinsically inferior. Again, there is no evidence that the choice of a Standard form of any language is ever based on purely linguistic factors. With that caveat, I will continue throughout the text to refer to certain morphological or syntactic forms as 'Standard' and 'Non-Standard'. I apply these labels as shorthand to indicate that a usage is more or less widespread, rather than more or less 'correct' from a linguistic viewpoint.

This is not to say that linguists have an all-out anything goes attitude when it comes to language grammar; far from it. The work of syntacticians, linguists who study sentence structure, depends on determinations of what is **grammatical**. In linguistics this is a technical term which differs from the layperson's concept of 'good' grammar.

1.2 Grammaticality

Consider if we rephrase our query about wool as in (2).

(2)   a. *Any you wool have?
       b. *Have you any wool do?
       c. *Got have any wool you?
       d. *Any wool got you do?

The examples in (2) have exactly the same words as the ones in (1), but the reordering of these words makes them extremely difficult, if not impossible, to interpret. We call any ordered group of words like this a

string.[1] The contrast between the two sets of strings, with those in (1) representing possible sentences of English and those in (2) not, allows us to make an initial distinction between what is grammatical and what is **ungrammatical**.

By the time you reach this book you may already have had it drummed into you that the study of language conducted by linguists is not **prescriptive**. It is a point worth emphasising. Linguists make no judgements with respect to what is 'right' or 'wrong', other than in terms of what a native speaker can or cannot say. Regardless of our personal feelings about whether they all sound 'correct', each of the strings in (1) is constructed according to a systematic set of **rules**, and could be uttered by at least some subset of English native speakers. The strings in (2) are ungrammatical word salad: they have been put together at random, and no speaker of English would produce these spontaneously.

Like 'grammar' and '(un)grammatical', the term 'rule' has a special sense for linguists. Rather than proscriptions such as 'don't end sentences with prepositions', or 'don't split infinitives', rules in syntax are what is possible within the grammar of a given language (or crosslinguistically). A basic rule of English would be that simple declarative sentences have subject-verb-object (SVO) word order. While a majority of English speakers could thus readily produce the sentence-final preposition in (3)a, they would never use the VOS word order in (3)b.

(3)   a.   I read the book he talked about
      b.   *read the book he talked about I

Sometimes the most natural form of a sentence for a native speaker is one that violates a prescriptive rule. In (4) the placement of *not* between infinitival *to* and the verb *move* is the clearest way of expressing that there was a requirement that the subject not move. Putting the negation elsewhere results in ungrammaticality, ambiguity or a complete change in meaning: (4)b is not possible for many speakers, and (4)c implies that there was no requirement for the subject to move, rather than a requirement that he not move.[2]

---

[1]   Most of the examples in this book will be unpunctuated, because they are strings rather than sentences, although quite a lot of these strings represent sentences as well. Punctuation and grammar get lumped together in pedagogical settings and common parlance, but they are seen as distinct within the domain of linguistics. Syntacticians see spoken language as primary, and therefore do not view the placement of apostrophes and commas as directly relevant to their work.

[2]   Speakers who are wedded to not splitting infinitives may argue that the solution here is to rephrase, e.g. *he was required to keep still while the paint dried*. The origin of this proscription is the impossibility of splitting infinitives in Latin, which has these

(4)   a.   He had to not move while the paint dried
      b.   ^{??}He had not to move while the paint dried
      c.   He did not have to move while the paint dried

The **asterisks** (*) preceding the strings in (2) and (3)b mark that they are ungrammatical; the additional superscript question marks on (4)b indicate that it may be marginally or questionably grammatical (more on this example in §1.2.1).

Although I described our initial set of ungrammatical strings in (2) as potentially impossible to interpret, there are still ungrammatical sentences that we can understand, and grammatical ones that we cannot. The syntactic structure of sentences is just one component that contributes to our ability to interpret them. The sentence in (5), for example, is **semantically anomalous**: our real-world knowledge tells us that trees do not consume beverages, and apples are not potable. At the same time, the string has SVO word order, and conforms to a number of other syntactic rules of English, making it grammatically unproblematic. Such semantically anomalous sentences are marked with a **hash** sign (#).

(5)   #The tree drank an apple

There are other grammatical sentences that our brains cannot **parse**, or analyse and comprehend linguistically. In (6)a the amount of syntactic material between the sentence-final adverb *quickly* and *ate*, the verb that it modifies, makes it difficult to figure out how the adverb applies. If we replace the intervening object of the verb with a shorter, less complex one, as in (6)b, there is no problem with understanding and processing the relationship between the adverb and the verb.

(6)   a.   The boy ate a delicious red apple that had fallen off an enor-
           mous tree in the orchard next to his house when it unexpect-
           edly rained just after midday yesterday quickly
      b.   The boy ate an apple quickly

One could argue that the unparsability of the string in (6)a renders it ungrammatical. It is after all something that an English speaker would not actually say although, time permitting, it is much easier to come up with a sentence like this than the same group of words in a totally random order. It also does not convey the intended message, inasmuch as a hearer will be unable to understand the sentence in its entirety.

verb forms as single words. English is not Latin, so while there are certainly viable alternatives to the sentence in (4), the time spent finding them could, I think, be better spent on other pursuits.

The counterargument to the claim that such a sentence is ungrammatical is that these limitations on parsing do not come from our **language faculty**, the part(s) of the brain responsible for linguistic computation. They instead reflect larger restrictions on cognitive capacity and memory, unrelated to the rules of our grammar themselves. That is to say that many linguists view the capacity to produce language as separate from other cognitive functions, even if the actual production and comprehension of language may ultimately be constrained by them. A string may therefore be grammatical but **unacceptable** for reasons not arising from violation of grammar rules.

In contrast to (6), it is not hard to figure out what the strings in (7) are meant to mean, despite their ungrammaticality: (7)a has VSO word order instead of the SVO word order that is grammatical for English; the use of *the* and *my* together before *apple* in (7)b makes the string ungrammatical by violating the rule in English that nouns do not have both a definite article and a possessive pronouns.[3]

(7) a. *Ate the boy his apple
     b. *The boy ate the his apple

Instances such as these bring us to the gap between **competence** and **performance**, or between **I-language**, a speaker's internal linguistic system, and **E-language**, their externally produced utterances. It is not unimaginable that a speaker could, by some slip of the tongue or mid-sentence change of heart, produce (7)b. Mistakes of this kind are in fact extremely common, but syntacticians argue that they do not reflect the underlying grammatical system. Speakers' ungrammatical utterances are therefore explained in a similar way to hearers' inability to parse certain grammatical strings: factors beyond the realm of the language faculty (memory, confusion, inattention) interfere with their production.

Language-external factors also limit the length of our utterances. The rules of Language are such that we could, time permitting, have infinite different sentences, and infinitely long sentences. We can demonstrate the first notion in a trivial way. If we have a sentence with a number in it, we can replace that number with another one, ad infinitum.

---

[3] This rule is not a universal one. Italian allows article-possessive sequences of this type.

(i) la sua partenza
     the his departure
     'his departure'

(8)   The boy ate {two/three/a gazillion/seven bajillion/ ...} apples[4]

To some extent this example represents a property of numbers rather than language specifically. We can also replace some of the words in the sentence with other ones.

(9)   a. The {dog/cat/unicorn/ ...} ate two apples
       b. The boy {dropped/squashed/picked/ ...} two apples
       c. The boy ate two {biscuits/pies/cakes/ ...}

Combining the four options for each of the four words here gives us 4^4 or 256 combinations for a sentence with this structure. Additional word substitutions would increase this number of possible sentences exponentially.

Taking into consideration that speakers have vocabularies of several thousand words, and that this is only one of many possible ways of arranging them, we get a very large number of potential utterances.

Based on this argument, we might still contend that while there are lots and lots of possible sentences, limitations on vocabulary and grammatical configurations make the number finite. The rules of our grammar, though, are also recursive. This **recursion** means that grammatical rules can be repeated in such a way that we can have elements of the same type inside each other. For instance, if we have a noun such as *tea*, we can replace it with a group of words that contains that noun and functions in the same way syntactically.

(10)   a. I bought [tea]
       b. I bought [a cup of tea]

We can repeat this process, putting *a cup of tea* inside a larger string that again functions as a noun.

(11)   a. I bought [a painting of a cup of tea]
       b. I bought [a photo of a painting of a cup of tea]
       c. I bought [a copy of a photo of a painting of cup of tea]

This recursive nesting of syntactic units is really what give us the potential for infinitely long sentences and, since we can always come up with one that is longer, an infinite number of them. Our limited brains and life-spans mean that we do not actually have infinite recursion, but our underlying grammars do not restrict this.

As (Minimalist) syntacticians we are interested in competence, the capacity of our syntax-specific cognitive systems (i.e. the rules of our grammar), rather than any other aspects of cognition outside of the

---

[4] Braces ('curly brackets') around a series of words separated by slashes indicate a set of alternatives within a particular string.

language faculty. Like social attitudes to language, performance, the actual production of language, is interesting in itself, but it is not our current object of study.

1.2.1 Determining grammaticality

The distinction between competence and performance creates a tension when it comes to studying grammar. On one hand, we want to understand the former; on the other hand, we truly have access only to the latter. Our language faculty is not a discrete area of the brain (although there are parts of the brain that appear to be specifically associated with language), and words and sentences arise from neural signals that cannot be directly decoded. Tools such as functional MRI offer indications about different areas of cerebral activity, but not on a level that can allow us to measure competence in any detailed or meaningful way.

Furthermore, our knowledge of a native language is **implicit**. In spontaneous speech sentences are produced with no conscious thought regarding the mechanics of their grammar. Producing sentences is in this sense like many other things we do in an automatic way without necessarily knowing how we do them. You may pick up a pen to make some notes on this chapter. If I ask you how you have done that, you can probably give me a basic description of moving your arm to reach for the pen, putting your fingers around it, and lifting it up. But unless you have studied anatomy and biomechanics, you will not be able to put into words all the muscles involved or how the signal to pick up the pen gets from the brain to the hand. To extend the analogy, except in cases of injury or disability, no one will have taught you specifically how to grasp small objects. Likewise, while you may have been drilled on particular (prescriptive) grammar points at school, your knowledge of your native language will have been acquired with essentially no explicit instruction, long before you ever set foot in a classroom

Determining grammaticality from a **descriptive** perspective requires us to access and make overt subconscious knowledge of syntax. Here, too, we see a contrast with prescriptive grammar, for which the rules must be imposed externally and explicitly. Descriptive grammarians have to set aside their individual prejudices and preferences to determine whether a particular string is something a native speaker would or could say.

There are various approaches to making this determination. Complicating the matter is that languages are not unitary, but consist of a number of **varieties**, spoken in different places by different people. Assorted varieties of a language may be more or less **mutually intelligible**, depending on the degree to which their speakers can understand each other.

In order to be considered the same language in more than a political or social sense, varieties must meet some (unspecified) threshold in terms of sharing rules of grammar. It is not enough for them to have the same vocabulary or **lexicon**; English words arranged according to French grammar do not an English sentence make. As such, the string in (12) is a better representation of a French sentence than an English one (although it is in fact neither) in that it perfectly obeys grammatical rules of French. The word-for-word **gloss** is a grammatical French sentence.

(12) *He goes it eat
       Il   va   le prendre
       (cf. He is going to eat it)

Varieties of a language have to have a certain amount of grammatical overlap, but will also be differentiated by *not* sharing certain rules. These divergences in English are of central interest to this book. Linguists take a comparative view of Language, for reasons to be outlined below, and while this is often crosslinguistic, there is much informative data to found among the varieties that make up a single language.

How do we determine what is grammatical? If you are a native speaker of the language under scrutiny you can consider whether you find a construction grammatical yourself. Theoretical syntax has a long tradition of **introspection** when it comes to deciding grammaticality; the reliance on researchers' own judgements is an area for which the field has faced deserved criticism. The obvious drawback to this approach is that one person's way of speaking will not capture every form of a language. If you are from York in the North of England, and I am from New York in the northeast United States, there will be inevitable contrasts regarding what sentences we can and do produce. Were I to rely solely on my own assessments of grammaticality, I would capture data about the grammar of my **idiolect**, my individual language, and to a certain extent the grammar of people who come from where I do, but I might miss or mischaracterise important aspects of your grammar.

The accuracy of introspection is also a fallacy. Because knowledge of one's native language is implicit, we cannot always judge what we can and cannot say. We **acquire** a first language rather than **learn** it. As anyone who has ever attempted to master a second language can attest, it is entirely possible to 'know' how a language works (e.g. what order to put words in, or how to conjugate verbs), yet be wholly unable to use it.

Conversely, you can use your native language with ease, but probably have to give a great deal of thought if asked why specific sentences are grammatical or not. Non-native speakers can sometimes give more detailed descriptions of how a language works than native ones, even if their mastery of the language is not perfect.

Introspection is also problematic because linguists evaluating their own grammars may be unintentionally influenced by a desire for certain facts to fit in with their hypotheses about the grammar. Some syntacticians report that studying grammar extensively has altered their ability to assess grammaticality, such that quite bizarre constructions begin to sound 'good', or quite normal constructions begin to sound a bit odd. There is evidence that professional linguists make different determinations about grammaticality from laypeople, perhaps for this reason.

A common alternative to introspection has been to seek **grammaticality judgements** from native speakers. Judgement tasks involve presenting participants with strings to be rated on some measure of acceptability. Asking speakers whether they find particular sentences or constructions acceptable has the advantage of garnering a wider array of opinion. Again, though, many people are not able to report accurately what they can or cannot say, often because they simply do not know. The literature is rife with examples of speakers claiming they would never use a syntactic construction and then, quite unconsciously, turning round and producing it minutes later, but continuing to deny it is something they can say.

It can also be difficult to ensure that non-linguists approach a grammaticality judgement task in the manner intended by researchers. Usually every effort is made to tell participants that they are to report on what they actually say, but being asked by an academic about their language has the undesirable effect for people used to tests with right and wrong answers of leading them to reproduce prescriptive norms. Speakers will also reject semantically anomalous sentences. Judgement fatigue can set in: it is tricky for anyone to evaluate the grammaticality of string after string. In this sense grammaticality judgements may reflect some of the same social and psychological factors that affect performance, when researchers are trying to measure competence in the domain of language structure.

The gold standard is to find examples of what speakers do say 'in the wild'. Sometimes a researcher gets lucky and happens upon the syntactic construction they are looking for, uttered as they go about their lives. A more systematic way to find 'natural' examples is to use a **corpus**, a collection of written and/or spoken language assembled for the purpose of linguistic investigation. The problem with corpora is that they exclude not only examples of ungrammatical language, but also a lot of grammatical ones. This finiteness means that forms which are unusual but acceptable may not show up in a corpus search, or may only appear in certain corpora. In short, a corpus gives us positive evidence of what is grammatical, but can never be exhaustive. If we want to know what is ungrammatical, essential for constraining our description of the language to grammatical rules that do not overproduce, then the lack of negative evidence a corpus provides means it is not sufficient.

Case study: *Had not to*

To get a better idea of the (in)effectiveness of different methods for determining grammaticality, we can return to the sentence in (4), repeated in (13), which was labelled with a couple of superscript question marks to indicate that it might be marginally acceptable.

(13) ??He had not to move while the paint dried

Introspection tells me that this sentence is not possible in my grammar, but it is quite likely that as a linguist I have an inability to make accurate grammaticality judgements. Other speakers I consulted for informal grammaticality judgements described it as 'weird', 'old-fashioned', or sounding like something a non-native speaker might say. One person insisted that they would use this form, to the exclusion of the *had to not* alternative.

A search of the British National Corpus (BNC), a collection of 100 million words, for *had not to* yields five results, four of which have the intended interpretation of *had to* meaning 'was required to'. Of these four examples, two come from novels set in historical periods, one from a golf digest and one from a history of copper mines. It has only three relevant results for *had to not*.

A search of the iWeb Corpus, a collection of language from 22 million web pages containing 14 billion words, returns 346 examples of this string. Many of these also do not have the right interpretation and others appear to come from writing by non-native speakers. Several examples do, however, have the 'was required to' interpretation.

(14) a. He **had not to** hunt long, for soon the unicorn approached (Grimm's Fairy Stories)
      b. ... all parties would mutually agree that the Bill **had not to** operate, or at any rate that the extended franchise to the women **had not to** operate ... (UK Parliament House of Commons Orders of the Day 29 March 1928)

c. It was true that she **had not to** charge herself ... with being the sole and original author of the mischief (*Emma* by Jane Austen, 1815)

d. I **had not to** wash the plates, which were done in the kitchen ... (*Down and Out in Paris and London* by George Orwell, 1933)

e. ... it was not ... introduced into the declaration, and the Jury **had not to** consider it ... (*The Kept Man-Mistress*, 1820)

I did not trawl through all of the examples, but it is notable that many of them, like those shown above, come from literature or archived documents, rather than contemporary use.

By comparison, there are 435 examples for *had to not* in the iWeb Corpus, almost all of which seem to have the 'was (not) required to' interpretation we are interested in.

I also consulted the British National Corpus of Spoken English, an 11.5-million-word collection of conversations. This search produced only one result for the string *had not to*, which does not have the requirement reading. It produced two results for *had to not* with the interpretation we are looking for.

What do these results mean for our sentence in (13)? We could argue that it is grammatical, based on the affirmation from a single speaker, along with the BNC and iWeb results. On the other hand, the preponderance of literary uses appears to indicate that this is an outdated form, in line with the comments of some of my respondents. The lack of *had not to* in the modern BNC Spoken corpus might point to this conclusion as well, but there are also very few instances of the alternative *had to not*. The paucity of examples may therefore be down to a general infrequency of these forms, rather than ungrammaticality.

We might need to re-evaluate, too, the reliability of the single speaker who claimed to say *had not to*: should we trust the self-report of someone who gives a different answer from everyone else? Could this person be giving an inaccurate report of their own speech, perhaps influenced by knowledge of prescriptive grammar? This respondent also happened to be the oldest person I asked: not a contemporary of Austen or Orwell, certainly, but maybe a user of grammatical forms that are on the decline.

Another point to consider here is that speakers were asked about only a single sentence, perhaps encouraging carefully considered rather than spontaneous assessments. For this reason, linguists often ask for grammaticality judgements for several sentences or constructions at a time. This approach not only allows them to gather more data, but can be helpful in concealing the exact form of interest. My one anomalous respondent may have been influenced unconsciously by the idea that I was looking for a particular answer, or at least that a particular answer would be (prescriptively) 'correct'. Overall the findings suggest that the *had not to* form has in the past been grammatical in English. It is harder to pin down whether it is grammatical now. To be sure I would need to ask more speakers and look at the corpus results in more detail. In this instance nothing hinges on the answer, but if we want to indicate that it is grammatical for some speakers (such as my informant) but not others (such as me), we could mark it with a **percentage** (%) symbol, to show that some proportion of speakers find it grammatical. Ultimately, we do not usually look at grammatical constructions or sentences in isolation as we have here, but rather in terms of a larger data set, where we may try to identify certain correlations (e.g. if someone can say *had not to* can they also ask the question in (1)a?). What often matters is not just whether a sentence is (un)grammatical, but what else speakers who use that sentence can say. These determinations help us build up a broader picture of how different aspects of an individual's grammar fit together, and in turn how grammar works as a whole.

Measurements of (un)grammaticality shape syntactic analysis and theory. Inaccurate or incomplete data on grammaticality can lead researchers to incorrect conclusions not only about what is possible in a specific language, but what is possible in Language more generally. The ideal way to determine grammaticality draws on a mixture of speakers' knowledge of their own language and instances of real-life language production in order to provide a reliable foundation for syntactic theory, but grammaticality can be very difficult to gauge with absolute certainty.

The data used in this book come from a number of different forms of English. Even if you are a native speaker you will find some of them strange. Nevertheless, they are all forms produced by native speakers of English, as verified by either my own experience or the work of other researchers, and so are grammatical in some variety of English. Where a form is known to be regional or Non-Standard, and therefore grammatical only for some subset of speakers, it will be marked with % symbol. There may be others not marked this way that are nevertheless ungrammatical for you.

1.3 What is syntax?

Our discussion of grammar and grammaticality gives us a starting point for more precisely defining what is meant by **syntax**. Etymologically, it comes from a coupling of Greek *syn* 'together', as in *synthesis* and *synchronise*, with *taxis* 'order', as in *taxonomy*. The origins of this word thus give us a very accurate picture of its meaning: putting words together in an ordered way.

More specifically, we can say that syntax is the system that determines how grammatical sentences are assembled in natural language. We assume that the structures and operations that make up this system are independent not only of other cognitive processes, but also of other aspects of language, although they do interact with these on some level. 'Syntax' is therefore in some sense synonymous with 'grammar', but many linguists also use the latter term to refer to all the pieces that make up a language, from phonetics to pragmatics. We will stick to the narrower, syntax-specific sense in this text.

Linguists' study of syntax relies on data about grammaticality, as discussed above. Our goal is to model the computational processes that our brains undergo when we produce grammatical sentences. In the same way that, pending further advances in microscopy, physicists cannot look inside atoms but can nevertheless develop theories about how they are arranged internally, we can attempt to represent our internal grammar without seeing it directly. Scientists do not actually believe that atoms are composed of the little coloured circles and rings that you might see in a textbook diagram, but these are a useful representation.[5] Similarly, our brains do not literally contain syntax trees or words labelled with their lexical categories, but these are a helpful way of illustrating our theories about grammar.

What makes a good (model of) grammar? Linguists characterise grammars in terms of levels of adequacy. If we have a set of data that tells us what is possible or impossible in a given language, our grammar is **observationally adequate**. In other words, our observationally adequate grammar of a language consists of a list of all its grammatical strings, or at least constructions. Such an enumeration is a necessary starting point – it is what we are trying to establish in determining grammaticality – but our observationally adequate model does not really tell us anything about how the syntax of our language *works*.

---

[5] I have been informed by a reliable source that this kind of model is in fact at least a century out of date.

Building on our group of data points, we can formulate a set of rules that lets us form grammatical sentences and excludes ungrammatical ones for a language, matching up with native speaker intuitions. In doing so we achieve **descriptive adequacy**. This kind of grammatical model is also useful in allowing us to characterise the particularities of the language in question, but it does not get to the heart of **Language** (uppercase 'L'), the human capacity for acquiring and speaking languages. In studying syntax we are fundamentally trying to say something about the design and function of our brains that goes beyond determining grammatical sentences or grammar rules for any given tongue. The ultimate, overarching goal is to create a grammar that is **explanatorily adequate**: abstracting away from the quirks of individual languages, it lays out a set of rules that explain more broadly how Language works, in turn helping us to achieve descriptive adequacy for individual languages by giving us a principled way to choose between different hypotheses about their grammars. While they all have their own idiosyncracies, each language is expected to have grammatical properties that are possible within the scope of natural language syntax. A good descriptively adequate grammar will feed into an explanatorily adequate one by contributing rules that the latter must encompass, while the explanatorily adequate grammar will constrain what kinds of descriptive grammars we can produce.

Underpinning the quest for explanatory adequacy is the theory of **Universal Grammar** or **UG**, a set of syntactic structures and/or operations shared by all languages. Human infants are able to acquire without conscious effort whatever language is spoken around them, a feat that no other animal comes close to matching. It is thought that this unique ability is the result of a specific hard-wired language faculty in our brains (which is nevertheless abstract rather than existing as a pinpointable piece of cerebral anatomy). In effect, we do not acquire a language from scratch, but are born with a UG that gives us a foundation onto which to map the input we receive from our environments. UG does not mean that we have the individual grammars of English and Cantonese and Manx imprinted on our brains. Rather, it assumes that there are overarching properties that these and all other languages share, and that their individual 'grammars' are not discrete systems in themselves, but simply represent various alternatives within the boundaries that UG imposes.

We could think of UG as a bit like a pick-and-mix sweet shop. You can choose any number of combinations from an array of bins containing different sweets. These are all placed in single bag to make up a particular mixture. A particular language is like this bag of sweets, picked from the broader set of available options. Your selection may be quite similar to someone else's (perhaps you share a fondness for smarties and liquorice) or might have no overlap at all. Likewise, related languages or varieties of a single language will share lots of grammatical characteristics, while others will have almost none in common. We may investigate individual languages or varieties, but it is with the larger goal of seeing how they fit in with this bigger UG picture. Looking at a single bag of sweets will tell you some of what is sold at the sweet shop, but it is only by comparing several bags that you will be able to get a sense of the whole range on offer.

Humans are believed not to be able to acquire language that does not conform to UG, in the same way that you cannot buy fish or shoes or washing-up liquid at the sweet shop. There are instances of 'imperfect learning', which may lead to language change through re-analysis of linguistic input. But Non-Standard syntax does not represent a failure to 'get' grammar. Non-Standard input is also not grammatically below par. As noted above, we frequently make errors in speech, so in this sense all children get 'faulty' input. Therefore, in the same way that comparing languages shows us different possibilities within the realm of UG, comparing varieties of a language can provide insight into facets of Language that are not encompassed in a single, Standard form.

1.4 What is Minimalism?

While the study of grammar is a very old one, the approach outlined in this book has grown from a movement that began in the 1950s with Chomsky's *Syntactic structures*. During its development this way of examining syntax has had various names and concomitant acronyms, some of which you may be familiar with.

Essential to this approach to syntax is the concept of **Principles and Parameters (P&P)**. As touched upon above in relation to UG, the P&P model says that there are some properties, the **Principles**, that all languages have in common: these are what make Language what it is. The **Parameters** are those aspects that differ by language, in the limited way circumscribed by UG.

One example of a universal characteristic shared by languages is the **Principle of Structure Dependency**, which says that syntactic operations apply to hierarchical syntactic structures rather than linear strings. We can see this Principle in the formation of English *yes-no* **questions**. Based on the data in (15) we could conclude that these questions are formed by taking the first verb (in this instance a form of *be*) and moving it to the beginning of the sentence.

(15) a. The girl is happy when she is baking cake
     b. Is the girl happy when she is baking cake?
     c. The girl is baking a cake because it makes her happy
     d. Is the girl baking a cake because it makes her happy?

The rule we proposed, however, gives us an ungrammatical question in (16)b.

(16) a. The girl who is baking a cake is happy
     b. *Is the girl who baking a cake is happy?

In treating our sentence as only a linear string we have failed to take into account that the sentence has a complex subject which acts as a single syntactic unit, or **constituent** (more on these in Chapter 2). In forming questions by moving a verb to the beginning of the sentence, we must therefore bypass the first *is*, which cannot be extracted from the complex subject.

(17) a. [The girl who is baking a cake] is happy
     b. Is [the girl who is baking a cake] happy?

This sensitivity to structure when it comes to syntactic operations applies no matter what the language, meaning that a rule such as 'move the first verb in the sentence to the beginning' is always impossible. The Principle of Structure Dependency therefore gives us insight into how UG shapes the way that languages work.

We can also see parameterisation in the formation of **wh-questions**. In English, typical *wh*-questions are formed by moving the question word (*who, what, when,* etc.) to the beginning of the sentence.

(18) a. She will bake a cake
     b. **What** will she bake? (A cake)

As an alternative, the *wh*-word may stay in the position where the word(s) it replaces would otherwise be in a statement. In English this **wh-in-situ** configuration occurs in **echo questions**, which repeat a previous statement and require prosodic stress on the *wh*-word.

(19) She will bake what?

For other languages, such as Japanese and Mandarin, all *wh*-questions have the question word in situ.[6]

---

[6] The *wh*-Movement versus *wh*-in-situ discussion here is very much a surface-level description of this Parameter. We will see as the book progresses how Parameters operate on a deeper syntactic level.

These two options represent the only two possibilities for *wh*-words crosslinguistically, notwithstanding other syntactic properties of questions. There are no languages in which the *wh*-word swaps places with the subject, moves to a position preceding the penultimate word in the question, or is inserted into the middle of the first word containing a fricative. Therefore, even though there is variation in the behaviour of *wh*-questions' formation, it is still constrained by UG within a limited set of options.

Infants start with the Principles of Universal Grammar and then 'set' the Parameters of the language they are exposed to. Parameter setting for *wh*-questions, for instance, would involve figuring out whether the *wh*-word moves to the beginning of sentence or not based on the questions the child hears. This subconscious decision is much easier than if there were infinite alternative ways to ask such questions.

In elucidating what these Principles and Parameters are, we can attempt to achieve explanatory adequacy, going beyond the catalogue of rules for each language to the mechanisms by which Language works, regardless of the specific tongue.

Minimalism is a programme of research which has grown out of this idea of P&P, and latterly its most recent incarnation **Government and Binding** (**GB**) (you will often see mention of **GB/Minimalism**). In many ways Minimalist syntax is a direct extension of these previous ways of looking at grammar. It gives especial emphasis to creating a model of grammar that is as simple as possible, and so has pared down and eliminated many elements of the previous approaches that were seen as redundant or computationally uneconomical. Minimalism does not get rid of syntactic architecture arbitrarily, but it seeks to represent our linguistic systems in an optimal way, under the assumption that the system itself functions optimally.

The notion of **Economy** at the heart of Minimalism is not necessarily a straightforward one. There may be competing ways to account for particular data, with one having certain advantages over another but introducing complications in other respects. There will therefore not always be definitive answers given in this book, but rather a look at the comparative pros and cons of feasible analyses.

Throughout this text I will highlight some elements of pre-Minimalist grammars that are no longer used. You are welcome to skip these sections, but they are intended to provide insight into the development of this approach to syntax, giving a sense of what makes Minimalism 'minimalist' beyond the brief, general characterisation in this chapter. The pre-Minimalist sections may also provide help with 'translating' terms and devices that you come across in older literature.

GB/Minimalism is not the only way to approach the study of syntax, nor is it necessarily superior. You may have seen references to Lexical Functional Grammar, Combinatorial Categorial Grammar, Generalised Phrase Structure Grammar, Head-Driven Phrase Structure Grammar, or Dynamic Syntax. In operating within a Minimalist framework, this text will present just one way of looking at grammar, and makes no claims about other approaches to syntax, other than to present the Minimalist model as a theoretically plausible alternative.

One essential component of Minimalism is that it assumes a **generative grammar**, one in which sentences are built up piece by piece. A potential counterargument to this approach is that it entirely excludes utterances that are ungrammatical. While we want to rule out ungrammatical sentences for the most part, it is problematic that speakers do utter things such as (7)b in error.

A generative grammar in theory generates only grammatical strings and leaves no room for producing slightly ungrammatical ones. All errors must therefore be attributed to the interference of external factors. The generative grammar presumably still constrains grammatical mistakes to a certain extent; our sentence with two determiners can be seen as a plausible instance of sentence generation being interrupted and restarted. In contrast, it is totally implausible that a speaker would make the 'mistake' of uttering an entire sentence backwards, perhaps because the grammar does not generate even an approximation of this construction. The existence of ungrammatical utterances therefore does not rule out this kind of sentence generation, and the theory of generative grammar does not rule out speakers' producing ungrammatical utterances in actual speech

1.5 Variation in English

This text will introduce you to the main aspects of Minimalist syntax through use of data from a number of varieties of English. The essential aim of the book is twofold: to give readers a firm grounding in tools of Minimalist syntactic analysis, and in doing so to highlight the potential for variationist linguistics and theoretical syntax to feed into each other.

As in most areas of linguistic study, English has been the subject of exhaustive syntactic investigation. Historically syntactic study focused on fairly Standard English because this was the language of the academics in the field, who based their analysis on their own introspective judgements. The philosophy behind this approach was the idea that a single speaker of a language (Chomsky's 'ideal speaker-hearer') has perfect implicit knowledge of that language, and can therefore represent all speakers of that language. Sociolinguistic research, along with a certain amount of common sense, tells us that such an assumption is flawed. We can certainly study linguistic structure independently of social factors, and much significant work has been done this way. But in ignoring variation some theoretical linguists have successfully described only a small slice of the linguistic pie that is English.

Many contemporary syntacticians are now tapping into the potential for Non-Standard varieties to contribute to our understanding of syntax and the development of syntactic theory. Thus, although researchers in theoretical syntax have long emphasised the importance of descriptive linguistics, coverage of English in use within theoretical frameworks has at times been patchy.

Each chapter of this book will centre on a set of 'puzzling' syntactic phenomenon in some variety of English. Some of these may be Non-Standard constructions with which you are unfamiliar, and others will include more widely-used forms that nevertheless present surprising characteristics when examined closely. The hope is that you will emerge not only with knowledge of the Minimalist Programme, but also with an understanding that all varieties of language are rule based and can be observed and described systematically, regardless of how Standard or socially valued they are.

The book is structured as follows. Chapter 2 will consider verbs that vary crossvarietally in what objects they take (e.g. *I learned him a lesson*), as part of a review of syntactic architecture, and an introduction to the Minimalist Bare Phrase Structure model. Readers will also be introduced to the Minimalist **Y-model**, in which lexical items are Merged, or added into the syntactic derivation, followed by Spell Out, output to semantic and phonological systems of the language.

Chapter 3 will consider the behaviour of different types of English verbs, introducing an expanded notion of Verb Phrases.

Building upon the previous chapter, Chapter 4 will look at auxiliary verbs such as *be* and *have*, allowing us to expand the syntactic architecture of the clause outside the main Verb Phrase. There will also be consideration of the 'double modal' constructions found in some dialects (e.g. *I might can do that*).

Chapter 5 will look at embedded clauses and questions, returning to, among other examples, the ones given at the beginning of this introductory chapter.

In Chapter 6 we will discuss various phenomena related to negation, including so-called 'double negation', and Non-Standard negation markers such as Scottish *-nae*, which differs in behaviour from Standard *-n't*.

There will also be consideration of **Negative Raising**, in which negation appears to apply across a clause boundary (e.g. *I don't think he is happy*).

Chapter 7 will explore the distinction between different types of *non-finite* complements beginning with *to* (e.g. *I want to go* versus *I want for to go*). There will also be discussion of different dialect variants of embedded passive (e.g. *the cat needs fed* or *the cat needs feeding*, as opposed to *the cat needs to be fed*).

In Chapter 8 we will examine characteristics of nominals, giving consideration to different categories of nouns, including special uses of reflexive pronouns (e.g. *She said that he saw herself*), and the unexpected case on coordinated pronouns (e.g. *Me and him went*) as a point of discussion.

Chapter 9 will look at adjectives and adverbs, considering the distinction between attributive and predicative adjectives, as well as the behaviour of zero-adverbials in certain dialects, which may only occur post-verbally (e.g. *He ate it up quick* versus **He quick ate it up*).

Finally, Chapter 10 will conclude with a look at how Minimalist syntax applies in instances of variation and beyond English.

This book also contains a glossary, where definitions for all terms introduced in bold throughout the text can be found.

1.6 Further reading

For discussion of implications of prescriptivism within and outside of the field of Linguistics see Milroy and Milroy (2012). To learn more about grammaticality and grammaticality judgments see Schütze (2016).

Strazny (2013) has an entry on UG, and Mintz (2010) discusses UG in the context of language development. Dąbrowska (2015) also outlines a number of the most fundamental arguments for UG (while also arguing against this concept).

Åfarli and Mæhlum (2014) give some general discussion of differing approaches to grammar, contrasting structural and sociolinguistic views. For a brief, relatively dense overview of the Minimalist Programme see Lasnik (2002).

1.7 Exercises

1. All of the sentences here are grammatical for some speakers of English. For each one, consider whether it is grammatical in the

variety of English that you speak. If not, see if you can identify why it is not grammatical for you. What would you say instead?
a. %Which book have you?
b. %She's getting a big girl
c. %I'm going to write her
d. %He showed it me yesterday
e. %He might could talk to you
f. %What did you say all you want?
g. %I'm just after eating my breakfast
h. %I'm not wanting to eat now
i. %He needs it doing
j. %She speaks different to me

2. The following sentences are ungrammatical for all speakers of English. Describe what makes them ungrammatical. What would be the grammatical alternative?
   a. *He will clean up it
   b. *Who do you think what saw?
   c. *She will sleep the baby
   d. *I not have had breakfast
   e. *He ate this morning with a silver spoon cornflakes
   f. *She may walks to the shops
   g. *Made you pancakes this morning?
   h. *I walking quickly
   i. *He sang the tune his friends
   j. *Him to she pudding offered

3. Choose one of the sentences in either of the previous exercises and employ some of the methods in §1.2.1 to confirm whether it is grammatical or not.

For Answers see edinburghuniversitypress.com/englishsyntax.

2 Phrase structure

Soon after I moved to Scotland, I was surprised to hear one friend tell another:

(1)   You really suit green

I agreed with the sentiment – the addressee did look good in green – but I was puzzled by its form. For this string to be grammatical in my native variety of US English the subject and object would have to be reversed.

(2)   Green really suits you

In one sense the difference between these two utterances is purely a lexical or semantic one. For the speaker in (1) the verb *suit* in this context means 'look good wearing', while for me it means 'look good worn by'. There is arguably a difference in emphasis, but when taken in its entirety each utterance expresses the same **proposition**, or (falsifiable) idea about the world. They encapsulate this proposition, here the assertion that a particular person has an aesthetic affinity for a particular colour, in disparate, albeit quite similar ways.

There is thus no ultimate effect on interpretation, but the two forms of *suit* alter the word order of the utterances of which they form a central part. This difference points to one important assumption of the Minimalist approach to syntax, which is that the generation of sentences occurs not by the application of external syntactic rules to elements taken from the lexicon, or mental dictionary. Rather, syntactic derivation is driven by properties of the **lexical items** themselves: elements taken from the lexicon impose certain requirements on other elements as sentences are generated. The grammar of each individual language constrains these properties, and that grammar is in itself bounded by Universal Grammar.

In this chapter we will look at how these lexical items, usually words, combine to form larger syntactic units, as well as the ways in which these syntactic units are represented and described in a Minimalist model. We will also consider which properties of a sentence are determined by the syntax, and which may be fixed by other components of the language faculty.

2.1 C-selection and Merge

The word *suit* has a number of characteristics that are presumably encoded in a speaker's lexicon. It is pronounced [suːt] or [sjuːt], depending on the variety of English you speak, but this phonological information is irrelevant to the syntax. As elucidated by the nineteenth-century linguist Ferdinand de Saussure, the connection between a word's meaning and the sounds that represent it is arbitrary. Two words may differ in their phonological representation but otherwise have exactly the same interpretation and syntactic distribution. The Scottish term *shoogly*, for instance, can stand in for the Standard English *wobbly*, without unseating the proposition expressed.[1]

(3)   a.   She sat on a {wobbly/shoogly} chair
        b.   The chair was {wobbly/shoogly}

In generating sentences our brains ignore information about phonology, which has no bearing on how syntactic structures are put together. The syntax instead treats lexical items as abstract bundles of properties rather than words in the way that we speak or write them (recall from Chapter 1 that we could produce a sentence with English words which was otherwise syntactically French). Both *shoogly* and *wobbly* are adjectives that can come before a noun or after a linking verb, and so from the perspective of the syntax are identical: it does not care whether the pronunciation of that word ends up as /ʃuɡli/ or /wɒbli/ or indeed /blɔrk/. Of course, in order to represent these bundles of syntactic properties it is easiest to use the conventionalised phonological/orthographic form of words, rather than assigning each one a special symbol or shade of blue. As discussed in Chapter 1 this choice is a question of modelling, in much the same way scientists might represent atoms as little circles.

Our syntax is also not concerned that *shoogly* and *wobbly* both mean 'not very steady'. We can easily replace these with any number of other adjectives (e.g. *sturdy, lovely, cheerful*), and while the meaning changes

---

[1]   There is an argument that absolute synonyms do not exist – certainly *shoogly* evokes connotations that its counterpart does not – but syntactic behaviour is immune to these slight gradations in meaning (and indeed much larger ones).

(sometimes leading to semantic anomaly), the syntax remains the same.

(4) a. She sat on a {sturdy/lovely/#cheerful} chair
    a. The chair was {sturdy/lovely/#cheerful}

There are instances where meaning appears to play a more significant role in the syntactic construction of sentences, but syntacticians disagree to what extent. We will revisit this question in §2.6 and later chapters. Returning to *suit*, one property of this lexical item which does matter to the syntax is that it is a verb. This **lexical category**, a group of words which behave in a similar way grammatically, has certain implications for how it functions in the syntax, distinct from nouns, adjectives, adverbs, prepositions, and so on. Moreover, *suit* belongs to a subcategory of **linking** or **transitive** verbs that require an object.[2] These **categorial** (e.g. verb) and **subcategorial** (e.g. transitive) properties influence how this word combines with other words as an utterance is generated.

The verb *suit* does not just require an object: it *selects* one. *Selection* describes what types of restrictions a word imposes on other words it combines with. There are two types of selection: syntactic selection and semantic selection. We will concentrate on the former for the moment, and return to the latter in §2.6.

Syntactic selection, also known as **categorial selection** or **c-selection**, is concerned with the lexical category of the entity that a particular lexical item combines with. In our example, the lexical item in question, the verb *suit* (we will assume the Scottish version for the moment), c-selects a noun. If *suit* combines with another lexical category, such as an adjective, a preposition, or an adverb, the resulting string will be ungrammatical.

(5) a. *You suit shoogly[3]
    b. *You suit up
    c. *You suit giddily

The element that a lexical item c-selects is its **complement**. The lexical item that is the selector is called a **head**. A head and its complement

---

[2] The word that follows a linking verb such as *suit* or *be* is not a true object in the way the word that follows a transitive verb such as *hit* is. For current purposes we will ignore this distinction.

[3] Some speakers may find a sentence like (5)a marginally acceptable. It can only be understood as such if the adjective after *suit* is understood as a noun (e.g. *shoogliness*), in the same way that *green* functions as a noun rather than an adjective in this context.

combine syntactically through an operation called **Merge**. Merge is not limited to heads and complements, but can combine any two syntactic units under the right circumstances.

When two elements Merge, they form a **constituent**. A constituent is a piece or 'chunk' of syntax that is syntactically well-formed (adheres to a language's grammatical rules) and meaningful; it can be as small as a single word or as large as an entire clause. This meaningfulness does not require that the constituent is semantically coherent: we can have semantically anomalous constituents just as we can have semantically anomalous clauses. For instance, the bracketed strings in (6) are both constituents, but only one makes real-world sense.

(6)   a.   #I will be [drinking haggis]
      b.   I will be [drinking whisky]

The well-formedness of a constituent also does not require that it can stand alone as an independent utterance.

(7)   *drinking whisky

Constituents are in themselves **phrases**. The term **phrase** indicates that the word or group of words that makes up the constituent has a head that determines its overall category and behaviour. This headedness makes phrases **endocentric**, with their syntactic properties coming from within, so that nouns are the heads of Noun Phrases (NPs), verbs the heads of Verb Phrases (VPs), prepositions the heads of Prepositional Phrases (PPs), adjectives the heads of Adjective Phrases (APs), and so on.

If you look closely at sentences you can get a sense of what words hang together just by intuition, but there are systematic ways to determine whether a particular string constitutes a phrase. Numerous **constituency tests** can be used depending on the context. Here we will employ three: **substitution** (also known as replacement), **fronting** (also known as topicalisation), and **question-answer** (also known as question-fragment).

The first test involves using a single word in place of the string being tested, based on the notion that single words are themselves constituents, and that a phrase may comprise only a head. The substitute word depends on the type of constituent/string being tested. For the sentence in (8) we can do substitution of several different types of phrases.

(8)   Alastair will have the extra incredibly delicious haggis at teatime

- NPs can be replaced with pronouns
  [the extra incredibly delicious haggis] →
  Alastair will have [it] at teatime

- VPs can be replaced with *do (so)*[4]
  [have the extra incredibly delicious haggis] →
  Alastair will [do (so)] at teatime

- PPs can be replaced with *then* or *there*
  [at teatime] →
  Alastair will have the extra incredibly delicious haggis [then]

- **Attributive** APs, which are part of an NP, can be replaced by a single adjective
  [extra incredibly delicious] →
  Alastair will have the [scrummdiddlyumptious] haggis at teatime

- APs that are **predicative**, following a linking verb, can be replaced with *so*
  The haggis was [extra incredibly delicious], and the whisky was [so] too

Fronting involves moving a constituent to the beginning of a sentence. This test cannot be employed for elements that are already sentence-initial (e.g. subjects), or ones that cannot be extracted from larger constituents (e.g. adjectives within NPs).

- NP fronting
  [The extra incredibly delicious haggis], Alastair will have at teatime

- VP fronting
  [Have the extra incredibly delicious haggis], Alastair will at teatime

- PP fronting
  [At teatime], Alastair will have the extra incredibly delicious haggis

The question-answer test is a combination of the other two. The string being tested is replaced with a *wh*-word, which is moved to the beginning of the sentence. If the string is a constituent, it will be possible to answer the question with it as a sentence fragment. This is a special case where a constituent can stand on its own, regardless of whether it is a whole clause or not.

- Q: What will Alastair have at teatime?
  A: The extra incredibly delicious haggis

---

[4] Parentheses ('rounded brackets') around an element indicate it is optional in that string. Where *do so* is used to replace a VP the string in question is still considered to pass the substitution constituency test, even though this technically uses two words, because some speakers simply cannot say sentences such as *I will do* for reasons unrelated to constituency.

- Q: What will Alastair do at teatime?
  A: Have the extra incredibly delicious haggis
  (Note that in the case of VPs we must use *do* in conjunction with the *wh*-word.)

- Q: When will Alastair have the haggis?
  A: At teatime

- Q: How was the haggis?
  A: Extra incredibly delicious

In our original sentence in (1) the *you* and *green* both have a semantic relationship to *suit*. However, the verb *suit* and its object *green* form a constituent that excludes the subject *you*, as evidenced by the possibility of replacing them with a single word of the same lexical category as the head, in this instance a verb.

(9) a. You (really) suit green
    b. You (really) belong/exist/do
    c. *belong/exist/do green

We can also front the string *suit green*, although in this instance fronting requires insertion of an auxiliary *do*; we will return to the reason for this addition in Chapter 4.

(10) Suit green, you really do

We can ask a question that corresponds to this sentence, but it is perhaps semantically anomalous given that *suit* is a **static** verb, denoting a state, making replacement by *do* sound odd.

(11) ??Q:What do you really do? A: Suit green

Use of *do* in a question such as this tends to call for an answer with a **dynamic** verb, which denotes an action. For instance, in (12) the semantically anomalous *drink apples* is a constituent, as evidenced by the fact that it can be replaced by a single word of the same lexical category as its head.

(12) a. The tree will drink apples
    b. The tree will fall/shake/do (so)

When any two elements Merge, the resulting constituent is given the label of one of them. In the case of a head and its complement, the overall constituent has the label of its head. This labelling represents that the head **projects** certain properties to the overall constituent formed by Merge. This constituent therefore shares these properties with its head.

The label we give to any constituent is not in itself a distinct entity, but rather serves in our model as a way of indicating certain characteristics of the constituent that is labelled.

The projection of the label of one element (and the properties that label represents) means that while Merge involves putting two things together to form a whole, it is not a straightforward addition operation. Instead, it is a little like cooking porridge (or rice or pasta). The porridge oats require water in order to fulfil their function as a nutritious breakfast. A special operation (cooking) combines the porridge with the water to make it edible. The result of this absorption of the water by the porridge is called porridge, rather than porridge-with-water: although the water contributes to the function of the oats, it is the porridge oats that make the porridge what it is.

In our example the verb *suit* selects the noun *green* to form the Verb Phrase (VP) *suit green*. We represent this operation (or, perhaps more accurately, its results) with a **syntax tree** as in (13).

(13)   VP

       V   N
     suit   green

It is also possible to represent Merge of syntactic constituents by enclosing them in brackets – syntax trees are really just a shorthand for these – but doing so becomes unwieldy and unreadable once there are more than two or three pairs of brackets. In bracketing notation the label for each constituent is tucked into the opening (left) bracket. Where trees use lines or branches to connect Merged elements under a single label, bracketing puts brackets around the Merged elements.

(14)   [$_{VP}$ [$_V$ suit] [$_N$ green]]

That *suit* rather than *green* projects its label in this instance arises from its status as the selector (head). It does not matter to the complement (*green* here) what it is selected by, and it does not contribute properties to the overall constituent, apart from fulfilling some requirement of the head.

There is also no meaningful reason for the complement *green* to appear to the right of the head *suit*, other than that this is a condition specific to English, which is largely a **head-initial** language. In **head-final** languages a complement Merges to the left of a selecting head, so that it is the element on the right that projects its label to the entire phrase. In such a language the tree for this constituent would be a mirror image of the English one, as in (15).

(15)   VP

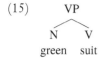

N   V
green suit

These differences in **(head) directionality** are parameterised, i.e. whether complements (and other elements) occur to the left or right of their heads differs by language. Languages may also have a mixture of head-initial and head-final constituents, depending on factors such as the lexical category of the head. Knowledge of directionality is acquired by children according to the input they receive from a particular language. The way languages order their heads and complements is arbitrary in an analogous way to the relationship between the form of a word and its sense. It is significant because this is the Parameter setting for a particular language, but there is nothing intrinsically more meaningful about having a complement come before or after its head, any more than using the sounds /ʃugli/ rather than /wɒbli/ to represent the concept of being not very steady.

English is an SVO (subject-verb-object) language because VPs are head-initial: verbs come before their complements. Languages such as Japanese have SOV word order because VPs are head-final: verbs come after their complements. **Head-directionality** therefore has an impact on sentence construction and grammaticality. However, many linguists argue that directionality is not determined by the syntactic systems of the language at all, but applies post-syntactically once all syntactic operations are complete. In this view *suit* and *green* would Merge as described, with *suit* projecting its label and the properties that represents, but whether the string is ultimately pronounced as *suit green* or *green suit* would be determined at the same point as the sound sequences /suːt/ and /griːn/ are instantiated.

Again, for ease of representation, I will continue to illustrate Merge with items ordered as they are in actual output, leaving aside the question of at what point in the derivation this word order becomes fixed. We will reconsider **linearisation**, the translation of hierarchical syntactic structure to linear strings, in Chapter 9.

2.2 Adjuncts and specifiers

Having established the relationship between the verb *suit* and its complement *green* we can now turn to the other elements in our original utterance (1). Unlike the complement noun *green*, the adverb *really* is optional. It does not form a constituent with the verb *suit* on its own, but rather with the VP *suit green*. We can again demonstrate this relationship by using a substitution constituency test. A single verb can stand in for *suit green*, to the exclusion of *really*, as we saw in (9), but not for *really suit* to the exclusion of *green*, as shown in (16). It is possible to replace *really suit green* with a single word, indicating that this three-word string is a constituent that contains the smaller constituent [$_{VP}$ suit green].

(16) a. You really suit green
      b. *You belong/exist/DO green
      c. You belong/exist/DO

Merge is a **recursive** process that can apply to syntactic constituents already formed by Merge. Thus *really* will Merge with the VP *suit green* to form a larger VP *really suit green*. Because the verb *suit* is still the head, the driving lexical item in the larger constituent formed, this phrase also is labelled VP.

(17)

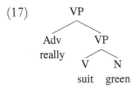

Merge of an optional element of this type is called **adjunction**. **Adjuncts** are formally distinguishable from complements inasmuch as they are not selected by the head of the phrase. In this instance the verb *suit* is grammatical only if it has a complement, but remains grammatical regardless of whether it has an adverb adjunct.

(18) a. *You really suit
      b. You suit green

The final element to be Merged in this sentence is the noun *you*. As with the adjunct adverb *really*, when the subject *you* is Merged the resulting constituent is a VP, with *suit* as its head.

(19)

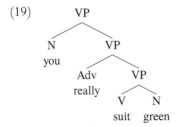

The constituent that Merges to complete the phrase, as *you* does here, is called a **specifier**. Specifiers differ from adjuncts in that they sometimes are required or selected by the head. We will look at the implications of this selectional distinction in the next section. We now have a basic illustration of how our sentence in (1) is generated. As the text progresses we will see that according to our Minimalist framework even a short utterance such as this one has much more extensive structure than is shown here. This tree therefore represents a good first attempt, allowing us to consider how it can be approached in terms of structural description.

2.3 Talking about trees

At this point we have seen lexical items Merge to form increasingly complex constituents. Each lexical item is labelled with its lexical category, and represents a **node** of the tree. As you might expect, the lines extending from these nodes are **branches**; the points where branches meet (labelled with phrasal categories, VP in our example) are also nodes. Nodes formed by Merge (i.e. those having two branches extending from them) are **non-terminal**, while the 'leaves' at the ends of the branches of our (upside-down) tree are **terminal** nodes.

English-speaking linguists often describe syntax trees in terms of female familial relationships. Two nodes Merged to form a constituent are **sisters**. The node formed by this Merge operation is their **mother**.

Let us apply these descriptors to our tree in (20). It has four terminal nodes: [$_N$ you], [$_{ADV}$ really], [$_V$ suit], and [$_N$ green]. Each of our three VP nodes is non-terminal (these have been labelled VP$_{(1)}$, VP$_{(2)}$ and VP$_{(3)}$ for ease of reference; the numbers do not represent anything in our syntactic derivation).

(20)

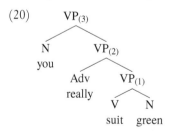

Apart from motherhood/daughterhood and sisterhood, there are two possible relationships between any two nodes in a tree. The first is **dominance**: one node **dominates** another if it is 'above' it in the tree, i.e. if it is its mother, grandmother, great-grandmother, etc. In our tree VP$_{(1)}$ dominates [$_V$ suit] and [$_N$ green]; VP$_{(2)}$ dominates [$_{ADV}$ really], VP$_{(1)}$,

[$_V$ suit] and [$_N$ green]; and VP$_{(3)}$ dominates [$_N$ you], VP$_{(2)}$, [$_{ADV}$ really], VP$_{(1)}$, [$_V$ suit] and [$_N$ green].

As will be apparent from these increasingly long lists, dominance is a transitive property, such that if one node dominates another, it dominates all other nodes dominated by that node. In familial terms, a mother node dominates not only its (her?) daughters, but also its grand-daughters, great-granddaughters, etc.

Dominance gives us a more precise definition of constituency in terms of our tree structure as well: all nodes dominated by a single node make up a constituent. In (20) we can see that [$_V$ suit] and [$_N$ green] form a constituent because they are both dominated by VP$_{(1)}$; [$_{VP(1)}$ suit green] forms a constituent with [$_{ADV}$ really] because they are both dominated by VP$_{(2)}$; and [$_{VP(2)}$ really suit green] forms a constituent with [$_N$ you] because they are both dominated by VP$_{(3)}$. These structures correspond with the results of our constituency tests.

If one node is directly above another in a tree, with no other nodes in between, it is said to **immediately dominate** that node below it. In our tree in (20), VP$_{(1)}$ immediately dominates [$_V$ suit] and [$_N$ green]; VP$_{(2)}$ immediately dominates [$_{ADV}$ really] and VP$_{(1)}$; and VP$_{(3)}$ immediately dominates [$_N$ you] and VP$_{(2)}$. **Immediate dominance** is, in essence, a formal term for motherhood. Two nodes immediately dominated by the same 'mother' are sisters.

Nodes that are not in a dominance relationship are in a **precedence** relationship. One node **precedes** another if it comes 'before' it (to its left) in the tree. In our example [$_V$ suit] precedes [$_N$ green]; [$_{ADV}$ really] precedes VP$_{(1)}$, [$_V$ suit] and [$_N$ green]; and [$_N$ you] precedes VP$_{(2)}$, [$_{ADV}$ really], VP$_{(1)}$, [$_V$ suit] and [$_N$ green]. This is a relationship between sisters and their offspring (aunts/nieces), and again it is transitive. As with dominance, we can have **immediate precedence**, wherein one node precedes another with no other nodes intervening. A sister on a left branch will immediately precede a sister on a right branch. Of course, if directionality is determined post-syntactically then prece-dence is not strictly a property of trees, but it remains a useful descriptor regardless.

Note that VP$_{(3)}$ does not enter into any precedence relationships because it dominates every other node in the tree; dominance and prec-edence are mutually exclusive. This highest VP node is also a **maximal projection**, meaning that it dominates every other node of the phrase projected by its head [$_V$ suit].

While in this instance VP$_{(3)}$ has no mother, a maximal projection may Merge with another syntactic unit, provided that the other unit is the one that projects (otherwise the maximal projection ceases to be maximal). For example, if we replace our complement *green* with *dark green*, Merging [$_{ADJ}$ dark] and [$_N$ green], it creates a Noun Phrase (NP) with *green* as its head. This maximal projection NP can Merge with [$_V$ suit] as [$_N$ green] did. Thus, in the same way that we have seen constituents within constituents, we get phrases within phrases. This aspect of elements of the same type being within each other is another example of the way in which Language is **recursive**.

(21)

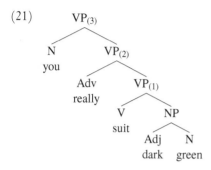

The relationship between nodes can also be described in terms of **c-command**, a description that applies to sisters and aunts/nieces. Sister nodes (e.g. [$_{ADJ}$ dark] and [$_N$ green] above) **symmetrically c-command** each other: the node that immediately dominates (is mother of) one also dominates the other, and vice versa. Aunts **asymmetrically c-command** nieces: the node that immediately dominates the aunt also dominates the niece (or great-niece, etc.), but not vice versa. [$_N$ you] in the above tree c-commands [$_N$ green] because the mother of [$_N$ you], the node VP$_{(3)}$, also dominates [$_N$ green]. But the node that immediately dominates [$_N$ green] (the NP node) does not dominate [$_N$ you], so [$_N$ green] does not c-command [$_N$ you], putting them in an asymmetric c-command configuration.

The c-command relationship arises from the Merge operation. Nodes Merged as sisters will be visible to each other as they have come into the derivation at the same point. Previous parts of the derivation will also be visible to nodes Merged higher up in the tree, but new parts of the derivation will not be accessible to nodes already Merged.

We can think of this limitation a little like a group of people going into a theatre from a back entrance, where they are seated so that the rows are filled front to back. If you get there and join a friend in the third row, you will be able to see that person, as well as the other people in the first and second rows; your friend will be able to see you when you sit down next to them. Assuming you are a well-behaved audience member facing the stage, you will not be able to see people who come in behind you afterwards and sit in the fourth and fifth rows, but they will be able to see you. You and your friend are therefore in a sort of symmetric c-command relationship, while you are asymmetrically c-commanded by the people sitting behind you.

Looking back to our consideration of c-selection and Merge, we can now partially translate the relationship between heads and other elements into structural descriptions. A complement will always be the sister of the head. Our directionality Parameter can be characterised in terms of precedence: in a head-initial language such as English, heads precede their complements.

Adjuncts, in many instances, will be sisters of non-terminal nodes. However, if a head does not select a complement, it may have its adjunct as a sister. This contrast can be seen in (21): $[_N$ green], the head of the NP, does not select for a complement, and thus the adjunct $[_{ADJ}$ dark] Merges directly with $[_N$ green]; on the other hand, $[_V$ suit] already has its complement $[_{NP}$ dark green] as its sister, and therefore the adjunct $[_{ADV}$ really] Merges with $[_{VP1}$ suit dark green].

The subject $[_N$ you] can be called a specifier, meaning that it is **immediately dominated** by, or daughter of, a maximal projection. Unlike adjuncts, specifiers do seem to be selected by the head. Specifiers and heads also **Agree**, or share certain properties, as evidenced by the change in the verb ending depending on person and number (e.g. *you suit* versus *he suits*), but the impoverishment of English morphology means that this relationship is often invisible.

In the absence of a specifier it is possible for an adjunct (or, in certain circumstances, a complement) to appear in the same configuration as a specifier. In (21), for example, the adjunct ADJ *dark* is the daughter of the maximal projection NP.

2.4 What happened to X-bar?

The syntactic representations I have outlined thus far are instantiations of **Bare Phrase Structure** (BPS). This Minimalist approach to syntactic representation supersedes many aspects of its forerunner, X-bar structure, elements of which remain present in much work on syntax, and are still used in many syntax textbooks. This section will outline the differences between BPS and X-bar in order to clarify the (dis)advantages of this newer approach for those readers who are already familiar with the older one, and to highlight points of difference for readers who are unfamiliar with X-bar but are likely to encounter it at some point in other linguistic literature.

As structural descriptions, the terms *complement*, *adjunct* and *specifier* are holdovers from X-bar syntax. As discussed in §2.3, complements and specifiers have certain structural requirements: a complement must be sister to a head; a specifier must be the daughter of a maximal projection. In BPS, though, these structural configurations can also occur with, e.g., adjuncts, raising the question of whether such descriptions are still relevant.

In X-bar structure, **intermediate projections**, those nodes that dominate the head and are dominated by the maximal projections, are specially labelled with the category of the head followed by a prime (called a 'bar' for historical reasons having to do with changes in typography). As a result, all phrases are structurally identical, along the lines of (22).

(22)

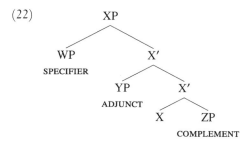

The X in (22) is a variable standing in for any lexical category label: V(erb), N(oun), P(reposition), A(djective), etc. Likewise the other letters in (22). We can therefore describe complements, adjuncts and specifiers in relation to maximal projections (XP), intermediate projections (X′) and heads (X).

(23)   Complement: sister of X, daughter of X′
       Adjunct: sister of X′, daughter of X′
       Specifier: sister of X′, daughter of XP

Note that the rule for adjuncts is recursive: we can have infinite intermediate (X′) projections, allowing for infinite adjunction.

When X′ is eliminated these definitions become untenable. Complements are still sisters of X, selected by X, as they Merge directly with the head of the phrase. But it becomes difficult, if not impossible, to distinguish between adjuncts and specifiers. Both are typically sister of XP, daughter of XP in BPS. We might still differentiate them in terms of agreement or selection, taking into account that specifiers, like complements, tend to be required by the head of the phrase, and share certain properties with that phrase. Without X′, though, these are no longer structural descriptions.

Some linguists argue in fact that there is no structural difference between specifiers and adjuncts, a point of view that has significant consequences in terms of how optional constituents such as adverbs and adjectives are incorporated in clauses and nominals. We will return to this issue in Chapters 8 and 9.

In order to consider other changes from X-bar to BPS, it is useful to juxtapose an X-bar version of one of the trees we have already produced in BPS.

(24)

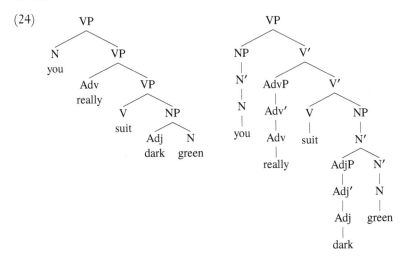

The comparatively pared down aesthetic of the BPS tree reflects the elimination of a number of artefacts deemed un-Minimalist. The lack of X′ is the most obvious of these. We can distinguish terminal nodes, which are taken from the lexicon, from non-terminal nodes, which result from Merge of lexical items and/or larger constituents. The lexical category of a phrase comes from its head. There is no way, however, to differentiate intermediate projections from each other, or from maximal projections, other than by imposition of some external syntactic classification. Because the Minimalist approach specifies that every part of syntactic structure is projected by a lexical item head, we cannot justify the insertion of an intermediate bar level.

In our BPS tree, lexical items do not project their lexical categories, and there is no branch between a word and the label corresponding to its lexical category because there is no separation between them. The terminal node represents all of the properties of the lexical item, including those that are not instantiated in the syntax, rather than an element that is inserted into a pre-existing syntactic derivation or structure.

Separation of a lexical item from its lexical category is also impossible because all branching in Minimalism is **binary**, meaning that any non-terminal node dominates two and only two non-terminal nodes. The binary branching requirement is a result of how derivations proceed in Minimalist syntax: the only way to create a new node is by Merge of two constituents. Consider, also, other types of mental computation. Try doing the following calculation:

(25) 5 + 3 + 2 + 7

Even if you are enormously adept at arithmetic, it is unlikely that you arrived at the answer (it's 17) by totting up all the digits in one fell swoop. Rather, you will have proceeded by adding up pairs, e.g. 5 + 3 = 8, then 8 + 2 = 10, then 10 + 7 = 17. Although this sum differs in many respects from a sentence (among other things, its parts are re-orderable), we can see Merge as analogous to this computation, inasmuch as it involves dealing with only two elements at once. It is indeed not so much that *two* is the magic number as *one*: after initial Merge of the first two elements, only a single constituent is Merged into the derivation at any given point. Anything more than binary branching would require simultaneous Merge of multiple lexical items. In the other direction, unary branching is like an equation such as 2 = 2. It is not inaccurate, but it does not give us any information about the value of 2 that we do not get from the number on its own. The same can be said for X′ and XP levels that dominate a head with no dependents, as in the structure for *you* or *dark* in the second tree from (24).

One result of the elimination of X-bar and non-binary branching is that it is possible for a lexical item to function as both a head and maximal projection simultaneously. Thus the distinction we made between (20), in which the complement was the noun *green*, and (21) is not meaningful: *green* on its own has the same properties that are projected in the NP *dark green*, and so it could also be labelled NP. While they are labelled only with lexical categories, all the terminals in our BPS tree (with the exception of V *suit*) constitute phrases as well as lexical items. This is true for the X-bar structure as well, made explicit by the additional X′ and XP nodes. From a Minimalist perspective, though, these other levels of structure cannot be distinct from the terminal nodes.

2.5 Syntactic generation

As described in Chapter 1, Minimalism assumes a generative grammar. The X-bar model does not represent the generation of a sentence in the same way as its BPS counterpart, because it requires the introduction of a property, intermediacy, that comes neither from the lexicon nor the Merge operation.

Summing up what we have seen so far, we can now present a model of how a Minimalist derivation proceeds. A set of lexical items for a given sentence, called a **lexical array**, is taken as input. Driven by the properties of these lexical items, Merge applies in order to form increasingly larger syntactic constituents. When this syntactic process is complete the resulting structure is sent to **Spell Out**, meaning that it is no longer accessible to any kind of syntactic operations. Spell Out has two components: **Phonological Form** (PF) and **Logical Form** (LF). This kind of derivation can be illustrated using the so-called **Y-model**.

(26)

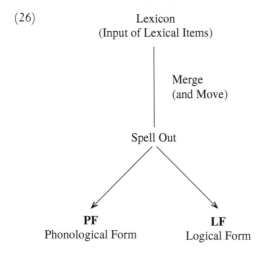

The Y-model represents a departure from previous approaches, which framed sentences in terms of **D(eep)-Structure**, their underlying syntactic form, and **S(urface)-Structure**, the sentence that was ultimately pronounced. Mediating between these were **transformations**, syntactic rules imposed on the underlying structure to produce the eventual sentence and explain seeming mismatches between the proposition expressed and the actual word order of an utterance. For instance, the position of a *wh*-word at the beginning of a question when the word is also understood as, e.g., the object of a verb, would be accounted for with a Movement transformation.

(27) You will eat [an apple] →
    You will eat [what] →
    [What] will you eat?

Like the labelling of projections as intermediate, these transformation operations were external, rather than arising from the properties of lexical items themselves. As we will see in later chapters, Minimalist derivations can also capture apparent misalignments between form and meaning, including Movement, but they do so in a way that depends on the properties of lexical items themselves.

We have already touched on Spell Out to PF: this is the assignment of sounds to lexical items that occurs after the syntax has completed its generation of an utterance. The phonological component of the language reads off the output of the syntactic component, which has ignored the phonological properties of lexical items, to determine how an utterance will be pronounced.

LF pertains to the meaning of a sentence. This component of the language takes the output of the syntax and relates it to the proposition that that output represents. The extent to which semantics contributes to our syntactic derivation is a trickier question, which brings us back to our original puzzle regarding the difference between *you suit green* and *green suits you*.

2.6 S-selection

The first point to make about these two sentences is that it is not simply a difference in word order, but a difference in function. The two forms of *suit* genuinely mean different things, even though these utterances in their entirety express the same proposition. The alternative conclusion would be that one of these forms (e.g. *you suit green*) is basic, and that the other (e.g. *green suits you*) represents a special case of OVS word order. But there is no reason to think that a specific lexical item (here the verb *suit*) can alter the fundamental word order of a language. Such an idea would be counter to the larger picture of a unified grammar for any given language.

It is moreover evident from the verbal morphology on *suit* in each instance that it agrees with the subject (-*s* in the case of third person singular *green*, -Ø in the case of second person singular *you*) as we would expect. There is therefore nothing singular about either form of *suit* in terms of its syntactic behaviour.

In looking at the verb *suit* we established that it c-selects a noun. Although we were focusing on the form of the verb in (1), the same applies for the form of the verb in (2). The difference between them is therefore not one of c-selection, but rather of **semantic selection**. Scottish *suit*$_1$ s-selects the colour (or item of clothing, etc.) being worn as its complement, while *suit*$_2$ selects the person doing the wearing as its complement.

From a semantic perspective, a verb such as *suit* is not just the head of a syntactic phrase (constituent), but also a **predicate**, a semantic function that requires certain 'gaps' to be filled by **arguments**, entities that complete its propositional meaning. These are usually NPs, but in certain instances belong to other categories. Predication aligns to a certain extent with transitivity, the requirement that certain verbs have objects – for example, *suit* requires a complement syntactically, and a 'suitee' semantically – but encompasses subjects as well.

S-selection therefore represents this predicational relationship. *Suit*$_1$ s-selects the colour being worn as its object and the wearer as its subject, while *suit*$_2$ s-selects the wearer as its object and the colour as its subject.

If we define what is grammatical purely in terms of our syntax, then s-selection should play no role in syntactic derivations. It must be true that syntactic selection operates at least semi-independently of semantic selection, given the possibility of semantic anomaly. In fact, for a speaker who uses *suit*$_1$, the sentence in (2) is not ungrammatical, but semantically anomalous, and vice versa.

At the same time, it would be ungrammatical for the verb *suit* to have no subject or complement, or multiple objects. These limitations potentially go beyond c-selection, suggesting that semantic requirements do play some role in the syntax.

2.6.1 Thematic roles

Up to this point I have referred in a non-specific way to 'properties' encoded in and projected by the verb (or any lexical item). Because verbs are not just syntactic heads, but also act as predicates, some of their properties (or those of any predicate) must therefore pertain to the restrictions they impose on which arguments can satisfy their semantic requirements. These restrictions can be captured by **theta roles**, which occupy a space between syntax and semantics.

Theta roles stand for the thematic relationship between a verb and the NP arguments that it selects for. Every verb has a certain number of theta roles to assign, and each potential argument must be assigned one and only one theta role, a restriction known as the **theta-criterion**. For instance, the verb *give* must have a giver, who does the giving, an entity given, and a givee, who receives the entity given. These thematic roles specific to *give* can be defined in more general terms as an **agent** (giver), a **theme** (given) and a **recipient** (givee). Every theta role is associated with certain semantic requirements. Agents, in particular, must at minimum be sentient and capable of intention. Assignment of an agent theta role to a non-sentient argument is possible on a syntactic level, but results in semantic anomaly.

(28) #The tree gave me a drink

There are a number of other semantic or thematic relationships that can be described in similar terms, but the syntax is not concerned with the interpretation of theta roles. In one sense, then, c-selection and s-selection are simultaneous, but the potential for grammatical but semantically anomalous outputs indicates that the semantic component does not restrict the construction of sentences beyond the syntactic requirement that theta roles be assigned exhaustively, with each argument receiving its theta role at the point when it is Merged. Theta roles also do not encompass all aspects of meaning within a sentence, as there are various semantic and/or pragmatic relationships which may go behind the relatively narrow confines of theta role assignment.

Each form of *suit* has two theta roles: one assigned to the person wearing the colour (who in more general terms might be called an **experiencer**) and one to the colour worn (a theme). With Scottish *suit*₁ the experiencer theta role is assigned to the subject, and the theme to the object; with *suit*₂ the theme theta role is assigned to the subject, and the experiencer theta role to the object. These theta roles are not interpreted until after the syntax has been spelled out to LF. It is thus important for the syntax only that they are assigned. We can therefore say that theta roles do operate on a syntactic level but are not realised within the syntactic component of the language.

2.6.2 Other types of selection?

While we have so far concentrated on verbal complementation, other heads select complements as well. We will see more of these in later chapters. These complements may also differ depending on what form of English you speak. For example, there are certain adjectives that can be followed by a variety of prepositions.

(29) a. He is different {%to/%from/%than} my brother
     b. I was bored {%of/%with} the film
     c. She was enamoured {%of/%with} him

In all of these instances the adjective head c-selects a Prepositional Phrase. You cannot use any preposition with these adjectives (e.g. *He was bored among my brother)*, but, contrary to the assertions of prescriptive grammar guardians who claim that replacing *from* with *to* or *than* after *different* affects clarity, the available options carry very little meaning in themselves. These prepositions are **function words** that act to mediate certain relationships in the syntax without giving us the temporal or spatial information that we might get from prepositions in other contexts. For the Adjective Phrases in (29) the important semantic information comes from the head of the phrase, the adjective itself.

It is therefore possible that the adjective c-selects a preposition without specifying which one, and that the form of the preposition is decided at PF according to speakers' preferences for particular **collocations**, strings of words that typically occur together. This idea has the advantage of shifting aspects of lexical items external to the syntax (i.e. their pronunciation) out of syntactic derivations. Such an analysis is in another sense controversial, considering that in other contexts prepositions do contribute semantic rather than just grammatical information. The alternative approach would be to say that the syntax, without being affected by the pronunciation of these prepositions per se, is nevertheless sensitive to the properties that distinguish one preposition from another when it comes to selection by an adjective, even when the differences between these prepositions apparently have no particular significance in terms of underlying syntactic structure or semantics.

2.7 Conclusion

In this chapter we have looked at how syntactic structures are built up, taking a very simple sentence, with contrasting forms of the same verb, as our starting point. Merge, selection and projection by lexical items are cornerstones of our Minimalist approach to syntax. As sentences become more complex it becomes necessary to consider whether they can still be accounted for using only these operations, and whether our view of these operations must be amended. In Chapter 3 we will look at other subcategories of verbs, expanding our conception of the VP.

2.8 Further reading

For more discussion of constituency tests see Miller (2016). Strazny (2013) also provides entries on constituency tests and phrase structure.

For extensive discussion of different kinds of syntactic representations, including X-bar structure and BPS, see Carnie (2010). Chametzky (2003) explores phrase structure in the context of Minimalism. Harley (2010) gives a broader overview of theta roles and Strazny (2013) again offers some in-depth discussion of thematic structure. For consideration of the interface between syntax and semantics see Lohndal (2014). See Collins and Stabler (2016) for formal definitions of Minimalist syntactic operations. For an extensive look at the development of Minimalism see Boeckx (2006).

2.9 Exercises

1. Determine whether the strings in brackets in the following sentences are constituents. If a string is a constituent identify what kind of phrase it is, and which word is the head of that phrase.
   a. [Maisie will run around] the park
   b. Maisie will run around [the park]
   c. Billy smacked [the man with his hand]
   d. Billy [smacked the man] with his hand.
   e. He gave me an extremely [confusing answer]
   f. He gave me an [extremely confusing] answer
   g. The book I found [on the table in the kitchen] was boring
   h. The book I found [at midnight in the kitchen] was boring
   i. Flora [ate an apple on Tuesday]
   j. Flora ate [an apple on Tuesday]
   k. Oscar poured Lucy [a glass] of wine
   l. Oscar poured Lucy a glass [of wine]

2. For each of the sentences in Exercise 1 decide which constituents the main verb selects. Is the selection syntactic, semantic or both?

3. Using Bare Phrase Structure, and keeping in mind the results of your constituency tests, draw syntax trees for Exercise 1 sentences (c) and (i).

4. What aspects of the rest of the sentences in Exercise 1 make them difficult to draw trees for in the model of syntactic structure we have outlined thus far?

For Answers see edinburghuniversitypress.com/englishsyntax.

3 Lexical verbs

Borrowing a pen from me recently, a friend from the North of England said (1).

(1) Hang on, I'll give it you back

If you are not a Northern English speaker the word order in this utterance may strike you as unexpected. Many varieties of English require that the **indirect object** (IO) precedes the **direct object** (DO) in **ditransitive** constructions, in which a verb selects for two objects. The majority of English speakers would therefore have the IO *you* before the DO *it*.

(2) I'll give you it back

The DO-IO order seen in (1) is permitted for speakers of most non-Northern English varieties only in **double object** constructions, where the indirect object is first Merged with the preposition *to* (or sometimes *for*) to form a Prepositional Phrase (PP). Most verbs with two objects allow both a ditransitive and double object form, although there are double object verbs such as *explain* and *introduce* which cannot be used ditransitively.

(3) a. I'll {give/show/offer/lend/etc.} you it (ditransitive)
     b. I'll {give/show/offer/lend/etc.} it to you (double object)
     c. *I'll {introduce/explain} you {him/it}
     d. I'll {introduce/explain} {him/it} to you

The difference in the order of the pronouns for ditransitive constructions represents a distinction between varieties of English. There are further complications, cutting across these crossvarietal differences, concerning the status of *back*. While they are typically homophonous with prepositions, elements such as this one function as a part of a verb, changing the meaning from use of the verb on its own.

44

(4) a. I looked the answer **up**
         (cf. *I looked the answer)
     b. I threw the rubbish **out**
         (cf. I threw the rubbish)
     c. We talked the idea **through**
         (cf. *We talked the idea)

In terms of word order, this **particle** must occur after any pronominal objects in a ditransitive construction.

(5) a. *I'll give you back it
     b. *I'll give back you it
     c. *I'll give back it you
     d. *I'll give it back you

In double object constructions the particle still follows the pronominal direct object, but must precede the PP containing the indirect object.

(6) a. I'll give it back to you
     b. *I'll give back it to you
     c. *I'll give it to you back

We must therefore account for these word order restrictions both within and across varieties. On a more fundamental level, any verb with both a direct and indirect object presents a conundrum for the conception of syntax outlined thus far. Given that Merge is binary, how can we explain a configuration in which a head appears to select multiple complements? Do the two objects and particle have equivalent status in terms of their relationship to the verb head of the VP?

In this chapter we will see that ditransitive verbs require an expansion of the simple VP structure shown in Chapter 2, and consider how this more complex structure accounts for an array of subcategories of **lexical verbs**, those that give a clause its core meaning. In doing so we will revisit issues pertaining to how much semantics contributes to the generation of syntactic structures.

3.1 Ditransitive and double object verbs

The first question in approaching verbs such as *give* is whether each of the two objects is a true complement. Neither the direct or indirect object is optional for the verb *give* (but see (11) below for other verbs), suggesting that both are required, and therefore selected, by the head. Our replacement constituency test does not allow us to isolate either object as forming a constituent with the head to the exclusion of the other.

(7) a. I will give him the haggis
     b. ?*I will give him
        (≠I will give him the haggis)
     c. ?*I will give the haggis
        (≠I will give him the haggis)
     d. *I will give her the haggis and you will do him
     e. ?*I will give her the whisky and you will do the haggis

Simultaneous syntactic selection of both objects is impossible for a number of reasons. Most obviously, it violates the requirement that Merge be binary. It also fails to differentiate between the two objects which, as evidenced by the ditransitive/double object alternation, are distinct in terms of function and behaviour.

Let us imagine for a moment that ternary branching is permitted in our model, and applies in instances of ditransitivity. If this were so it would be necessary to introduce additional directionality parameters to order the direct and indirect object in relation to each other.

(8) *

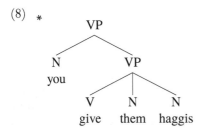

As noted in Chapter 2, some linguists argue that linear order is determined post-syntactically at PF. In order for the PF component to order the DO and IO of a ternary branching structure it would have to interpret not just properties of these lexical items, or the fact that they have been selected by a particular head, but also their specific semantic/thematic relationship to the verb. The information needed at Spell Out would therefore need to include specification that an NP was a direct or indirect object.

The DO/IO distinction is unlike properties such as lexical category and syntactic relationships such as complement/adjunct. Lexical category membership is an intrinsic property of lexical items. There are words that can belong to more than one category, and it is possible to identify from the syntactic context which of these categories the word fits into for a particular sentence. *Green* is an adjective in (9)a, and a noun in (9)b.

(9)   a. Green is a lovely colour

    b. Flora's lovely cardigan is green

This multi-category membership nevertheless comes from the word itself rather than being imposed externally by the syntax; we cannot put any word in any syntactic context and expect it to change category. Instead, the lexical category (or categories) of a lexical item must already be specified in the lexicon.

Unlike lexical category, the identification of constituents as complements or adjuncts is not inherent.[1] But rather than occurring as independent labels, these syntactic relationships arise as a result of selection and/or Merge operations. Thus, although they are not encoded in the lexicon, they still do not need to be imposed by any kind of labelling operation external to the syntax.

The direct or indirect object status of an NP, on the other hand, is a semantic property pertaining to that argument's relationship with the verb. It comes neither from the lexical item itself, nor any syntactic operation per se. The relationship between the DO and IO is also not a direct one, but instead is mediated through the verb. Which object is which would therefore need to be stipulated independently and externally for each NP whenever linearisation occurs.

Such specification of properties not inherent to lexical items or structural configurations is not in keeping with a lexically-driven approach. This solution to ditransitives is therefore fundamentally un-Minimalist and leads back to a larger argument against ternary branching in our model: unless three elements Merged together are freely ordered, a structure of this type cannot be accommodated without imposing properties from outside of the lexicon on lexical items and syntactic structures. In contrast, a binary structure may be inherently asymmetric, in that only one of the elements Merged will project its properties, allowing the grammar to differentiate between the two constituents (e.g. a head and complement) at the point when their linear order is determined, without any additional information about their semantic or sentential function.

An alternative solution to the puzzle of multiple objects would be to Merge the indirect object with the head, followed by subsequent Merge of the direct object to the VP constituent formed by the head and IO. This configuration gives us the correct word order, but the verb and indirect object form a constituent to the exclusion of the direct object, a relationship not borne out by our constituency tests in (7).

---

[1]   For the sake of the argument here we will ignore other potential problems with employing these terms in BPS.

(10) *

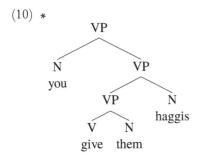

Certain ditransitive verbs can in fact also be (mono-)transitive, suggesting that if anything it is the direct object that has a closer relationship with the head.

(11) a. I brought (him) haggis
      b. I threw (her) a ball
      c. I made (him) a haggis

There is also evidence that indirect and direct objects are in an asymmetric relationship opposite to the configuration in (10). One example of this asymmetry can be seen in use of the reciprocal *each other*. As shown in (12), *each other* must be preceded by its **antecedent**, the entity or entities to which it refers.

(12) a. Alastair and Flora want each other's toys
      b. *Each other want Alastair and Flora's toys

This is not just a precedence but a c-command requirement. If we embed the compound subject NP *Alastair and Flora* in another NP so that it no longer c-commands *each other* we lose the reciprocal meaning.

(13) *[_{NP} The boy next to Alastair and Flora] wants each other's toys

Applying this c-command requirement for *each other* to ditransitive constructions we see that it is grammatical to have the antecedent *Alastair and Flora* as the IO, and reciprocal *each other* as the DO, but not vice versa. Given what we know about *each other* being c-commanded by its antecedent, these data indicate that the IO must c-command the DO, but the DO does not c-command the IO in such constructions.

(14) a. I gave Alastair and Flora each other's toys
      b. *I gave each other Alastair and Flora's toys

This asymmetry presents another argument against the configurations in (8) and (10). In the ternary branching structure the IO and DO symmetrically c-command each other; in the IO-as-complement structure the DO asymmetrically c-commands the IO. Both of these approaches therefore give us an inaccurate structural representation of the linguistic facts. We will return to further implications of c-command and elements such as *each other* in Chapter 8.

3.1.1 Splitting the Verb Phrase: ditransitives

The solution to the problem of multiple objects lies in a reconceptualisation of the head and its relationship to complements. From a structural perspective objects may not be complements at all. Without introducing additional mechanisms in generating syntactic structures, we can argue that a single lexical item can be **decomposed**, so that it Merges more than once in the course of a derivation. For verbs, this multi-part Merge creates a **split VP**.

We have already seen a structure with multiple VP layers, each created by Merge of additional elements and projection of the properties of V. What we will propose here involves not just projections of a single head. Rather, V will be split into multiple heads, each projecting a separate phrase.

As we said in Chapter 2, a lexical item is a bundle of properties, only some of which are relevant to the syntax. We can view repeated Merge of a verb as representing a division of this lexical item into its disparate (syntactic) properties, with a subset of these projected from each head. While the resulting structure is more complex than one in which the verb comprises only a single projection, the split VP model is still at heart Minimalist because no properties are present that do not arise from the lexicon. Selection of one verbal projection by another is also straightforward because it consistently occurs in the same configuration(s): the properties of each head of the split VP will always be the same within a language.[2]

Our split VP structure can therefore be represented as the **VP shell** configuration in (15). For the moment each projection is labelled VP (with subscripts for reference), but we will ultimately give them labels that more accurately reflect their specific properties.

---

[2] It is possible that which properties correspond to which heads is parameterised crosslinguistically; discussion of this possibility is beyond the scope of this text.

(15)

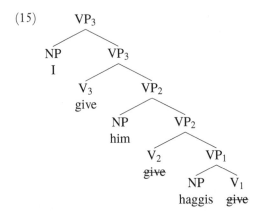

This tripartite structure allows us to account for the syntactic relationship between indirect and direct objects. In (15) the indirect object c-commands the direct object, but the direct object does not c-command the indirect object; this structure is consistent with the evidence from use of *each other*, as seen in (14), as well as a raft of other instances where the indirect and direct object appear to be in an asymmetric configuration.

Of course, not all of the heads in this configuration are pronounced, as we would get a gobbledygook (and rather repetitive) sentence if that were so: *I give him give haggis give*. The lower instances of *give* are scored out in (15) to represent that they are silent. How can we model the apparent discrepancy between our proposed structure and actual linguistic output? There are at least three approaches, which may be seen as more or less Minimalist in their requirements:

- The most traditional analysis would be to say that the verb 'Moves' from its initial position in the lowest V head to each subsequent verbal head position. This Movement explanation captures the notion that the verb is, structurally, in three places at once. As we saw in the previous chapter, though, the Minimalist framework assumes that there is a fairly strict separation between syntax and Phonological Form (PF). In this sense the pronunciation of the lexical item is not present in any of these heads during the syntactic derivation, which means that we would have to see this Movement of the verb from one head position to the other as displacement of (phonological) properties that are not realised until after Spell Out.

- As an alternative, if each verbal head represents only some properties of the lexical item *give*, then we could hypothesise that the parts of the verb encoding its pronunciation exist only in the highest verbal projection, and that other properties of the verb make up the other verbal heads, but they do not contain information on pronunciation. As with the other proposal, this information would be ignored by the syntax, but instantiated at PF. Such an analysis is more Minimalist than the Movement account because it assumes less redundancy. Each verbal projection has only a certain subset of properties, Merged in particular positions, rather than these properties starting in V and then Remerging in other head positions.

- Another approach would be to say that pronunciation, while still invisible to the syntax, is encoded in every verbal head (regardless of what other properties are encoded in each head). Which head is actually uttered would be determined post-syntactically at the point of Spell Out by some rule of PF, such as 'pronounce the first instance of a word, and leave all subsequent instances silent'. From a purely syntactic point of view this explanation is perhaps the simplest, as it does not require any determination by the syntax of where the verb will be pronounced. It may not be any more economical overall, because it shifts decisions about word order to the PF component. Whether these word order generalisations can be captured by straightforward rules along the lines of the one given here becomes a complicated question if we look at other instances of apparent displacement of constituents.

For the moment we will represent the structure of the split VP as in (15), with the unpronounced heads crossed out. We will return to the issue of possible Movement or Remerge of heads and other constituents in Chapter 5.

Putting aside pronunciation, we are now in a position to consider which properties of the verb are projected by, or at least instantiated in, each verbal head. A verb such as *give* is a predicate with three thematic roles that must be assigned to arguments: roughly, a 'giver' (or agent), a 'given' (or theme) and a 'givee' (or recipient). We can illustrate the assignment of these theta roles within our split Verb Phrase by recreating our derivation step by step. The verb *give* initially Merges with a direct object, assigning a theta role: in this instance, the 'given' theme argument. The direct object is classed as an **internal argument**, meaning that it is dominated by the maximal projection of the verb, i.e. it is internal to the Verb Phrase.

(16)   VP$_1$

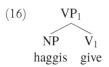

NP   V$_1$
haggis give

The VP formed by this Merge operation is then selected by another instantiation of *give*, forming another VP (labelled VP$_2$ for ease of reference). The head of this second VP selects for an indirect object, also an internal argument, discharging an additional theta role to the 'givee' recipient argument.

(17)

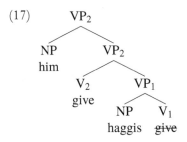

Another instantiation of *give* then Merges with VP$_2$. This head selects for a subject, which can also be described as an **external argument**. Traditionally, this designation meant that the subject was outside the maximal projection of the verb (a state of affairs which is still thought to apply for English, as we will see in Chapter 4). More relevant for our discussion here, external arguments tend to be agentive or causative. The highest V head is therefore represented as *v*, called '**little v**', to indicate its special status as an assigner of an agent/cause theta role to an external argument, in this instance the 'giver'. We will see in later chapters that this causative head *v*(P), as the instantiation of the verb Merged highest in the tree, has additional special properties that distinguish it from the other verbal heads.

(18)

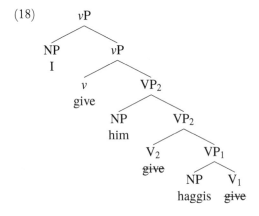

This structure for ditransitives creates consistency in the relationship between the verb and subjects and objects: each manifestation of the verb Merges with an NP to its left, assigning a theta role to an argument in this sisterhood configuration. Each of the upper heads also selects for another verbal projection as its complement. Thus, while it is more complex than a unitary VP, our split VP structure is advantageous in not requiring mechanisms particular to each object.

3.1.2 Double object verbs

Having established a split VP structure for ditransitives, we can consider whether it is generalisable to other types of verbs. The closest comparable form is the double object construction, as in (19).

(19) I give haggis to him

That the IO follows the DO in this configuration suggests that one or both of these objects must Merge in different positions from the ones in ditransitives. We could accomplish this change in word order by simply switching their positions in our split VP structure.

(20) *

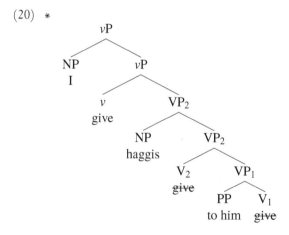

This potential solution has the undesirable result that our objects are assigned the same theta roles by different heads for the same verb (here *give*), depending on whether it is being used in a ditransitive or double object form. Under this approach sometimes V_1 assigns the 'givee' theta role to an indirect object, and sometimes the 'given' theta role to a direct object; V_2 sometimes assigns the 'given' theta role, and sometimes the 'givee' theta role. An inconsistency of this type is un-Minimalist, as it changes the properties of our structure (which heads assign which theta roles), based on factors external to the lexicon. Ideally we would want each verbal head to have the same properties regardless of whether it is used in a ditransitive or double object construction, or indeed for any other subcategory of verb.

We could instead argue that the indirect object PP in a double object construction is a complement of the lowest V head, resulting in a configuration along the lines of (21) (to be amended below).

(21)

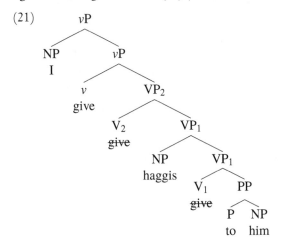

Under this approach the direct object is always Merged in VP_1 (cf. (18)), which also consistently assigns it the same theta role (for *give* 'given' or theme). We can extend this consistency of Merge position to the IO as well if we assume that V_1 assigns a theta role to both objects.

If Merged directly as the complement of VP, the IO will get a theta role from V_1 rather than the higher V_2 head. In order to precede the DO, however, it must Remerge with the higher verbal head V_2, resulting in the configuration in (22). This structure represents an amendment of what we proposed for ditransitives in (18): specifically, the IO Moves to a specifier position in VP_2, rather than Merging in this position initially.

(22)

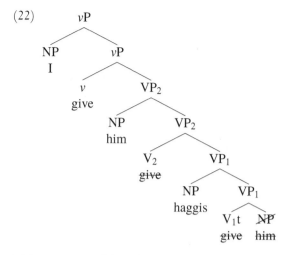

This Remerge of the IO in a position above the DO can be explained as resulting from a Case assignment requirement. Modern English is a morphologically impoverished language. Among other types of inflection that English lacks, **case**, which marks the grammatical function of nouns within a sentence, is typically not overt. Roles such as subject and object are instead indicated by word order. The sentences in (23) do not have the same meaning: the element preceding the verb is the subject, and therefore the 'biter'; the element following the verb is the object, and therefore the 'bitee'.

(23) a. The dog bit the man
      b. The man bit the dog

We do see overt case marking on English pronouns. In (24) the subject must have **Nominative** case, and the object **Accusative** case.[3]

(24) a. He saw her
      b. *Him saw her
      c. *He saw she

Since English has relatively strict SVO word order, case seems to be assigned to pronouns in specific positions. Like the assignment of theta roles, then, case assignment seems to be a property of particular projections. A given pronoun must therefore be in a Case position to be assigned case. Without case it cannot be sent to Spell Out, as there will be no instructions at PF regarding which form of the pronoun to use.

---

[3] There are interesting exceptions to this case marking for compound subjects, e.g. *Him and I went out*, which will be addressed in Chapter 8.

Case is not pronounced on non-pronominal NPs, but we will assume that they are nevertheless assigned abstract **Case**, which is equivalent to the case on pronouns in all but phonological realisation. This notion of abstract Case (capitalised to distinguish it from overt morphological case) is predicated on a broader idea of maximal consistency in the treatment of constituents of the same type. Given that pronouns and non-pronominal NPs are in most instances (and certainly in the current context) interchangeable, we would expect them not to differ in terms of fundamental properties such as Case assignment. For instance, each of the pronouns in (24) can be replaced with another noun (or NP) with no effect on the syntax of the sentence.

(25) a. The little boy saw her
      b. He saw the dog
      c. The little boy saw the dog

Although it may seem counterintuitive to have 'silent' morphology, in terms of interaction with the syntax this is the simplest explanation, and thus most fitting with a Minimalist approach.

Lest readers find the idea of abstract Case morphology unconvincing, it should be noted that there are other instances of unpronounced inflection in English. For example, so-called zero morpheme plurals such as *sheep* lack the typical plural -*s* inflection, yet behave syntactically and semantically as plural: they must therefore be plural at some abstract level of mental representation, even though they have no overt plural morpheme.

(26) a. The sheep {was/were} in the barn
      b. Two sheep {*was/were} in the barn

Likewise, English present tense is unmarked morphologically in all but third person singular, but is still understood as present regardless of overt morphology (e.g. *I go* and *you go* versus *he goes*).

Alternatively, we can reframe the requirement that NPs be assigned Case as one that they be in a 'Case position'. This approach makes no commitment to the presence of unpronounced morphology (but see the discussion of features in Chapter 4).

NPs are subject to a **Visibility Condition**, which requires that an argument has Case, or be in a Case position, in order to be 'visible' for assignment of a theta role. We can see this Condition as a sort of entrance requirement: if you are matriculating at a university, for instance, you cannot sign up for individual classes until you have fully registered as a student. You might be able to make some initial choices, but if you have not paid your tuition and picked up your ID card you will not be able to have those selections confirmed, because you will not be visible to the university's systems as a student.

This Visibility Condition applies not just to individual instances of an NP, but to **chains**, which are formed by Merge and Remerge of a constituent. It may therefore be satisfied when the NP is assigned a theta role in a non-Case position, as long as the NP is Merged in a Case position at some point in the derivation. We will see below what one of these chains looks like.

Returning to our verbal structure, VP_1 does not appear to be a Case assigner, as it only allows an indirect object as a complement if that IO is assigned Case by a preposition.

(27) 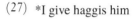 *I give haggis him   I give haggis to him

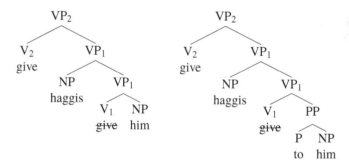

We have already suggested that, in the absence of a preposition, an indirect object Remerges in the specifier of VP_2. Taking the specifier of V_2 to be a Case position, we then have a principled way to relate our ditransitive and double object structures. If the IO is assigned Case by a preposition within a PP selected by V_1, it will appear after the direct object in the specifier of VP_1; if it is selected directly by V_1, which is not a Case assigner, as a complement, it will Move to the specifier of VP_2, which is a Case position.

The DO does not appear to undergo a similar Movement, indicating that the specifier of VP_1 is also a Case position. But if V_1 cannot assign Case to an indirect object in its complement, it would be unexpected for it to assign Case to a direct object in its specifier, as it Merges with the IO first, and there would be no reason for it to delay application of Case assignment. However, if V_2 is the locus of Case assignment, then it can assign Case to the DO that is in the specifier position of VP_1 by virtue of their close c-command relationship. The specifier of VP_1 is therefore a Case position because VP_1 is a complement of the Case assigner V_2.

Because of its special role in relation to objects, this VP$_2$ projection can be relabelled AgrO, short for Object Agreement.

Let us now give a derivation for double object constructions, as well as review our derivation for ditransitive constructions. A verb such as *give* can select a PP complement or NP. If it selects a PP the IO within the PP receives its Case from P. The theta role (here 'givee') is also discharged in the process of this selection. If it selects an NP, the IO receives a theta role from V, but no Case.

(28)

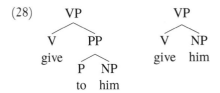

The direct object then Merges in the specifier of VP, where it also receives a theta role from V.

(29)

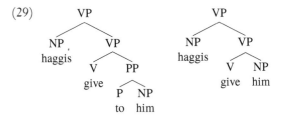

VP is then selected by AgrO, which assigns Case to the DO in the specifier of VP.

(30)

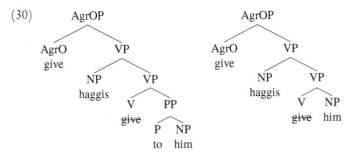

At this point the derivations diverge. If the indirect object does not already have Case from a preposition, it Remerges in the specifier of AgrOP.

(31)

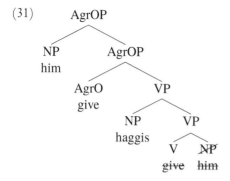

In both instances AgrOP is then selected by *v*.

(32)

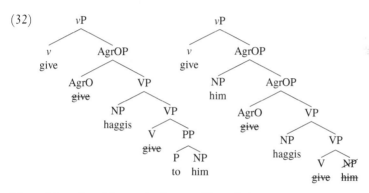

The subject then Merges in the specifier of *v*P.

(33)

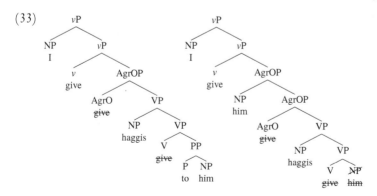

These parallel derivations leave us with two outstanding questions. First, what makes the specifier of AgrOP a Case position? In terms of consistency alone, we might argue that *v* assigns Case to an object in the specifier of AgrOP in the same configuration as AgrO assigns Case to an object in the specifier of VP.

(34)

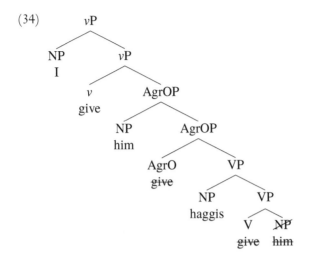

We will revisit this question in §3.2.

Second, can we have a Case position in which there is no NP? This occurs in our derivation for the double object construction when the IO does not Move to the specifier of AgrOP. We would also have to assume that it occurs when there is no IO.

Transitive verbs, those taking a single object, may also be represented using our split VP structure. Again, the DO will be Merged in the specifier of VP, where it assigned a theta role by V. Because *v* can assign Case to an NP in the specifier of its complement, we could argue that for these Verbs VP is selected directly by *v*.

(35)

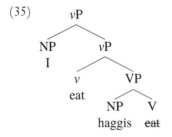

Transitive verbs would otherwise have a structure with a seemingly vacuous AgrO projection.

(36) ??

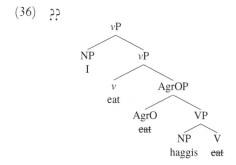

For straightforward transitive verbs this additional structure thus appears to be unnecessary, but we will see in §3.3 that it may be required to account for other, more complex types of transitives. Recall from the examples in (11) that certain ditransitive verbs may also be monotransitive, excluding the IO. This alternation follows from the proposed structure: monotransitive verbs differ only from double object verbs according to whether V selects for a complement. It is notable that, in contrast to omission of an indirect object, omission of a direct object is typically ungrammatical.[4]

(37) a. I brought him *(haggis)
   b. I threw her *(a ball)
   c. I made him *(a haggis)

There are instances in which a DO can be left out, but these are likely to be highly idiomatic. The example (38)a can only have an interpretation in which the thing written is some sort of correspondence; it cannot be interpreted as meaning that the writer has authored an essay or a book for the recipient. The example (38)b can only have an interpretation in which the subject is a teacher in some capacity, rather than one in which she happens to teach things to children every once in a while.

(38) a. %Billy wrote me
      (cf. He wrote me a letter)
   b. Martha teaches children
      (cf. Martha teaches children reading)

---

[4] Where an asterisk is inside the parentheses around a word or string it means that inclusion of that element is ungrammatical. Where an asterisk is outside of the parentheses, as it is for these examples, it means that it is ungrammatical for the word(s) within to be omitted. In fact the strings without the direct objects would be grammatical here, but only if the indirect object is reinterpreted as a direct object.

The fixed meaning of examples of this type suggests that the direct object is not structurally absent, but rather can be elided because it is understood, in the same way a speaker may state *I will* in response to a request, leaving out the main verb because it has already been established.

In §3.2 we will see how our split VP structure applies for instransitive verbs.

3.1.3 Variation in theta role assignment again

The classic American novel *Huckleberry Finn* features a number of examples of the verb *learn* used to mean *teach*:

(39) a. 'Why, she tried to learn you your book, she tried to learn you your manners'
      b. 'This is the speech— I learned$_{(1)}$ it easy enough, while he was learning$_{(2)}$ it to the king.'

The examples in (39) give us three versions of *learn*. In its transitive (and Standard) use, as in (39)b$_{(1)}$, it is followed by a single NP direct object (*it*). In its ditransitive use in (39)a it is followed by an NP indirect object and an NP direct object (*you* and *your book/manners*, respectively). And in its double object use, as (39)b$_{(2)}$, it is followed by an NP direct object (*it*) and a PP headed by *to* which contains an indirect object NP (*the king*).

The Non-Standard use of *learn* is a shibboleth for some prescriptive grammarians, but there are Standard forms of verbs that essentially act as antonyms to themselves. For instance, *rent* is something one does as both owner and occupier. In the first instance it is a ditransitive or double object verb (e.g. *I rented him my flat*), while in the second it is a transitive verb with a single object (e.g. *He rented my flat*). As we said in Chapter 1, the syntax is unconcerned with what sounds correspond to which lexical item, even if in certain instances the result is homophony of words representing opposite ends of a single process.

Many verbs belong to more than one subcategory. The prototypical example is *eat*, which can be **intransitive**, as in (10)a, or select for a direct object complement, as in (10)b.

(40) a. When he arrived, I was eating (intransitive)
      b. When he arrived, I was eating haggis (transitive)

Like *suit* in Chapter 2, then, *learn* alternates which theta roles it assigns to which arguments. It differs from *suit* in that this fluctuation occurs within a single variety, rather than changing depending on which variety is being spoken. In the next section we will further explore the impact the split VP has on our view of verbs that do not take multiple objects.

3.2 Transitive and intransitive verbs

As noted above, verbs such as *eat* are optionally transitive: they may have one object, or none at all. Intransitive verbs, as well as those that alternate between intransitivity and (mono-)transitivity, exhibit a number of disparate behaviours, depending on the lexical item in question.

While *eat* is agentive, and would therefore be assumed to have a *v* projection, there are a number of intransitive verbs that do not seem to assign external theta roles to their subjects. A simple test for these special intransitives is to use them with the adverb (*un*)*intentionally*; those verbs that do not work are so-called **unaccusatives**.

(41) */#He intentionally {arrived/disappeared/departed}[5]

In contrast, intransitive **unergative** verbs do have agentive subjects.

(42) He intentionally {jumped/clapped/quit}

Unergatives can sometimes have **cognate complements**, NP objects that share the root of the otherwise intransitive verb, whereas unaccusatives generally cannot.

(43) a. Nancy smiled a lovely smile
     b. *Charlie arrived a sudden arrival

A certain class of unaccusative verbs may also be transitive. This unaccusative-transitive alternation differs from that seen with *eat*, which simply takes an object or not, because the subject of the intransitive form corresponds to the object of the transitive form.

(44) a. Alec cooks haggis
     b. Haggis cooks (in a pot)

As we saw in §3.1, *v* appears to assign an agent/cause theta role to an external argument in its specifier. In instances such as (44)b the subject is not an agent/cause (the haggis does not cook itself). The lack of this type of theta role is explained if the causative head *v* is absent from our

---

[5] Use of *intentionally* with these verbs becomes grammatical if they are followed by some other adjunct, e.g. *He intentionally arrived late*, but in this instance the intentionality appears to apply to the other adjunct rather than the verb itself. We will return to such constructions in Chapter 9.

split VP structure. Moreover, there appears to be no function for AgrOP here either, as the would-be DO is not assigned Accusative Case but as a subject must have other Case properties (we will discuss in Chapter 4 where Case for subjects is assigned). Unaccusative verbs may therefore be argued to consist of only a VP.

(45)

```
        VP
       /  \
     NP    V
    haggis cooks
```

Comparing the structure in (45) to the transitive alternative, we can see that the unaccusative form is in effect the transitive form with *v*P (and AgrOP) stripped away.

(46)

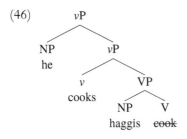

```
          vP
         /  \
       NP    vP
       he    /  \
            v    VP
          cooks  /  \
               NP    V
             haggis  cook
```

The unaccusative-transitive alternation is in some respects like that between active verbs, in which an agent is the subject, and passive verbs, in which a theme or patient is the subject, and the agent/cause appears in a *by*-PP or is omitted altogether.

(47) a. I bought a haggis (active)
b. The haggis was bought (by me) (passive)

We can again explain this configuration, involving demotion/exclusion of an external argument, as resulting from the absence of the causative *v*P projection. This explanation does not account for the auxiliary *be*, which appears between the subject and passive participle form of the verb. We will return to the question of passives in Chapter 4.

3.3 Back to *give back*

Having established a structure for our split VP, we can now return to consideration of our original examples. Our first question concerns the syntactic identity of the particle *back*. It clearly bears some relationship to the verb, as it cannot be replaced by another particle without a change or breakdown in meaning, e.g. *I gave him it out.* It also does not form a Prepositional Phrase with either of the objects (as evidenced by mutability of word order) but at the same time does not obviously form a constituent with the *v* head in which the verb is pronounced, given that they can be separated by other constituents. As noted in the introduction to this chapter, particles such as *back* in *give back* must follow any pronominal objects. It is also possible for a particle of this type to appear between an indirect and direct object in a ditransitive construction if they are both full, non-pronominal NPs.

(48) a. I gave the boy the book back
      b. I gave the boy back the book
      c. ??I gave back the boy the book

These variants can be accounted for if the particle is a manifestation of one of the projections of the split VP. There is evidence, in fact, that particles make a particular semantic contribution by indicating an endpoint. Verbs which have a specified endpoint are said to be **telic**.

(49) a. Julian was eating the haggis
      b. Julian was eating the haggis up

While the propositions captured in (49) both involve consumption of the haggis, only (49)b, with the particle *up*, indicates that the haggis is being completely consumed. This outcome is also a possibility in (49)a, but it is not established in the sentence without the particle.

We can therefore assume that *give back* is a single lexical item which, unlike its counterpart *give*, is marked as having the property of telicity. This is not to say that *give* on its own is **atelic**, but that the endpoint is not determined by the verb itself. Given that the heads of our split VP represent different properties of the verb, one or more of them can be assumed to encode telicity.

Before we tackle ditransitive particle verbs, let us start with monotransitive ones. As we said before, a full NP can either precede or follow the particle, but a pronoun must precede it.

(50) a. The boy ate up the haggis
      b. The boy ate the haggis up
      c. *The boy ate up it
      d. The boy ate it up

From what we have proposed so far, there are two potential sources of this variation. The first one is the head in which the particle is realised. If it is pronounced in the V position it will follow a DO in the specifier of VP; if it is pronounced in the AgrO position it will precede a DO in this position.[6]

(51)

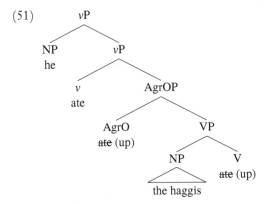

The other potential source of variation is the position of the object. We have suggested that AgrO need not be present in monotransitive verbal configurations, but if we allow this additional projection as we have in (51), at least for particle verbs, there is the possibility of direct object Movement. If the DO remains in its original Merge position in the specifier of VP it will follow the particle, as above. If it Moves to the specifier of AgrOP, it will precede a particle in AgrO.

(52)

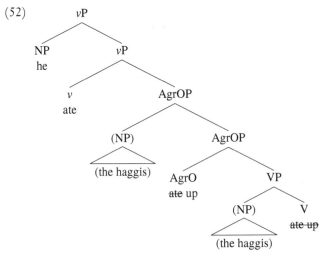

---

[6] A triangle is used in syntax trees to indicate that the structure of a particular constituent is not being shown. We will use triangles where the internal structure of a phrase is not relevant to our discussion, but you should avoid them as much as possible when practising drawing trees yourself.

Because any pronoun *must* precede a particle, this Movement appears to be a requirement for pronominal NPs. It remains possible that the particle itself could be instantiated in more than one verbal head, as in (51), but that analysis does not on its own rule out the ungrammatical instances of a particle preceding an object. We must therefore conclude that at least some NP objects Remerge in the specifier of AgrOP, and that for pronouns Remerge in this position is obligatory.

(53)

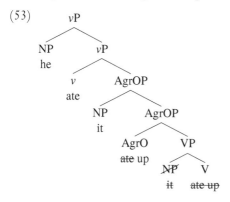

We can now consider the more complicated case of particle verbs with two objects. As with monotransitive verbs, a full NP may follow the particle, but any pronominal object must precede it.

(54) a. He gave the boy back the haggis
     b. He gave him back the haggis
     c. *He gave the boy back it
     d. He gave the boy it back
     e. *He gave him back it
     f. He gave him it back

These data indicate that both a pronominal DO and IO must Move over the particle in order to precede it if they are pronouns. In order to allow this Movement of both objects, we must permit them to successively Merge in the specifier of AgrOP.

(55)

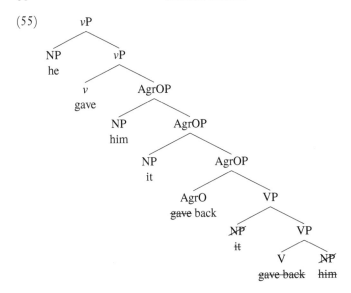

We have previously said that the IO Moves to the specifier of AgrOP for Case assignment. The hypothesis outlined here means that this cannot be the only reason for an object, particularly a pronoun, to Move to this position. There would otherwise be no reason for an object Merged in the specifier of VP, which is also a Case position, to Remerge in the specifier of AgrOP.

This question about reasons for Movement of the pronoun points to a broader one about the relationship between ditransitive and double object constructions. We have been able to relate them syntactically, but are they semantically identical? We could argue, in fact, that although the two forms encapsulate identical propositions, they differ in terms of **information structure**. According to this view of how information is packaged, an entity can be a **topic**, old, known information, or it can be **focused** if it is new information. This distinction is apparent in terms of how one might answer particular questions.

(56) Q: What happened to the book?
      A1: I gave the book to Alec
      A2: I gave Alec the book

Both answers in (57) are grammatical, but A1 is perhaps more acceptable, because it foregrounds the new information that Alec was the recipient of the book. *The book* is a topic, already mentioned in the question. The contrast becomes even more prominent if this topic is replaced by a pronoun.

(57) Q: What happened to the book?
    A1: I gave it to Alec
    A2: I gave Alec it

Pronouns are intrinsically topical, in that they refer to entities previously mentioned in the discourse, and therefore must be known to the interlocuters. We can thus view the specifier of AgrOP as not only a Case position, but a topical one.

For ditransitive verbs we now have two properties that can be discharged to NPs in the specifier of AgrOP: we will call these [+CASE] (for Accusative Case), and [+TOPIC]. A pronoun in the specifier of V may be **Attracted** to Remerge in the specifier of AgrOP, as the closest NP able to satisfy its [+TOPIC] property; however, because the DO has already been assigned Accusative Case in its original Merge position, this 'Movement' does not allow the [+CASE] property to be discharged. The IO object (pronoun or not) can therefore subsequently also Remerge with AgrOP, receiving the [+CASE] property. If it is a pronoun, its requirement for the [+TOPIC] property will also be satisfied by this Remerge (in other words, the [+TOPIC] property may be discharged multiple times).

In terms of conceiving of the specifier of AgrOP as a [+TOPIC] position, it is notable that a pronoun can follow a particle if it is stressed phonologically. This emphasis on pronunciation is an indicator of focus, overriding the inherent topicality of the pronoun. For instance, in (58) *me* is new information in response to the previous discourse.

(58) Q: Did he phone Julian up?
    A: No, he phoned up ME

3.3.1 Give it you back

We now have a hypothesis regarding the structure of a variety of verb types with and without particles. What, then, to make of our Northern English DO-IO ditransitive? It is tempting to argue that this is an instance of phonological ellipsis and that these are actually identical to double object constructions, with the *to* preposition left unpronounced.

(59) I'll give it ~~to~~ you

Many Northern English speakers elide *to* in other contexts, suggesting this could be an across-the-board type of omission.

(60) %I'm going the shops

However, the presence of a particle makes this explanation problematic. Recall from (6), repeated in (61), that for Standard double object constructions the particle must appear between the pronominal direct object and the indirect object PP.

(61) a. I'll give it back to you
     b. *I'll give back it to you
     c. *I'll give it to you back

The Non-Standard ditransitive construction is also largely limited to pronominal NPs. Speakers who use this form find it decreasingly acceptable if one or both objects are a full NP.

(62) a. %I gave it him
     b. %?I gave it the boy
     c. %??I gave the book him
     d. %?*I gave the book the boy
        (cf. I gave the book to the boy)

The evidence from double object constructions with particles tells us that DO-IO order cannot simply result from non-pronunciation of a preposition. If this were so we would expect the grammaticality of this construction not to be sensitive to use of pronouns or full NPs.

It instead appears that the difference depends on the order in which the [+CASE] and [+TOPIC] properties are discharged by Merge to AgrOP. In Northern English varieties the [+CASE] property may be discharged first, bypassing the DO, which is already in a Case position, to Attract, or prompt Remerge of, the IO. As before, the [+TOPIC] property may still be discharged, such that the DO may Remerge to AgrOP after the IO in order to be assigned this property as well.

(63)

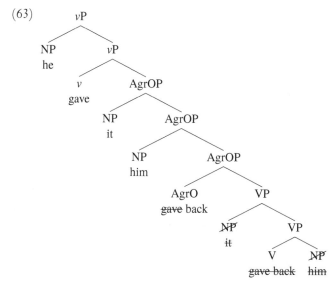

This construction is more acceptable with pronouns because pronouns require Merge in a position where they can receive the [+TOPIC] property. A topical full NP object may have this [+TOPIC] property, but does not require it. Therefore, if this property has already been discharged by Merge of an IO in AgrOP for Case reasons, it is less likely that [+TOPIC] will also be discharged by Merge of a full NP DO in AgrOP, since this property is not obligatory for full NPs.

These Northern English ditransitives give us a nice example of a minimal difference between varieties. In Standard English the [+TOPIC] property on AgrOP is discharged first. Because it is closer to this position that the IO, the DO will Remerge in AgrOP to satisfy this [+TOPIC] property if it is a pronoun or an emphasised full NP.[7] In Northern English the [+CASE] property is discharged first. It cannot be satisfied by the DO, which already has (Accusative) Case, and therefore it is the IO that Remerges with AgrOP initially. The difference therefore boils down to which property is discharged first, with this order encoded in the structure of ditransitive verbs for each variety.

For some speakers the order in which these properties must be discharged may also be freely ordered, allowing them both the Standard and Non-Standard constructions.

---

[7] In later chapters we will revisit this idea of 'closeness' and its implications for Movement/Remerge.

3.4 Conclusion

This chapter has introduced an expanded split VP and its consequences for ditransitive and double objects verbs, monotransitive and unaccusative verbs, and particle verbs. Each of these has been argued to represent a configuration of three possible verbal projections, vP, AgrOP and VP, along with Remerge of NPs to meet particular Case and/or information structure requirements. We have also seen how a single difference in the order in which particular properties must be discharged can result in a crossvarietal distinction in word order.

While the expansion of the VP accounts for a number of different constructions, it still does not allow space for multiple verbs, such as the passive auxiliary *be*. In the next chapter we will see that the use of auxiliaries necessitates further extension of the types of projections present in our clause structure, taking us beyond lexical verbs and the Verb Phrase.

3.5 Further reading

Further arguments regarding the asymmetry of the two objects in ditransitive constructions can be found in Barss and Lasnik (1986). Larson (1988) is another classic paper on this topic, and Hudson (1992) also tackles the differences between direct and indirect objects in ditransitives.

The introduction to Dehé et al. (2002) gives an overview of issues related to verb-particle configurations, with the other chapters in that volume providing a range of viewpoints on these constructions. McIntyre (2007) and Goldberg (2016) offer more analysis of verb-particle forms in English. Haddican and Johnson (2012) look at verb-particle constructions from a variationist perspective.

For discussion of DO-IO ditransitives see Haddican (2010) and Gerwin (2013). Gerwin (2014) provides a broader discussion of ditransitive constructions.

3.6 Exercises

1. Trees
   Based on the structures proposed in this chapter draw trees for the following sentences.
   a. The boy handed him the book
   b. I gave the other book to the other boy
   c. He dropped his donation off

   d. Hazel bought a slice of cake
   e. A rabbit appeared from the hat
   f. Jack drank up the coffee

2. Further analysis

   a. In this chapter the requirement that pronouns precede a particle has been explained by Remerge of direct and indirect object pronouns in the specifier of AgrOP. Does this analysis also account for all possible configurations of full NPs in relation to the particle?

   b. In the beginning of §3.3 we proposed that there was potential for the particle to be realised (pronounced) in more than one position. Is this source of variation with respect to the order of objects and particles necessary, or is Remerge of objects in AgrOP sufficient?

   c. In our analysis, both objects can Merge as specifiers of AgrOP. As an alternative, we could split AgrO into two heads, one for direct and one for indirect objects, as in the tree below. How does this new structure potentially affect our analysis? What are potential advantages or disadvantages to this further expanded structure?

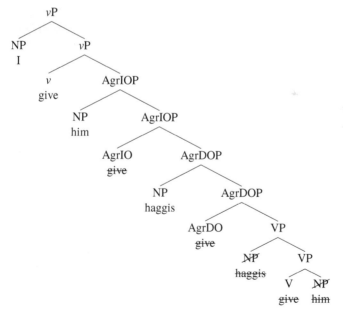

For Answers see edinburghuniversitypress.com/englishsyntax.

4 Auxiliary verbs and functional structure

Use of constructions such as (1) has been noted in disparate localities, from the southern United States to many parts of Scotland (a Scottish colleague of mine confirms that these are grammatical for him).

(1)   I might could do that

For non-users this co-occurrence of **modal** verbs provokes everything from confusion to outrage (one blog I found describes it as 'bad grammar and redundant'). Yet even though this particular configuration is unheard of in many localities, use of more than one verb together is a characteristic of all varieties of English. Modal verbs always co-occur with non-modals because a modal on its own cannot function independently as a main verb. Utterances such as (2)c are only possible for discourse contexts in which there is **ellipsis**, phonological omission of a VP that can be understood from context, as in answer to the question *Will you do that?*

(2)   I might *(do that)

It is therefore necessary that our Minimalist approach accommodates **functional verbs** in multi-verb configurations, regardless of the acceptability of **multiple modal constructions**. Having split our Verb Phrase in Chapter 3 we must now look to structure outside the core verbal domain in order to account for the entirety of the clause. This chapter will begin by revisiting passives, giving consideration to the status of the *be* verb in these constructions, as well as the alternative *get*. This discussion will lead to examination of other **auxiliary** verbs, and how these fit into an expanded syntactic architecture.

4.1 Passive auxiliaries

Recall that a passive construction consists of a form of *be* followed by a participle form of the verb.

(3)   The haggis was eaten (by the boy)

In Chapter 3 we proposed that the verb itself was lacking a *v*P projection, thus rendering it unable to assign an external theta role to an agent/cause subject, which is then demoted to inclusion in a PP adjunct, or deleted altogether. The passive is marked not just by morphology on the verb, but also through the auxiliary *be*. This additional verb distinguishes passives from **perfect** constructions, which have the same participle forms, but the auxiliary *have*.

(4)   The boy has eaten the haggis.

The alternation between *have* and *be* is presumably a selectional one: *have* selects for *v*P, but *be* selects for a VP projection. While passive and perfect participles are thus identical on a superficial phonological level, they represent distinct structures. The auxiliary *be* does not select for 'intrinsically passive' unaccusative verbs in English, although historically it did. Some varieties continue to use *be* as an auxiliary with perfect participles.

(5)   a.   %He is arrived (at five o'clock)
      b.   %He is left school early

The form of the participle is also identical regardless of tense, which is marked only on the auxiliary verb.

(6)   a.   The children {are/were} given haggis regularly
      b.   The boy {has/had} eaten haggis

Passive or perfect auxiliary participles are sometimes referred to as *-en* forms, reflecting the morphology on e.g. *written, taken, shaken*, etc. There are also a number of verbs which have **syncretism**, identical surface morphology representing different morphosyntactic properties, for these participles and their **preterite** (past tense) forms. Instances where these *-ed* participles (e.g. *dined, offered, wobbled*) occur with an auxiliary verb do not represent marking of tense in two places. It is rather a quirk of English morphology that the *-en* form for these verbs happens to end in *-ed*. As discussed in previous chapters, the phonological realisation of constituent does not influence syntactic processing, so similarity in form should not be taken as an automatic indication of the representation of the same (morpho)syntactic properties.

(7)   a.   The boy offered me haggis [preterite]
      b.   The boy has offered me haggis [past perfect]
      c.   The boy was offered haggis [passive]

Like the main verb, tense is essential to the clause. It is impossible to have verbless clauses, and **non-finite** clauses, or those that do not have tense marked, cannot stand on their own. The sentence in (8)a contains a passive participle within a relative clause (*written*), but tense is marked on the main verb (*appeared*). While the string in (8)b is largely comprehensible, the lack of tense makes it ungrammatical as an independent clause. An auxiliary verb would be required to provide tense marking here, as in (8)c, where *was* is finite.

(8) a. His note, written in haste, appeared illegible
     b. *His note, written in haste
     c. His note was written in haste

As we have already seen, auxiliary verbs such as *be* and *have* do not have the same selectional properties as main verbs, selecting for participle forms rather than NPs or PPs. This difference in behaviour suggests that auxiliaries are syntactically distinct from other verbs, manifestations of tense rather than verbal projections.

Even in the absence of an auxiliary, we can tease apart a verb and its tense using our constituency tests. In (9)a the *v*P can be fronted, with *has* remaining in situ, while in (9)b fronting requires the addition of *did*.

(9) a. Alastair has eaten haggis
         → Eaten haggis, Alastair has
     b. Alastair ate haggis
         → Eat haggis, Alastair *(did)

Just as the auxiliary *have* shows tense being left behind by the *v*P, the auxiliary *did* inserted in (9)b represents a separation of tense from the verb.

Thus, although tense and a main verb are often encompassed in a single word, they are syntactically distinct. We can model this separation through the expansion of our syntactic structure to incorporate a T(ense) projection.[1]

(10)

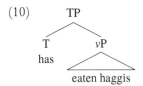

---

[1] Depending on the approach this is sometimes instead labelled I for Inflection, to reflect that it encompasses facets such as subject-verb agreement as well.

In sentences with an auxiliary, tense will be realised on the auxiliary in T. If an auxiliary is absent, tense will be instantiated on the main verb. The introduction of a T head leaves us with a discrepancy between the syntactic position of Tense independent of the verb and the pronunciation of tense morphology on the verb. For the moment we will say that the determination of where tense is pronounced is a post-syntactic operation. When a main verb selected by a T head with a particular value is sent to PF it will be realised with the corresponding morphology. The structure for a clause without an auxiliary will therefore look like (11), with a tense value rather than a word in the T position.

(11)

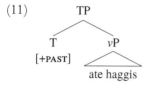

Tense in Standard English must be marked in finite clauses.

As a consequence, in sentences such as (9)b where the T head is not proximate to a verb or auxiliary an auxiliary *do* is inserted at PF to ensure that Tense is represented overtly. In later sections we will consider in more detail the syntactic factors that contribute to the way Tense is realised. We will also revisit auxiliary *do* in Chapter 5.

4.2 Whither the subject?

In introducing auxiliary verbs in T we are now faced with a logistical problem. If subjects are Merged within the split VP in the specifier of *v*P we would expect English to have auxiliary-initial sentences. English in fact always has SVO word order in declarative sentences. Auxiliaries can precede subjects, but only in questions.

(12) *Has Alastair eaten haggis

There must be a way, then, of the subject getting from its initial Merge position in a VP or *v*P to its position preceding an auxiliary verb. This outcome is achieved by **Movement**, displacement of a constituent to another part of the structure.

We have already seen Movement of objects from within the VP, where they are assigned a theta role, to the specifier of AgrOP, where they are assigned Case. In the previous chapter this Movement was characterised as sequential Merge and Remerge of a single lexical item in order to meet certain requirements (assignment of theta roles and Case) that can only be met at certain points in the derivation, specifically at particular positions of Merge. In this view 'Movement' is a misleading term, given that the Remerged constituent does not vacate any position in which it has previously Merged, but it may well be phonologically absent from all but its highest Merge position. The multiple instances of a Moved constituent form a chain. We will continue to employ the term Movement, which is prevalent in the syntactic literature, but with the understanding that it refers to a process of Remerge.

Like objects, then, the subject may Move from the position where it is initially Merged (or **base generated**), the specifier of *v*P (or VP), to a higher position in the structure, the specifier of TP, resulting in a structure such as (13).

(13)

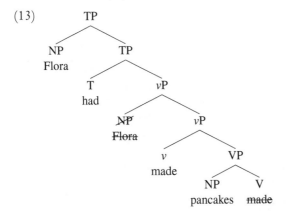

Why is the subject not simply Merged in TP in the first place? Recall that it is assigned a theta role in its initial Merge position within the *v*P. For this theta role assignment to happen the subject must be in a **local** relationship with the theta role assigner *v*.

Locality is the notion that syntactic operations cannot apply across arbitrarily long distances. What is defined as local depends on the type of constituent and/or syntactic operation involved. In the present context the local **domain** for theta role assignment is the phrase projected by the theta role assigner, the *v*P. To receive a theta role from the *v* head an NP argument must be Merged with *v* or some entity with the properties of *v*, because *v* cannot assign a theta role to an NP outside its maximal projection. Being the head of the phrase is in this sense a bit like sitting in a closed room: you can see and manipulate things in the room, but not anything outside.

Were the subject to Merge with T(P) directly, it would be too distant from *v* to be assigned a theta role, resulting in a violation of the **theta-criterion**. This criterion states that every argument must be assigned one and only one theta role; in structural terms it means that at some point in the derivation an NP must Merge in a theta-position, and once it has done so it may not Remerge in another theta-position.

Recall also our Visibility Condition, which specifies that an NP will be invisible for theta role assignment if it is not at some point Merged in a Case position. The subject therefore Moves to the specifier of TP, where Nominative Case is assigned. This Remerge of the subject in TP establishes another local relationship between the subject and the Case assigner. Again, T cannot assign Nominative Case to an NP at a distance. In our closed room analogy, this amounts to a person in one room (the head of the TP) reaching into a window of another room (the *v*P) to Move something (the NP) into their own room (the TP) in order to manipulate that thing.

Up to this point we have referred to lexical items having particular 'properties' which define their syntactic behaviour and relationship to each other. We can model many of these properties in terms of **features** that encode the requirements of a given lexical item. Features come in (at least) two flavours. **Uninterpretable** features are those that apply only in the syntax and cannot be processed post-syntactically, at the phonological level (PF) or the semantic level (LF). If an uninterpretable feature is present when the syntax is **Spelled Out**, the syntactic derivation will **crash**, failing to produce a grammatical utterance. The presence of uninterpretable features on lexical items can be resolved in the syntax by matching them with **interpretable** features, ones that *can* be interpreted post-syntactically. This matching, or **checking**, eliminates the uninterpretable features, so that they will no longer be active in the derivation when it goes to Spell Out. Once all uninterpretable features have been checked by interpretable ones, the derivation can proceed to PF and LF without crashing.

We can frame the Movement of our subject in terms of features of T and the subject NP. T has an uninterpretable Case feature: it can assign Case, but Case cannot be expressed on the T head itself. Case is determined by the functional structure of the verb, but it is not a verbal property. Instead, Case is expressed on NPs, even if not always overtly. The interpretable feature on the NP subject can therefore check the uninterpretable feature on T by Merging as part of the TP.

This need for feature-checking **motivates** the Movement of the NP to a position within the TP, thereby satisfying both of their requirements by putting them in a local configuration where the [uCASE] feature on T can be matched with the [iCASE] feature on the subject.

The Movement within the split VP that we saw in Chapter 3 has a similar motivation: an object NP with an interpretable Case feature will Remerge in AgrOP to check an uninterpretable Case feature. They differ in that the [*u*CASE] feature in TP is valued [+NOM], but [*u*CASE] features elsewhere are valued [+ACC].

In light of this feature-checking approach and the introduction of auxiliary verbs, let us revisit how we might derive a sentence such as (14).

(14) Flora had made pancakes

The initial derivation precedes as before: the object NP *pancakes* Merges with V *made*, receiving a theme theta role. We will mark the NP as having an interpretable Case feature [*i*CASE].

(15)

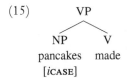

The VP formed by this Merge operation is then Merged with *v*, to form a *v*P. This *v* is another instantiation of the verb *made*, which will ultimately be pronounced in this *v* head position. The *v* head has an uninterpretable Case feature which can be checked immediately by the interpretable one on the NP *pancakes* in the specifier of VP. While they are not in the same phrase, this is a close enough configuration to allow this feature-checking (in our analogy, the VP is a smaller room or cupboard inside the *v*P room, with the NP in its specifier like something easily accessed sitting immediately in its doorway).

(16)

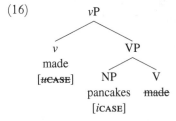

The subject NP *Flora* then Merges with the *v*P, where it receives its agent theta role. This NP also has an interpretable Case feature, but it does not check the uninterpretable Case feature on *v*, because it has already been checked with the one on the object NP.

(17)

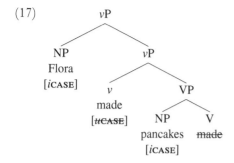

The auxiliary verb *had*, in T, then Merges with this *v*P to form a TP. As well as marking past tense (which is expressed on the auxiliary verb *had*), T has an uninterpretable Case feature. Unlike *v*P, it cannot immediately check this uninterpretable feature with the NP in the specifier of the phrase with which it has Merged, for reasons that will become clear in §4.4.

(18)

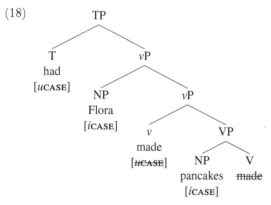

At this point T must find an NP to check its uninterpretable Case feature; if it does not the derivation will crash at Spell Out. It does this by looking down the tree to previous parts of the derivation to find the closest element with a matching interpretable feature, in this instance the NP *Flora*. This NP then Remerges with the TP so that its uninterpretable Case feature can be checked in a local configuration. The process by which one element causes another to Move in this way in order to check its features is called Attract.

(19)

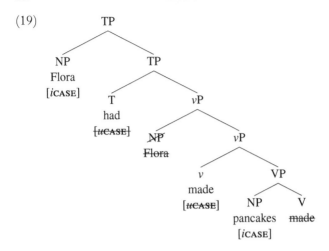

Our feature-based model accounts for why elements with a variety of theta roles can act as subjects or, in other words, why syntactic and semantic functions do not consistently align. In typical active sentences the subject receives its theta role when it Merges initially within the *v*P. As we have noted previously, this projection appears to s-select for an agentive/causative external argument. The subject then Remerges within TP in order to be assigned Nominative Case.

Objects are also assigned a theta role at their initial point of Merge. The assignment of theta roles to NPs in their position of base generation is crucial to (semantic) selection. Where this initial Merge position is not a Case position, as with Indirect Objects Merged with V rather than the Preposition *to/for*, they may then Move to the specifier of AgrOP, where they will ultimately be assigned Accusative Case by checking the [*u*CASE] feature on *v*.

It appears that verbs which do not assign an agent theta role, either because they are passive or unaccusative, also do not assign Accusative Case, as evidenced by Movement of NP that would otherwise be an object to Merge in TP. This connection has led to the proposal that *v* determines both of these properties. We can maintain this theory even though we have said that AgrOP sometimes also assigns Accusative Case on the basis that it can only occur in conjunction with *v*P. As a result, if *v*P is not present, then an NP cannot receive Accusative Case, and must Move to TP for Case assignment, as in the passive sentence illustrated in (20).

(20)

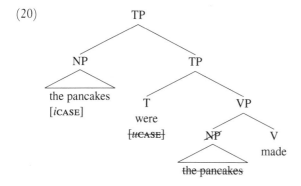

If *v*P or AgrOP is present an object NP checks the uninterpretable Case feature on these projections, and does not undergo Movement to TP; a subject in *v*P will Move to this position instead, as seen in the active sentence (19). Expanding on our discussion in Chapter 3 we can illustrate a similar difference between unaccusatives and their transitive counterparts. As we said before, this difference amounts structurally to the presence/absence of the causative head *v*. Here we have the addition of a TP.

(21)

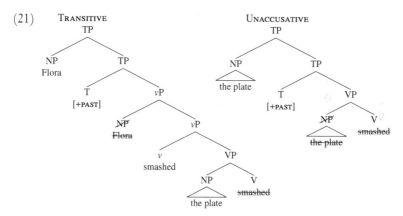

The connection between assigning an external theta role and assigning Accusative Case is known as the **Unaccusative Hypothesis**.

4.2.1 Evidence for subject Movement

At this stage we have a proposal for subject Movement based on theoretical considerations. A subject Merges in two positions because it has a dual function, as an argument of the verb and subject of the sentence. The initial Merge position puts the subject in a local relationship with some verbal projection for theta role assignment, with subsequent Merge putting it in a local relationship with T for Nominative Case assignment. This hypothesis solves our word order problem, but remains abstract. Explicit evidence for Movement of the subject can be seen in the behaviour of **floating quantifiers** such as *all* and *each* that modify NPs. These particular quantifiers can appear adjacent to the NPs they modify, but may also show up in another part of the sentence.

(22) a. All the children have eaten haggis
     b. The children have all eaten haggis

The separation of the quantifier and the NP, in this instance *all* and *the children*, can be explained if they initially form a single constituent *all the children*. Fitting the **VP-internal Subject Hypothesis** we have just outlined, this constituent is Merged directly before the verb, in the specifier of *v*P, but then Moves to the subject position. The associated quantifier is not subject to the same restrictions as a Moved NP, and may be pronounced at any point where it has been Merged. As a result, some quantifiers may be 'left behind' or **stranded**, so that they are instantiated separately from their corresponding NPs at PF. Floating quantifiers therefore can mark the initial position of Merge for the subject, indicating that it has at some point in the derivation been lower down than its final position in the specifier of TP.

4.2.2 What happened to traces?

Displacements of the type we have been discussing historically fell under **Move Alpha**, a rule which broadly stated that a syntactic constituent could be Moved anywhere at any point in the derivation. In Minimalism, Movement is not an independent operation applied to an existing **D(eep)-Structure**, but must be motivated by feature-checking, proceeding as part of a step-by-step derivation.

Traces, represented as *t*, were used in previous approaches to indicate that an element previously occupied a position in the syntactic structure. From a Minimalist viewpoint the insertion of a trace as a placeholder is superfluous. Instead of viewing a Moved constituent as having vacated its original point of Merge, we can argue that it has simply Merged again elsewhere. Rather than having a trace in the element's original position, we have a scored out instantiation of the element itself. That it is not pronounced probably comes down to a rule of PF (which may be as simple as 'pronounce the first instance of a constituent'). In essence, the original instantiation of the element functions as its own trace, so no additional indicator is needed.

4.3 Get-passives

Although *be* is the typical auxiliary for passive verbs, many English speakers can also produce passives with *get*, which are often viewed as more informal than *be*-passives.

(23) The haggis got eaten

The verb *get* has undergone an evolution in meaning which underpins this usage. Originally having the sense 'to obtain', it has shifted to mean 'to possess', as well as 'to become'. *Get* can be used in the latter sense with an adjectival complement, especially if the adjective is in a comparative form. Speakers of some varieties of English (including many in Scotland) can extend this usage to nominal complements as well.

(24) a. The little boy is getting big(ger)
      b. He's getting a big boy
          'He's becoming a big boy'

The *get* in the passive form could also be read as meaning 'become'. In this interpretation the passive participle may be analysed as an adjective describing a resultative state. Certainly such participles can be used adjectivally in other contexts.

(25) a. The fence got painted (blue)
      b. The painted (*blue) fence looked nice

In other respects participles in *get* passives behave differently from comparable *get* + adjective constructions. Note that the participle in a *get*-passive can have an additional object, not available when it is unambiguously adjectival, as in (25). Participles with the adjectival prefix *un*- are also ruled out for *get*-passives.[2]

(26) *The fence got unpainted

Like *be*-passives, *get*-passives can have an agent in a *by*-phrase, but *get* + adjective constructions cannot. *Get* + adjective constructions are not agentive at all, as evidenced by the use of these with inanimate (and therefore non-agentive) subjects.

(27) a. The fence got painted (by Alastair)
      b. The boy got happier (*by Alastair)

---

[2] Participles with verbal *un*-, as in *The parcel got unwrapped*, are fine. While something without paint can be *unpainted*, though, there is no verb *unpaint* representing a reversal of the painting process.

   c. The balloon got bigger (as I blew it up)
   d. The bag got heavier (as I filled it)

Agency is also not necessarily required for *get*-passives; again, they can be used with inanimate subjects (see (23)). At the same time, many speakers report that these have an agentive flavour. In (28)b there is more of a sense that it was Lucy's fault than in (28)a; likewise for (28)c and (28)d.

(28) a. Lucy was fired from her job
    b. Lucy got fired from her job
    c. My neighbour was arrested yesterday
    d. My neighbour got arrested yesterday

This sense of agency or causation comes into relief if we compare *get*-passives with corresponding causative constructions with *get*. These *get*-causatives superficially differ only in the addition of an object, but are unequivocally agentive.

(29) a. Lucy got {herself/her colleague} fired
    b. My neighbour got {himself/the postman} arrested

Here we again see the connection between agency (or causation) and the assignment of Accusative Case. An inanimate subject cannot be used in this construction with a DO, because the presence of the DO, and concomitant assignment of Case that this implies, means that the subject must be assigned an agent theta role.

(30) #The haggis got itself eaten

We could treat *get*-passives as structurally identical to *be*-passives, but this solution misses the apparent connection between causative and passive *get*. *Get* is also unlike the passive auxiliary *be* inasmuch as it does not precede negation or invert with the subject in questions.

(31) a. The haggis was not eaten
    b. *The haggis got not eaten
      (cf. The haggis did not get eaten)
    c. Was the haggis eaten?
    d. *Got the haggis eaten?
      (cf. Did the haggis get eaten?)

This evidence indicates that *get* is not an auxiliary verb, but its similarity to the passive *be* auxiliary, in terms of selection for a passive participle and interpretation, suggests that it is also not a full lexical verb.

We will instead argue that *get* is semi-lexical, acting as an instantiation of *v*. In causative constructions this *get v* behaves as we have seen elsewhere, assigning Accusative Case to an object in the specifier of the VP, and a theta role to the subject in the specifier of *vP*. In passives *get* is in the same position, but *v* is defective, no longer assigning an external theta role or Case. The presence of this head, however, means that *get*-passives retain a causative feeling not present in *be*-passives.

(32)

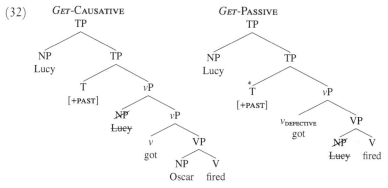

This analysis ties together *get*-passives and causatives, and is also consistent with the notion that *v* is the locus of agency/causativity for any verb.

4.4 Other auxiliaries

In §4.1 we saw that the passive auxiliary *be* and the perfect auxiliary *have* can be accounted for with the addition of a Tense projection. English auxiliary *be* can also select for a progressive *-ing* participle. This *be* is syntactically identical to other auxiliaries. It is marked for **tense**, which gives us information about a point in time, while the participle denotes **aspect**, information about the temporal structure of the event rather than when the event took place.

(33) The boy {is/was} eating haggis

In addition to *have* and *be* English has a set of modal verbs which express necessity, possibility, obligation or permission: *can, could, may, might, must, shall, should, will* and *would*.[3] Modals differ from other auxiliaries and the overall class of verbs in that they are morphologically defective. They cannot be marked for tense or co-occur with it.

---

[3] *Have to, dare* and *ought* are sometimes classed as 'semi-modals' because they have similar semantic characteristics, but not identical syntactic ones.

(34) a. He might like haggis
      b. *He mights like haggis
      c. *He might likes haggis[4]

In other respects modals behave similarly to other auxiliaries, selecting for **bare** (uninflected) forms of other auxiliaries or lexical verbs.
Based on the **complementary distribution** of modals and tense, the
limitation to either one or the other, we will posit that modal verbs are
in fact an alternative instantiation of the T head, occurring in place of
tense.

Unlike the auxiliaries *have* and *be*, modal verbs also lack non-finite
forms with *to*.

(35) a. He seems to have eaten already
      b. He seems to be eating now
      c. *He seems to might eat later

Taking *to* to represent the realisation of T for non-finite (untensed)
verbs, this difference again indicates that modal verbs are manifestations
of T itself.

At the moment our only functional projection outside the split VP is
T, but the possibility of having multiple auxiliaries means our picture
must be more complicated than this, literally and figuratively.

(36) The haggis might have been being eaten

As demonstrated in (36), we can string a number of auxiliaries together.
They always adhere to the same sequence.

(37) modal > *have*$_{\text{PERFECT}}$ > *be*$_{\text{PROGRESSIVE}}$ > *be*$_{\text{PASSIVE}}$

Tense is consistently realised on the highest auxiliary, giving us reason
to maintain a unique Tense head. We can accommodate the presence
of further auxiliaries with the introduction of an Aux category in our
structure, appearing between T and the main verb structure. Every
auxiliary projects separately, which can result in multiple AuxPs; each
of these has its own properties and has as the head of the phrase that is
its complement a participle that corresponds to its relevant aspect. For
the moment we will put modal verbs directly in T, although in the next
section we will consider whether they merit an additional, separate
functional projection.

---

[4] Sentences of this type are used to humourous effect in Internet memes, as in *I can
     haz cheeseburger*. Whether they will become grammatical beyond the realm of lolcats
     remains to be seen.

(38)

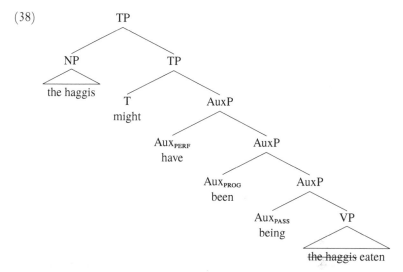

The introduction of these additional functional heads raises a tricky question about how their strict order is determined. There are several ways to address this problem, none of which is an entirely satisfactory explanation.

One approach is to frame this sequencing in terms of selection. Having introduced the concept of features as a way to motivate Movement, we can extend this notion to selection as well, since both are really just types of Merge.

As an example, we can see selection in terms of feature-checking in instances where there are no auxiliaries, and tense is expressed on a lexical verb. In this instance an uninterpretable tense feature is checked by an interpretable one projected by the verb that is the head of its complement vP at the point when they are Merged. At Spell Out this feature-checking configuration means that tense is expressed on the verb, rather than separately in the Tense head.

We have already seen marking of a tense value [+PAST] in T to represent past tense. The only other tense that can be realised on main verbs in English is present. Past and present tenses are in complementary distribution with each other (a clause cannot simultaneously be both), which means we can collapse them into a single feature value [±PAST], where [+PAST] represents past tense and [−PAST] represents present tense.

(39)

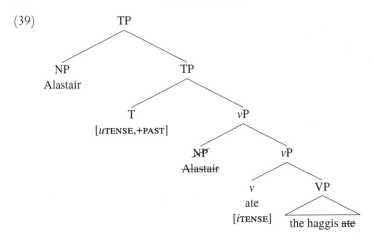

If we consider the beginning of our string of auxiliaries, we can see that a Modal verb can be followed be any other lexical verb or auxiliary.

(40) a. The haggis might be eaten
b. The boy might be eating the haggis
c. The boy might have eaten the haggis
d. The boy might eat the haggis

This property of modal verbs is another one that it shares with Tense, suggesting again that modal verbs are really an expression of T (but see §4.4.1 for discussion of alternatives). Framing this characteristic in terms of feature-checking, we could argue that a modal/T can Merge with any verb that can check its uninterpretable tense feature. Moreover, any verb, lexical or auxiliary, can have an [*i*TENSE] feature. Selection by and Merge with modals/T will therefore be unconstrained with respect to the type of verb that follows a modal auxiliary or is tensed.

The behaviour of the passive auxiliary *be* will be similarly straightforward if we assume this selectional approach. As stated previously, passive *be* appears to select for a VP lacking additional vP and AgrOP projections. Assuming that V has some unique feature [*i*V] that checks an uninterpretable feature [*u*V] on the passive auxiliary, we can explain why passive *be* does not select for other auxiliaries.

(41) a. The haggis was eaten
b. The haggis had been eaten
c. *The haggis was had eaten

Problems arise for our selectional account of auxiliary ordering when we consider auxiliaries that have neither the freedom of modals nor the singular limitations of passive *be* in terms of what they may be followed by. Progressive *be* can have either a lexical verb or passive *be* as its complement, but not the perfect auxiliary *have* or a modal verb.

(42) a. The boy is eating haggis
b. The haggis is being eaten
c. *The boy is having eaten haggis
d. *The boy is shoulding eat haggis

In order to explain these limitations on progressive *be* in terms of selection we would have to argue that lexical verbs and passive *be* share a feature not possible on auxiliary *have* or modals. Given their tense-like properties and general defectiveness, it is not hard to argue that modals lack a feature or features found on other verbs. But unlike auxiliaries or lexical verbs, which have certain similar characteristics that group them together, passive *be* and lexical verbs do not form an obvious natural class to the exclusion of perfective *have*. This absence of other shared properties makes it difficult to argue that they have a specific possible feature in common for reasons other than the need to restrict selection by progressive *be*.

The perfect auxiliary *have* is also restricted: it can be followed by lexical verbs and passive *be*, as well as progressive *be*, but not modal auxiliaries.

(43) a. The boy has eaten haggis
b. The haggis has been eaten
c. The boy has been eating haggis
d. *The boy has mighten eat haggis

Here we might again reasonably argue that there is some feature possible on auxiliary and lexical verbs, selected by *have*, that excludes modals. If so, our problem boils down to progressive *be*. More broadly, however, it is notable that the set of verbs selected by progressive *be* is a subset of those selected by *have*, and that those selected by passive *be* are a subset of those selected by progressive *be*. In this respect a selectional account in which each auxiliary selects for a different feature appears to miss some larger generalisation. The set of auxiliaries in other languages is different and sometimes more numerous, which also means that this approach is uncomfortably English-specific.

As an alternative, some linguists have proposed that the syntactic structure of functional projections is fixed. Under this theory, all of the Aux heads are always present in the structure of the clause, regardless of which auxiliaries are used. The auxiliary verbs in a particular utterance are slotted into this pre-existing structure, which would look something like (44).

(44)

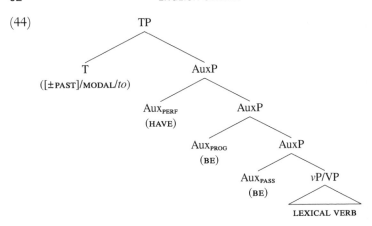

This solution overcomes some of the drawbacks of the selectional one: each Aux head can have only a single type of AuxP or VP as its complement, meaning each selects for a single feature. Taking this idea a step further, we can eliminate selection altogether by proposing that our fixed syntactic structure is not generated by successive Merge of the functional heads in question, but exists as a fundamental entity in our Universal Grammar. From this perspective having an unvarying functional structure is computationally efficient, but the architecture of a clause with a number of empty heads appears rather baroque.

On the other hand, this fixed structure approach is not lexically driven, and in this sense is un-Minimalist. Given the system we have argued for thus far, we expect each phrase to be projected by some lexical item or feature (e.g. Tense). It is therefore not clear what the status of these functional projections would be in the absence of the auxiliaries that correspond to them. It is also potentially problematic that when present an auxiliary could be at some distance from the next auxiliary it precedes. As we have seen with tense, overt morphology can be realised in a complement verb. In this proposal, however, it is not apparent how the feature required to instantiate the overt morphology would be transmitted to a verb at some structural distance across several intervening functional heads.

Another alternative proposal is that selection by auxiliaries is syntactically unrestricted. Under this approach our progressive and perfect auxiliaries could have their features checked by Merge with any verbal head (not including modals, which we will continue to assume are distinct). Ungrammatical instances such as (45) would be ruled out at LF when the derivation is sent to Spell Out.

(45) *Lucy was having made tea
      (cf. Lucy had been making tea)

Underlying this approach is the notion that it is semantically anomalous to have a perfect form interpreted within a progressive one. Progressive aspect (*be* + V-*ing*) gives us the event as having a continuous temporal structure; perfect aspect (*have* + V-*en*) gives us an event as a completed whole. The ongoing temporal nature of the progressive means that it applies typically to verbs denoting dynamic processes. It can also be used with stative verbs, but only if they are interpreted as processes in some sense. **Semelfactive** verbs that denote instantaneous events (e.g. *flashed*, *sneezed*, *blinked*) can be used in the progressive as well, but only with the reading that the event referred to is happening repeatedly.

(46) a. Maisie is {running/laughing/eating}
      b. Martha is {thinking of a number/enjoying her sandwich/
          feeling sad}
      c. The light was {flashing/blinking} when I walked in

In all instances the progressive covers an event at more than a single point in time, with no intrinsic specification of endpoint. The perfect represents an endstate with no depiction of previous temporal progression. While such temporal progression may still be understood from the properties of the verb used, this interpretation does not come from the perfect aspect. It can thus apply to dynamic, stative and instantaneous events.

(47) a. Maisie has {run/laughed/eaten}
      b. Martha has {thought of a number/enjoyed her sandwich/felt
          sad}
      c. The light has {flashed/blinked}

It is therefore reasonable to suppose that the state of completion indicated by the perfect cannot have a sense of ongoing temporal progression: it comes into being at only a single point in time, and while it continues to exist it can never be a dynamic process because it is fixed at the point of its inception. In contrast, we can understand a process that was ongoing over time to have reached an endpoint or state of completion.

From these observations it follows that the progressive aspect can be encompassed semantically in the perfect, but not vice versa. We might also note that it is possible to have progressive morphology on a perfect auxiliary, although taking into consideration that the morpheme -*ing* has a number of functions it may be inaccurate to classify this as a true progressive construction.

(48) Having eaten the haggis, Lucy went out

It is also worth pointing out that while other sentences with a perfect following a progressive (e.g. (42)c and (45)) are ungrammatical they sound much better than sentences in which this morphology is applied to modal verbs (e.g. (42)d and (43)d). This consideration is in keeping with the proposal that such sentences are not actually ungrammatical but semantically anomalous.

Our meaning-based hypothesis about the ordering of auxiliaries requires a certain separation between syntactic generation and semantics, an assumption on which we have already been operating. Certain auxiliary orders are also still ruled out syntactically: the selectional properties of the passive auxiliary *be* remain the same, inasmuch as we might claim that VP has a unique feature chosen by passive *be*. Sticking with the notion that modal auxiliaries are syntactically distinct from other verbs, we can also exclude selection of these by any other auxiliary, even though other verb forms semantically equivalent to modals (e.g. *have to* for *must*) can be selected by perfect *have* or progressive *be*. As such this restriction must be syntactic rather than semantic.

(49) a. *Alec was musting to go
      b. *Alec has musted go
      c. Alec was having to leave
      d. Alec has had to leave

The main potential drawback to this semantics-based approach to auxiliary order is that, in shifting some of the ordering of auxiliaries to LF restrictions, it may require the interpretation of tense/aspect to be quite narrow in order to rule out some combinations semantically. There is in fact not always a one-to-one match between grammatical properties and meaning. For instance, the sentences in (50) both give us information about events at some future point in time, yet are in the present tense. Moreover, the progressive in (50)b does not necessarily have a sense of ongoing process.

(50) a. Julian leaves tomorrow
      b. Julian is leaving tomorrow

Notwithstanding these sorts of examples, the arguments that auxiliary ordering depends on semantics rather than syntactic selection still appear least problematic.

For this and the syntactic selectional approach outlined initially, the question of how to capture the sequencing of auxiliaries becomes even more complicated with the availability of more auxiliaries crosslinguistically. Standard English is limited to the ones outlined above, but in the next section we will consider this question in light of Non-Standard multiple modal constructions used in many varieties of English.

4.4.1 Multiple modals

In §4.1 auxiliaries were described as appearing in the Tense head. We amended this analysis in §4.4, arguing that there is an array of possible AuxP projections, each of them headed by a specific type of auxiliary. The highest auxiliary is selected by T and expresses tense by the same mechanism as lexical verbs (we will reconsider this approach again in Chapter 5, but our working model here makes no difference to the rest of the discussion in this section).

Should modal auxiliaries also be treated this way? As we have seen throughout this chapter, modals have properties that set them apart from other (auxiliary) verbs. They are in complementary distribution with tense, including non-finite *to*, indicating that they are in fact a manifestation of T. Modal verbs must also precede all other auxiliaries, indicating that they are relatively high in the structure of the clause. Similarly, tense is expressed on the highest verb in a clause, indicating that it occupies a similarly 'high' position.

While all modals are inflectionally defective, *could*, *might*, *should* and *would* can be interpreted as past tense forms of *can*, *may*, *shall* and *will*. If a past tense is required in an embedded clause to match a past tense in the main verb (a phenomenon known as **backshifting**), the first set of modals replaces the second.

(51) a. Hazel knew that Jack {*is/was} late
      b. Hazel knew that Jack {?*may/might/?*can/could/?*will/
          would} be late[5]

The modal auxiliary *must* has no 'past' form (although, as we have seen, it can periphrastically be replaced with *have to*). *Might*, etc., are also typically used with non-past meanings: without temporal context (real-world or syntactic), sentences such as do not by default have a past tense interpretation.

(52) He might read the book

---

[5] I find such forms ungrammatical, but there appears to be an ongoing change in progress whereby many speakers produce and accept e.g. *may* in contexts where for me only *might* will do, as in (i).
(i) %The train had left late but he thought it may still arrive on time

As seen in (50), though, grammatical tense does not consistently correspond to real-world time.

We could nevertheless argue that modal verbs are instantiated in their own head directly below T, with the caveat that a [+PAST] T cannot select for a Mod(al)P headed by *must*. Alternatively, we could argue that *must* is its own 'past' form, given that it is at least marginally acceptable in backshifting contexts, as in (53).

(53) ??He thought that she must do it
      (cf. He thought that she had to do it)

Here we must assume, too, that modal auxiliaries do appear in present tense, and their lack of third person singular agreement is down to a morphological quirk rather than some syntactic restriction. The absence of *to* forms for these verbs would be less easy to explain, assuming that non-finite *to* is itself an instantiation of T. We could argue instead that *to* has an uninterpretable (non-)finiteness feature that cannot be checked by selection of a modal verb.

The double modal constructions introduced at the beginning of the chapter also directly contradict any arguments about modals appearing in T that are based on the singularity of a modal auxiliary within a clause. Other types of auxiliaries occur only once per clause. We cannot, for instance, have multiple instances of perfect *have*, but this might result from redundancy rather than a syntactic limitation.

(54) *They have had eaten

One way to deal with multiple modals in a single clause is to posit that there is a Mod(al)P distinct from Tense, and that, for speakers who can have multiple modals auxiliaries in a single clause, this ModP is split into two projections.

Separating ModP from Tense complicates the problem of ordering functional heads, requiring either more complicated restrictions on syntactic selection, or further semantic constraints. Some evidence for the viability of this approach comes from limitations on double modal constructions, which allow modal auxiliaries only in particular orders.

(55) a. %Charlie might could do that
      b. *Charlie could might do that
      c. %Charlie may can do that
      d. *Charlie can may do that

In all of the grammatical instances in (55) the first modal is **epistemic**, denoting possibility or necessity, and the second **deontic**, denoting permission or obligation. Reversing the order of these types of modal leads to ungrammaticality. From a semantic perspective it is logical that permission/obligation can be interpreted as possible or necessary, but not that possibility/necessity (in terms of the state of the world) can be interpreted as permissible or obligatory. If we are looking for a syntactic explanation, this division can be modelled by specifying two ModPs, one epistemic and one deontic.

(56)

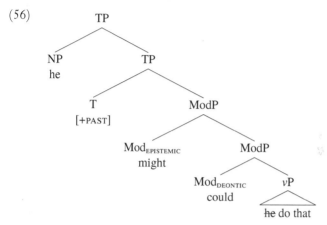

Some linguists have argued that instead the first modal should be treated as an adverb, because this first modal is almost always *may* or *might*, although sentences such as (57) are also possible for some speakers.

(57) He should oughta do that

In this analysis the first modal is equivalent to *maybe* in a sentence such as (58).

(58) He maybe could do it

This modal-as-adverb approach not only explains limitations on which modals occur in multiple modal constructions, but also explains why many speakers form questions by moving the second modal to the beginning of the clause rather than the first. If the first modal is not a true auxiliary, then we would not expect it to invert with the subject.

(59) %Could he might do that?

But certain characteristics of multiple modal constructions contradict this analysis. First, some speakers Move the first modal to the beginning of sentences in questions, rather than the second, suggesting that the highest modal verb (in this instance *might*) is a true auxiliary.

(60) %Might he could do that?

Second, for some speakers it is possible for negation to appear between the two modals; this configuration is not permitted with an adverb and a modal.

(61) %He might not could do that
      (cf. *He maybe not could do that)

Third, an adverb such as *maybe* or *possibly* may also follow a modal verb, meaning that the modal-as-adverb approach does not give a satisfactory explanation for why *may/might* must precede another modal.

(62) He could maybe do that

On a final note, some researchers have observed that it is possible to have more than two modals together, as in (63).

(63) %He'll might could do that

This array of data on multiple modals in English suggests that a mixed analysis may be required to account for this construction, or a different one altogether. It also raises the intriguing possibility that both the split modal head and modal-as-adverb hypotheses are correct, but not for the same speakers. In other words, distinct underlying grammars could produce a similar or overlapping set of surface forms.

4.5 Conclusion

This chapter has expanded beyond the split VP outlined in Chapter 3 by building up the 'functional' structure of the clause. We have proposed a number of additional projections to account for auxiliary verbs and tense, while also acknowledging some aspects of this model that remain difficult to explain. In the next chapter we will continue to expand our view of functional structure and Movement in the context of embedded clauses and questions, while also refining the proposals we have already made.

4.6 Further reading

Adger and Svenonius (2011) give a technical discussion of features in Minimalist syntax. For discussion of the structure of *get*-passives see Alexiadou (2006), Reed (2011) and Alexiadou (2012).

  To learn more about multiple modals see Battistella (1995) and Elsman and Dubinsky (2009), as well as Huang (2011) for a general overview of the data on these. Bour (2015a) and other works by the same author also give extensive coverage of the multiple modal phenomenon, primarily in a Scottish context.

4.7 Exercises

1. Trees

   Draw trees for the following sentences. You don't have to include features, but you should think about what they are.
   a. The milk has been spilled
   b. The butter has melted
   c. Nancy has burned the pancakes
   d. The sausages got overcooked
   e. Flora got everything muddled
   f. Breakfast may have been ruined
   e. You could be cleaning up the mess

2. Further analysis

   a. In §4.4 *have to, dare* and *ought* were mentioned in a footnote as 'semi-modals'. In what ways are these similar to typical modals? How do they differ? You should think about tense and negation.

   b. Consider the discussion of *get*-passives and causatives in §4.3. It is also possible to have passive and causative constructions for double object/ditransitive verbs.

      i.   The boy {got/was} given the book
      ii. The book {got/was} given to the boy
           (cf.*The book {got/was} given the boy)
      iii. I got the boy given a book
           (cf.*I got the boy a book given)
      iv. I got a book given to the boy
           (cf. *I got a book to the boy given)

      Do these examples fit with our analysis of the split VP from Chapter 3? Where would objects need to Merged? In what head positions would the participle need to be pronounced in order for these to have the correct word order?

   c. As an alternative to the two approaches outlined in §4.4.1, it has been proposed that the two modals in a double modal construction are the instantiation of a single modal head. In support of this hypothesis, some speakers form questions in double modal constructions by inverting both modal auxiliaries with the subject.

i. Might could he do that?
    How well does this single-head analysis account for the rest of
    the data on double/multiple modal constructions? Could either
    of the analyses in §4.4.1 account for (1)?

For Answers see edinburghuniversitypress.com/englishsyntax.

5 Embedded clauses and questions

The first chapter of this text introduced a number of ways to ask a particular question (repeated here), an enquiry about whether the addressee has wool.

(1)   a. Have you any wool?
      b. Do you have any wool?
      c. Have you got any wool?
      d. Do you got any wool?

This variation extends beyond these *yes-no* questions to *wh*-questions, those that have a question word *who, what, when, where, why* or *how*.

(2)   a. What have you?
      b. What do you have?
      c. What have you got?
      d. What do you got?

In all of these instances English questions involve moving a constituent (or constituents) to the beginning of a clause. As well as occurring in main clauses, questions can be embedded, introduced by *whether* or *if*, or by one of our *wh*-words.

(3)   a. I wondered {whether/if} you had any wool
      b. I wondered what you had

Speakers vary in terms of the shape of embedded questions. For many speakers these have the same SVO word order as declarative sentences. In some varieties, however, they have the **subject-auxiliary inversion** that characterises questions in main clauses.

(4)   a. I wondered what he had bought
      b. %I wondered what had he bought

On a superficial level the dissimilarity between questions in main and embedded clauses in most varieties of English is perhaps surprising: we might expect questions to be formed in the same way regardless of other syntactic context, as it is in some Non-Standard varieties. That they are not points to fundamental differences between main and embedded clauses.

In this chapter we will begin by looking at embedded clauses within VPs, followed by discussion of questions in a variety of syntactic contexts. Following considerations of question formation, we will consider the structure of relative clauses, embedded clauses within NPs.

5.1 Embedded clauses

As discussed in the preceding chapter, only tensed clauses can stand independently in English. Strings with untensed or non-finite verbs cannot be main clauses.

(5)   Looking bedraggled, *(Maisie came in from the rain)

As well as occurring on their own, finite clauses can be **embedded** as complements of certain verbs.

(6)   a. Alastair had eaten haggis
       b. Flora {saw/knew/believed/thought/wished} (that) [$_{TP}$ Alastair had eaten haggis]

The *that* which introduces embedded clauses is a **complementiser**, so named because it has the function of making the embedded clause a complement of the main verb (or other predicate). We can capture this additional category with a C(omplementiser) projection, which selects a TP as its complement, and itself is a complement of VP.

(7)

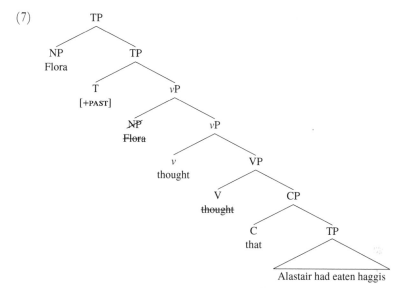

In essentially all instances the complementiser *that* can be omitted. There are two possible explanations for this optionality. On the one hand we could say that the CP projection is itself absent in these instances, with VP selecting directly for a TP. On the other hand we might say that the C(P) is present structurally, but unspoken, a silent **null complementiser** equivalent to *that* in all but pronunciation.

(8)   OPTION 1: SELECTION OF BARE TP

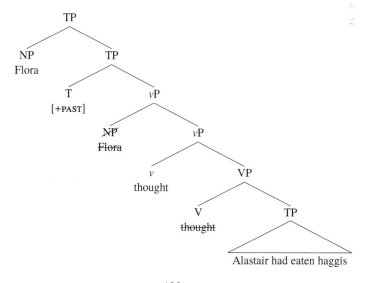

(9)   Option 2: Null Complementiser

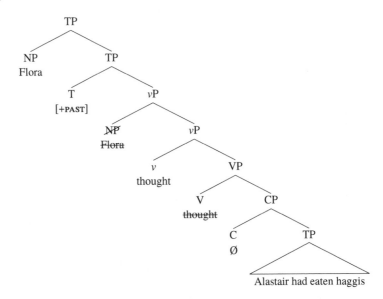

The first explanation is appealing in that it involves less structure, and assumes nothing in the syntax that is not also realised overtly at PF. However, it creates complications in terms of selection. If any verb that can select a CP headed by *that* can also select a finite TP, then we must specify for each individual lexical item that this is so: e.g. *see* can select a CP or tensed TP complement, *know* can select a CP or tensed TP complement, *think* can select a CP or tensed TP complement, etc. This analysis is therefore computationally inefficient, giving us massive replication of what should be the larger generalisation that any predicate that can have a *that* CP as a complement can also have the same complement without *that*.

  If we say that these verbs always select a CP, we can boil the optionality down to a single feature on C (something like [±PRONOUNCED]). Verbs that take embedded clauses as complements select for a C headed by *that*, and whether it is realised as an overt complementiser or a null one comes down to a feature that is not involved in this selection. This approach therefore requires much less storage in the lexicon, and so better meets our Minimalist requirement of cognitive simplicity.

  We can take this view a step further and argue that, given that the pronunciation of *that*/Ø has no apparent effect on the syntax, [±PRONOUNCED] is not a syntactic feature at all, and has relevance only at PF after Spell Out. This approach points to a more general conclusion about the nature of 'syntactic' variation, namely that in some instances its source is not the syntax at all, but some other level of production. A PF-relevant feature of the type we are suggesting here may be tied to a lexical item, but is essentially dormant until a point after the syntactic derivation is complete.

Turning to other types of embedded clause, there is further support for the latter analysis. A number of verbs can be followed by *if* or *whether*. There is a lot of overlap between these and the verbs that take *that* complements, but it is not exhaustive.

(10) a. I wondered {whether/if/that} he had eaten haggis
      b. I knew {whether/if/that} he had eaten haggis
      c. I asked {whether/if/*that} he had eaten haggis
      d. I investigated {whether/if/*that} he had eaten haggis
      e. I analysed {whether/if/*that} he had eaten haggis
      f. I assumed {*whether/*if/that} he had eaten haggis

In those instances where both types of complementiser are allowed, they introduce different **presuppositions**, or underlying assumptions about truth. *I know that X* takes as given that X is true (and if X is not true then the whole sentence is false). *I know whether X* makes no assumption about the truth of X, and the truth of the whole sentence remains the same regardless of whether X is true or not.

From a syntactic perspective, it is notable that the verbs above which cannot select for *that* also exclude a null complementiser.

(11) *I {asked/investigated/analysed} he had eaten haggis

The lack of overlap in the occurrence of the null complementiser in the same environment as *if/whether*, in contrast to the exact coincidence of where we can have *that* or no complementiser, provides another indication that the null complementiser is really just an alternative realisation or (non-)pronunciation of *that*.

There is also a class of verbs for which embedded clauses of this type can act as subjects. In these instances *that* is obligatory.

(12) (*That) Billy liked haggis {surprised/shocked/annoyed/puzzled/ intrigued} me

Verbs that allow CP subjects of this type can alternatively have *it* as a subject, with the CP in a post-verbal position.

(13) It surprised me (that) Billy liked haggis

The *it* subject in this example is an **expletive**: it has no semantic content of its own. These two forms of the sentence are therefore equivalent until a subject is required, at which point the CP may Move from the complement position of the VP. If the CP does not Remerge in the specifier of TP then the expletive *it* is inserted at PF as a **Last Resort** operation, a sort of back-up mechanism which applies to rescue a derivation that would otherwise crash at Spell Out.

(14)

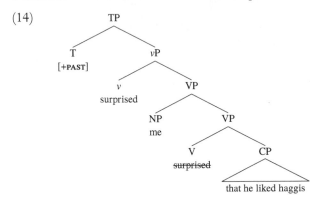

CP SUBJECT: That he liked haggis surprised me

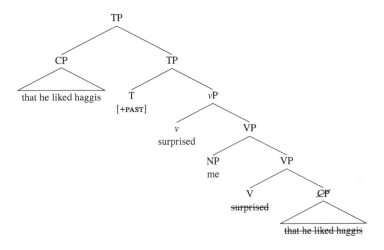

EXPLETIVE SUBJECT: It surprised me that he liked haggis

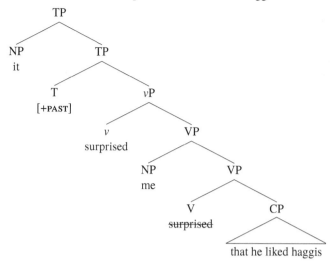

These alternatives mean we must amend our view of subject Movement. An embedded CP need not Move for Case assignment, the reason we have proposed for Movement of subjects out of the *v*P/VP, and therefore may remain in situ. When an embedded CP does Move this satisfies an apparent requirement of the TP, i.e. that its specifier be filled, which otherwise can be met through insertion of an expletive.

The need for English to have overt subjects is called the **Extended Projection Principle** (EPP). In our model we can represent this requirement as an [EPP] feature on T. This is not to say that Case requirements (i.e. the Visibility Condition) do not apply to NPs, but that Remerge of subjects in the specifier of TP is not exclusively motivated by Case assignment. Where there is an available NP, Movement to Remerge with TP will satisfy both Case assignment and the EPP. These requirements could also be satisfied for TP if an expletive *it* were inserted instead, but the derivation would crash because the NP would not be Merged in a Case position. A sentence such as (15) is therefore ungrammatical.

(15) *It has Martha cooked the haggis
      (cf. Martha has cooked the haggis)

A complement CP, however, need not be assigned Case. If it does Remerge with TP, the EPP is satisfied. If it does not, there is no violation of the Visibility Condition with respect to the CP (as opposed to an NP), and the EPP is instead satisfied by insertion of expletive *it*.

Returning to subject CPs, we must finally consider why these do not allow null complementisers. Given that an overt *that* is not required in the equivalent sentences with expletive subjects, it cannot be that verbs such as *surprise* impose some structural requirement on their CPs. If, as we have proposed, the *that*/Ø alternation is not syntactic we can reduce the need for *that* in a CP subject to a PF requirement that C be overt (pronounced) if sentence-initial.

This rule may in turn arise from processing limitations: without *that* speakers would inevitably have a **garden path** interpretation, in which the linear presentation of an underlyingly hierarchical sentence leads them to a misanalysis, requiring subsequent reparsing. For example, a speaker hearing the first part of the subject CP in (16) would interpret it as an independent main clause.

(16)   *[Billy likes haggis] surprised me

Examples such as these introduce a kind of chicken-and-egg question. Has the potential parsing problem led to a PF restriction that renders the sentence ungrammatical? Or is this utterance in fact structurally sound but unacceptable because the processing burden it introduces is too high? There is not a definite solution to this dilemma, but it indicates that (un)grammaticality may not be a purely syntactic phenomenon, and that the line between ungrammaticality and unacceptability may not always be as clear-cut as it is for some of the semantically anomalous sentences we have looked at in previous chapters.

5.1.1 Embedded questions

Verbs of the class that select for *if*/*whether* can also select clauses beginning with other *wh*-question words.

(17)   a.   Alastair wondered whether Jack had eaten haggis
       b.   Alastair wondered what Jack had eaten
       c.   Flora asked who had eaten haggis
       d.   Flora investigated {when/where/why/how} Hazel had eaten it

We can group all of these *if*/*whether*/*wh*-word clauses together as embedded questions. In terms of features this identification can be captured by a question feature [+Q] in C, with certain verbs selecting for C only if it has this feature. For the lexical items *if* and *whether* this feature is interpretable, meaning that the Merge of a question word is not required.

(18)

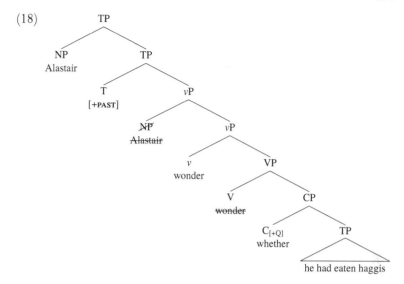

If a sentence has both an overt [+Q] complementiser and a *wh*-word the latter will remain **in situ** in its original Merge position, as the requirements of the [+Q] complementiser will have already been met. Such configurations can occur in echo questions, which repeat the form of a declarative sentence with the *wh*-word marked intonationally.

(19) I wondered if Jack ate haggis
    a. You wondered if Jack ate what
    b. *You wondered what if Jack ate

There also appears to be a null C with a question feature. Unlike the null equivalent of *that*, this complementiser is not freely interchangeable with overt forms. Instead, it has an uninterpretable question feature [*u*Q], which must be checked by Remerge of some *wh*-word.

(20)

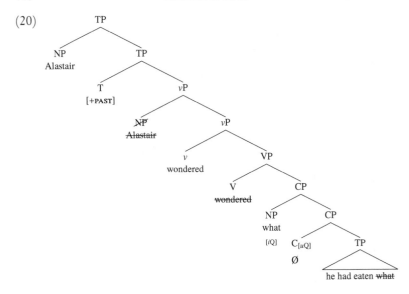

The Movement of the question word to Merge with CP that we see here is not dissimilar from the Movement of arguments (objects and subjects) that we have seen elsewhere in the clause. It differs in that an argument Moved to CP has already satisfied its own requirements in terms of theta role and Case assignment elsewhere, and Remerges specifically to check a feature on the CP. We say in circumstances such as these that the CP Attracts the question word for reasons of **Greed**: it motivates another element to Remerge in its specifier only to check its own features, rather than because that Moved element itself has any features that require checking.

Recall the concept of c-command, introduced in Chapter 2. A constituent can 'see' the constituent with which it Merges, its sister, as well as any elements dominated by its sister. A head can therefore only Attract elements that it c-commands, as it cannot 'see' constituents Merged higher up the tree, later in the derivation. 'Movement' is therefore always upwards. Given a bottom-up derivation, we cannot go back and Remerge an element in a lower position in the tree. Greed also falls out from c-command: an element with certain requirements (e.g. an NP needing to be assigned Case) cannot look to higher points in the derivation, but depends on Attraction by some c-commanding projection for its requirements to be checked. Thus, although Movement may happen to satisfy the needs of the attractee (sometimes called a **goal**), it is always motivated by the need to check features on the attractor (sometimes called a **probe**).

We know that *wh*-words are not generated directly in the CP because they must fulfil requirements elsewhere. *What* and *who* replace NPs, and therefore must have the same needs as any other NP in terms of theta role and Case assignment. Other instances of *wh*-Movement are less straightforward, in that *when, where, why* and *how* replace adjuncts (PPs or APs) rather than arguments. It is possible for an adjunct to be clause-initial in the presence of an overt complementiser, though it need not be. If it precedes that complementiser, however, it becomes an adjunct to the main rather than the embedded verb, indicating that it is not part of the embedded CP.

(21) a. Julian knew whether (on Tuesday) Alec ate haggis (on Tuesday)
 b. Julian knew on Tuesday whether Alec ate haggis

Moreover, a *wh*-word replacing an adjunct still cannot be used in direct proximity to an overt complementiser.

(22) Julian knew (*when) whether (*when) Alec ate haggis

Therefore, although the adjuncts that these other *wh*-words replace can potentially Merge in a variety of positions, like *who* and *what* they are Moved to the specifier of CP rather than being generated in that position.

As we have already proposed, it follows that *wh*-words do not Remerge in CP in the presence of *if/whether* because there is no uninterpretable question feature that must be checked, and so Movement to this position is not motivated. In addition, a *wh*-word cannot occur in the specifier of CP with a *that* complementiser.

(23) I know what (*that) he ate

This restriction occurs not because *what* and *that* fulfil exactly the same function, nor because they are in the same position (unlike, e.g., *whether, if* and *that*, which all occupy C). Instead, a head with a [Q] feature cannot be instantiated as *that*. However, a *wh*-word Merges in the specifier of CP in order to check an uninterpretable question feature projected by C. If the complementiser *that* is present, there will be no [Q] feature to motivate Movement of the *wh*-word to the CP.

(24)

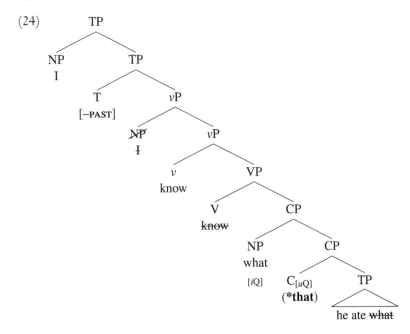

This restriction is called the **Doubly-Filled COMP Filter**: a *wh*-word cannot co-occur with an overt complementiser because Movement of the *wh*-word to the CP is motivated by a feature that either does not require checking if there is an overt interrogative complementiser *whether/if* already, or is not present on the declarative complementiser *that*. As we have seen for *whether/if*, however, it is not impossible for a *wh*-word to occur in situ in a clause introduced by *that*.

(25) Julian knows that Alec ate WHAT?

Here there is no conflict between the declarative complementiser and the embedded question word because there is no [*u*Q] feature in C, and as we would expect in the absence of this motivating feature, the *wh*-word therefore does not Move to CP.

(26)

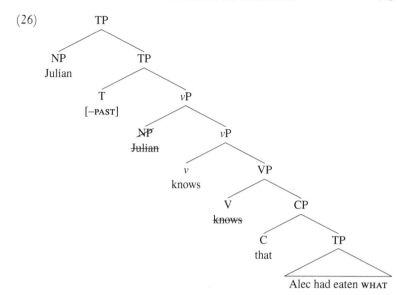

5.2 Questions

The introduction of CP has allowed us to account for the presence of complementisers and question words beginning embedded clauses. This additional functional projection can also help to explain the structure of main clause questions.

As noted in the introduction, English *yes-no* questions in main clauses are characterised by subject-auxiliary inversion, in which an auxiliary verb precedes the subject. We can account for this divergence from usual SVO word order through Movement of the auxiliary to C. This Remerge of a head in another head position is called **Head(-to-Head) Movement**.

(27)

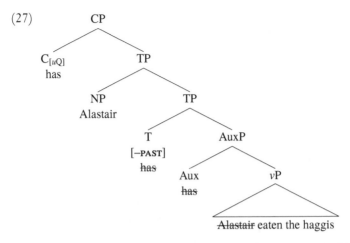

We have already seen something akin to Head Movement in Chapter 3, where the VP was split into several projections, only one of which was actually pronounced. In that instance each head was really a subset of features comprising a single lexical item, and it was suggested there that the overt position of the verb (and any particles) might actually come down to some rule of PF: either a general requirement that pronunciation occurs in the highest head position for a given lexical item, or a [+PRONOUNCE] feature present in a particular head.

Head Movement in questions appears more similar to other types of Movement we have already seen. Although it involves 'displacement' of a head rather than a phrase, on a fundamental level it is subject to similar mechanisms. In this instance T-to-C Movement is motivated by a feature in C that is checked by Remerge of the auxiliary. We will therefore assume that this Head Movement is not just a PF operation, but has syntactic underpinnings.

Head Movement is also subject to the **Minimal Link Condition** (**MLC**), a preference for the shortest possible Movement chains. In questions this means that it is the highest auxiliary in a series that Moves to C, even though any auxiliary can check its feature.

(28) a.   Nancy should have eaten haggis
      b.   Should Nancy have eaten haggis?
      c.   *Has Nancy should eaten haggis?

The MLC can be seen in terms of computational efficiency if Movement for feature-checking is again viewed in terms of Attract and Greed, whereby it is the requirements of the higher element (in this instance C) that motivate Remerge of some other element lower down in the derivation. The attractor must look down the part of the derivation that exists already in order to find a constituent with features that can check its uninterpretable features. Once the attractor has found an appropriate element to check those features, there is no need to look beyond that element. This process is analogous to, say, finding a pen to write down a piece of information: if there is one on the table next to you it is most convenient to use that one, rather than spending time digging through your stationery drawer or popping out to the shop to buy a new one. Likewise, it is most economical for the attractor to Attract the closest constituent that can meet its requirements. In our example this means that T (and subsequently C) will not overlook *should* in order to Attract *have*, which is lower down in the syntactic structure.

One leftover consideration from Chapter 4 was the position of auxiliaries, especially modals, in relation to T. Is the highest auxiliary generated in T, does it Move to this position from a separate Aux/Mod head, or does it remain in situ in an Aux/Mod head and get tense features post-syntactically in the way we have suggested for lexical verbs? Question formation gives a partial answer (and we will revisit this issue again in later chapters), in that it highlights the difference between auxiliaries and lexical verbs. Non-auxiliaries do not undergo Head Movement in questions in English.

(29) *Ate he haggis?

We can explain this contrast between lexical verbs and auxiliaries by looking to Head Movement further down in the clause. If inversion is accomplished by T-to-C Movement, then a verb must be present in T before it can Move to C. Lexical verbs do not Move to T, and therefore cannot undergo further Movement to C. The highest auxiliary in a series always ends up in T (either by base generation or Movement), and therefore can Move to C.

In our discussion of embedded questions we characterised the feature on C which is present when it is realised as *whether/if*, or when it prompts Movement of a *wh*-word, as a question feature. That it motivates T-to-C Movement for *yes-no* questions indicates that this question feature is in fact checked by some property of T quite specifically. We might thus characterise C as having an uninterpretable $[uT]$ feature in interrogative contexts. At the same time, we have already seen that embedded questions in Standard English do not have T-to-C Movement. These observations indicate that it may be too simplistic to characterise the feature on C that prompts subject-auxiliary inversion as $[uQ]$; instead, our 'question' feature may comprise a set of subfeatures which are not necessarily identical in all interrogative contexts. We will return to this idea in §5.2.2.

Where no verb is present in T it is of course possible to ask questions with lexical verbs through insertion of auxiliary *do.*

(30) Did he eat haggis?

Like insertion of expletive *it* subjects, *do*-**support** is a Last Resort operation, one that can apply to prevent the derivation from crashing when all other means of checking uninterpretable features are unavailable. If the features of T have Moved to C, Tense will be separated from the lexical verb in terms of both intervening structure and lexical material (the subject), making it impossible for them to be Merged post-syntactically.

In this respect insertion of auxiliary *do* provides evidence for the separation between the syntax and the realisation of sentences at PF after Spell Out. If there is no proximate verb on which tense features can be realised in C, it is instantiated as *do.* If the pronunciation of lexical items were already present during syntactic derivations, tense morphology would require post-syntactic re-analysis in order to allow for the separation and replacement of *-ed* (or equivalent past tense morphology) on the verb.

(31)

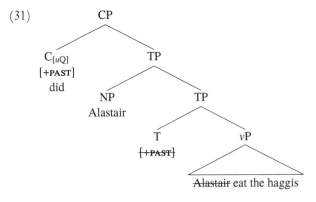

Note that in (31) it is only the syntactic feature of tense that originates in T, rather than *did.* This auxiliary is inserted at the point of Spell Out to rescue the derivation. By comparison, in (27) all the features of the auxiliary *has* are present in T prior to its Movement to C, so although its pronunciation is also not determined till PF (and in this respect it might be more accurate to only have *has* in C as well), it is present in the syntax proper in that it contributes features other than tense, indicating the perfective aspect, and selecting for a perfect participle. 'Dummy' *do,*

in contrast, represents only a tense feature, and only when this feature has no other possible realisation.

5.2.1 Lexical be, have and do

Although the majority of lexical verbs require *do*-support in questions, English has a few notable exceptions. Even when not used as an auxiliary, *be* Moves to T, and to C in questions.

(32) a. He is happy
    b. Is he happy?

Lexical *be* is similar to unaccusative and passive verbs in that it assigns no agent/cause theta role, and is therefore lacking the corresponding *v*P and AgrO structure. Indeed, in sentences such as (32)a, the subject is assigned a theta role by the adjective *happy*. *Be* carries little or no semantic content of its own, other than marking tense. Clear evidence for the lack of meaning contributed by lexical *be* comes from varieties such as African American Vernacular English, which allow this **copula**, a verb expressing equivalence, to be omitted entirely in the present.

(33) %He happy

More evidence for V-to-T Movement of *be* comes from the position of adverbs. Words such as *soon* typically cannot intervene between a lexical verb and its object in English (for reasons having to do with adverb placement, to be explored in Chapter 9), but it is unproblematic for an adverb to come between *be* and its complement.

(34) a. *Charlie ate soon haggis
    b. Charlie was soon happy

The adverb *soon* does not form a constituent with the adjective *happy* in the way that an intensifier such as *quite* does.

(35) a. Nancy soon was happy
    b. Nancy (*quite) was (quite) happy
    c. The {?*soon/quite} happy girl had haggis
    d. {?*Soon/Quite} happy, the girl was

The contrast between (34)a and (34)b can be explained if *was* has Moved over the adverb Merged in the VP into T, while *ate* (or any other lexical verb) does not. Here the subject initially Merges with a projection of the adjective rather than the verb, because it is *happy* not *be* which assigns it a theta role.

(36)

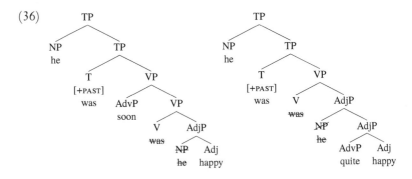

Returning to questions, not only can a lexical *be* verb in T can undergo Head Movement to C in interrogative contexts, but *do*-support in this instance is ungrammatical. In other words, our Last Resort operation not only applies when no other option is available, but cannot apply if other options are available.

(37) a.   Was he quite happy?
      b.   *Did he be quite happy?

As we have already seen in the introduction to this text, the behaviour of lexical *have* is more variable than that of *be* in questions. As opposed to the perfect-marking auxiliary *have*, lexical *have* denotes possession.

(38) I have wool

Some speakers exhibit V-to-T(-to-C) Movement of lexical *have*, resulting in the 'black sheep' form of questions, repeated in (39)a. For others it is treated as any other lexical verb, with *do*-support in questions, as in (39)b.

(39) a.   Have you any wool?
      b.   Do you have any wool?

The other forms of the question, repeated in (40), depend on the treatment of *got*. As discussed in Chapter 4, *get* has evolved from meaning 'to acquire' to, in its perfect form, meaning 'to possess' (presumably because possession is the logical outcome of acquisition). Typically, the *got* form is still used with the auxiliary *have*, with T-to-C Movement, as in (40).

(40) Have you got any wool?

Some varieties, however, treat *got* as an unalterable verb form requiring no auxiliary. For these speakers a sentence such as (41) will be ambiguous between a past tense statement about acquisition ('you have obtained wool'), and a present tense statement of possession ('you possess wool').[1]

(41) You got wool
(cf. You have got wool)

The possession interpretation of *got* in this instance represents omission of perfect *have*, in a similar way to that of *be* for some speakers: the *have* auxiliary marks only tense, and can therefore be elided. In questions, however, Movement of T-to-C must be marked overtly, and so *do* is inserted as in other instances where T features in C are not proximate to any verb on which they can be realised.

(42) a. %Do you got wool?
b. Have you got wool?

Do-support will also occur in question formation with the past tense 'acquisition' reading of (41), disambiguating the two interpretations.

(43) Did you get wool?

The different forms of our 'wool' question therefore provide insight into parameterisation. For speakers with the 'black sheep' form, lexical *have* is treated syntactically as an auxiliary, while for others it is treated as other lexical verbs. The difference between (39)a and (39)b therefore reduces to a single feature on *have*, which determines whether it undergoes Head Movement or not.

More precisely, we can describe the feature that motivates Movement of some verbs to T (auxiliaries, lexical *be*, sometimes lexical *have*) in terms of **strength**. A **strong feature** is one that requires Remerge with a projection of the relevant head for feature-checking. A **weak feature** allows checking in a local configuration without Movement, through selection or other means. In English lexical verbs (with the exceptions we have just described) generally have a weak $[iT]$ feature, and auxiliaries have a strong one. The variation for lexical *have* is thus not whether it has an interpretable tense feature or not, but whether that feature is strong or weak.

The difference between the sentences in (42) comes down to whether the participle *got* can be used to express possession without the *have*

---

[1] The ambiguity here arises partly from the syncretism, equivalence in morphological form, of the perfect participle and past tense forms of *get* as *got*. Many American speakers have *gotten* as the perfect participle for *get*, and indeed might use this form when speaking of acquisition and the other when speaking of possession.

auxiliary. In the absence of overtly pronounced *have*, *do* is inserted in C as a Last Resort. Again, then, the contrast between these sentences is reducible to a single feature on a lexical item, but in this instance it applies at PF, according to whether speakers can have a null equivalent to *have* in T.

Finally, although *do* is used as an auxiliary in all of the instances we have discussed, there is also a lexical form of *do*, which does not Move to T (or, subsequently, C).

(44) a. Flora did a dance
     b. *Did Flora a dance?
     c. Did Flora do a dance?

Unlike *be* and, for some speakers, *have*, *do* has two forms which are distinct not just in selection and feature strength, but also in position(s) of Merge.

Historically all verbs in English had a strong [*i*T] feature and underwent V-to-T and subsequent T-to-C Movement. For many languages both auxiliary and lexical verbs still have Head Movement. Nursery rhymes again provide a good source of relics of this process for lexical verbs in English.

(45) a. Little girl, little girl, what gave she you?
     b. Pussy cat, pussy cat, what did you there?

5.2.2 Wh-questions

For embedded clauses we argued that *wh*-question words Move to the specifier of CP in order to check a [*u*Q] feature. For main clause *yes-no* questions we noted that T-to-C Movement suggests that our question feature is checked in particular by the features of T. Main clause *wh*-questions appear to have both Movement of a *wh*-word to the specifier of CP, and T-to-C Movement, such that the question word appears clause-initially, and the verb undergoes subject-auxiliary inversion.

(46) What did he see?

The co-occurrence of these two operations raises a question regarding how we view the preference for the 'shortest' possible Movements in the syntax (recall the MLC), and the nature of feature-checking. If the uninterpretable question feature on C can be checked by Head Movement of features on T, what motivates Movement of the *wh*-word as well? And in our embedded questions, why would a (more distant) *wh*-word Move to check an uninterpretable question feature on C, when this checking could be accomplished by Head Movement of closer features in T?

A partial solution to this conundrum can be found in a quirk of English *wh*-questions. If the *wh*-word stands in for a subject, there is no T-to-C Movement. Tense is realised on any lexical verb, and *do*-support is ungrammatical.

(47) a. The storm destroyed the barn
     b. What did the storm destroy? [Object Question]
     c. What destroyed the barn? [Subject Question]
     d. *What did destroy the barn?[2]

In questions such as (47)c the preference for shorter Movements, or Movement of the nearest element to the attractor/probe, does seem to apply. A *wh*-word subject Merged in TP is closer to C than the head T, and therefore Remerges in C to check its uninterpretable question feature. Once this [*u*Q] feature has been checked, there is no motivation for subsequent T-to-C Movement.

(48)

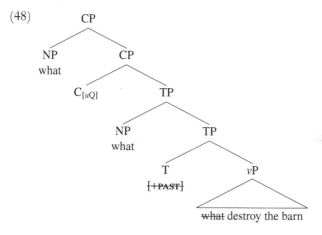

Movement of the *wh*-word to a clause-initial position in main clauses is thus sufficient to satisfy the requirements of a C head with an uninterpretable Question feature. However, this Movement also occurs when the [*u*Q] feature has already been checked by T-to-C Movement. We must therefore propose an additional uninterpretable *wh* feature

---

[2] *What did destroy the barn* is grammatical if *do* is stressed in pronunciation, but this is an instance of emphatic *do* (cf. *The storm* DID *destroy the barn*) distinct from *do*-support in questions.

[*u*WH] that is checked by an interpretable [*i*WH] feature on question words.

Consider as well that, with the exception of the subject questions outlined above, we do not get *wh*-Movement without T-to-C Movement in English main clauses. We can therefore propose that [*u*Q] is not unitary but can have [*u*WH] and [*u*T] subfeatures. In *wh*-questions checking of [*u*WH] by a *wh*-word is sufficient to check [*u*Q] overall, but even if the [*u*T] subfeature is checked, the [*u*WH] must still be checked as well, resulting in simultaneous T-to-C and *wh*-word Movement in many instances.

We can extend this analysis to embedded questions. The complementisers *whether*/*if* already have an interpretable question feature, 'filling' the C position so that Merge of other elements in the CP is not motivated. For embedded *wh*-questions, however, the C position cannot be occupied by an overt complementiser where there is a *wh*-word Merged in CP.

Embedded *wh*-questions therefore have two options. One is that they behave exactly as main clause *wh*-questions, which they do in some varieties of English. T-to-C Movement and overt complementisers are in complementary distribution, suggesting that they occupy the same head position (C).

(49) a.   Oscar knows whether Lucy ate haggis
     b.   %Oscar knows did Lucy eat haggis
     c.   %Oscar knows what did Lucy eat
     d.   *Oscar knows whether did Lucy eat haggis

The other option is that embedded *wh*-questions can have a null complementiser, distinct from the null equivalent of *that*, with a [*u*Q] feature with a [*u*WH] subfeature, but no [*u*T] subfeature. Merge of a *wh-word* in CP will check [*u*Q], which cannot be checked by T-to-C Movement in this instance, and its subfeature [*u*WH].

(50) Oscar knows what Lucy ate

We can sum up the possible Q features and subfeatures in C as follows:

- Main clause *yes-no* questions: [*u*Q] [*u*T]
- Main clause *wh*-questions: [*u*Q] [*u*WH] [*u*T]
- Embedded clause *if, whether*: [*i*Q]
- Embedded *wh*-questions: [*u*Q] [*u*WH]
- Embedded *yes*/*no* questions with subject-aux inversion: [*u*Q] [*u*T]
- Embedded *wh*-questions with subject-aux inversion: [*u*Q] [*u*WH] [*u*T]

The availability of subject-auxiliary inversion in embedded clauses is again reducible to a single feature. For speakers who allow these forms, a verb such as *know* may select for an embedded CP headed by a C with an uninterpretable question feature that has a [*u*T] subfeature. Other speakers may only select for a CP with a [*u*Q] lacking a [*u*T] subfeature. For speakers who do allow subject-auxiliary inversion in embedded questions, there is a preference for particular main verbs (e.g. *know*), confirming the idea that this difference is a selectional one.

5.2.3 Multi-clausal questions

Having looked at questions in embedded and main clauses, we can now examine instances where the *wh*-word appears to Move out of an embedded clause to Merge in the CP of the main clause. This Movement can occur over several embedded clauses, although as with any multi-clausal structure it may be more difficult to process the more clauses there are.

(51) a. What do you think Maisie ate?
      b. What do you think Martha knows I recalled Maisie ate?

It appears superficially that the question word simply Remerges in the highest CP, regardless of intervening structure. However, evidence from floating quantifiers in some varieties of Irish English indicates otherwise. Recall that quantifiers such as *all* may be stranded by Movement or, in more Minimalist terms, pronounced in any position in the derivation where the NP that they modified has Merged. For some speakers this stranding applies with question words as well.

(52) a. %What all do you think that he ate?
      b. %What do you think all that he ate?

The presence of *all* directly preceding the complementiser suggests that the question word *what* Remerges in the embedded CP before finally Remerging in the CP of the higher clause. Other varieties of English do not have floating quantifiers with *wh*-words in the same way, but we will assume that they adhere to the same pattern of successive Merge.

Why, then, does the *wh*-word not Move to check the [*u*WH] feature in the highest CP without Merge in intervening CP positions? From the perspective of motivating Movement, it appears that the highest CP in the main clause cannot 'see' a *wh*-word within an embedded clause to check its uninterpretable features, as otherwise there would be no reason for the question word to 'stop' at any point between its original and final position.

The embedded CP here acts as a sort of boundary, rendering the *wh*-word below it invisible to the higher CP. In Minimalism, this blocking effect can be reframed in terms of **phases**, pieces of the syntactic derivation that are sent to Spell Out successively, instead of the whole sentence going in one fell swoop. Once a phase has gone to Spell Out it will no longer be accessible for any further syntactic derivation. Because a CP is a phase, a *wh*-word within that phase cannot be Remerged in a higher position once the phase is complete, because it will no longer be an active part of the syntactic derivation. It is therefore not so much that the CP is in the way of another CP 'seeing' constituents within it, as it marks a point beyond which constituents have already been sent to Spell Out, and are therefore no longer available.

One way to view a phase is as a room with a single one-way door. While you are in the room you can rearrange the furniture and manipulate objects within it, but when you have left the room and the door has locked behind you, you will have no access to anything in that room. If before leaving you place something right outside the one-way door (or right inside next to a big enough cat-flap that you can reach through), it will be possible to take that thing with you to a subsequent room. The CP is in effect the door to the room. The rest of the CP phase is sent to Spell Out before the CP itself, so that elements Moved to the CP, or the **phase edge**, will continue to be accessible.

To extend the analogy, consider that when leaving a building of any size you typically have to go through multiple doors (unless you start out sitting next to the entrance). If each of these locks behind you, you will have to bring anything you want to take with you before proceeding to the next. A *wh*-word will therefore stop in each CP **escape hatch** in moving to the highest CP, in the same way you would go through each successive door on your way out.

As well as CPs, *v*Ps constitute phases. There is also evidence for the phasehood of *v*P from a variety of Irish English, in which *all* can be stranded at the *v*P phase edge.

(53) What did he all buy in town?

There is other, more complicated, evidence that CPs and *v*Ps are phases, but for now we will take these examples as sufficient indication.

In our one-way door analogy these stranded quantifiers are like markers left along the way as you exit. Let us say you have a flyer to post somewhere in the building as you leave. You are not just going to drop it on the floor somewhere, but you might stick it on one of the doors as you go through. Anybody who knows the flyer is yours will realise you have been that way, even if they have not seen you in the building. These left-behind quantifiers act in the same way to show an element has Moved through a particular syntactic position, even when this Movement is not always overtly visible in the syntax.

5.3 Relative clauses

We have so far looked at embedded clauses within VPs. English also has **relative clauses**, which modify nouns. Like other embedded clauses these begin with a complementiser or *wh*-word.

(54) a. The boy [who likes haggis] left already
      b. I bought haggis [that Alastair ate]

We can analyse relative clauses as having a CP, analogous to other types of embedded clauses. Instead of having a [*u*Q] feature in C they will have a [*u*REL] feature which motivates Movement of a **relative pronoun** such as *who, what, when, where, which, why* or *that* to Merge in the CP.

(55)

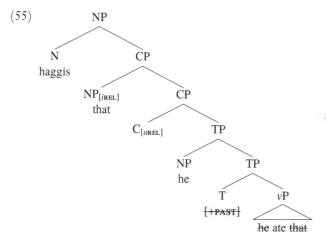

Unlike [*u*Q], [*u*REL] cannot be checked by T-to-C Movement: it has no [*i*T] subfeature.

(56) *I bought haggis that did he eat

Where relevant, relative pronouns match certain features to the head of the NP they modify, although each English relative pronoun is essentially invariant in morphological form. The verb in a subject relative clause will show the same agreement it would with the NP if that were the subject.

(57) a. I know a boy [CP who {*like/likes} haggis]

b. I know many people [CP who {like/*likes} haggis]

Like *that* in other types of embedded clauses, relative pronouns may be omitted, but for most speakers this elision is ungrammatical if the relative pronoun is referring to the subject of the clause.

(58) a. The haggis [I bought] was delicious

b. *The boy ate haggis left already

The ungrammaticality of omitting a subject relative pronoun is likely down to a parsing problem similar to the one we saw for omitting *that* in CP subjects: the directly preceding NP would be processed as the subject of the verb in the relative clause if there is no intervening relative pronoun or other subject. In the absence of a relative pronoun a sentence such as (60)a has a reading that is grammatical, but corresponds to (60)c, rather than (60)b with a relative clause.

(59) a. I saw the boy ate haggis

b. I saw the boy {that/who} ate haggis

c. I saw that the boy ate haggis

If the NP containing the relative clause is in a subject position, the absence of a subject relative pronoun leads to the expectation of a main clause, apparently rendering the sentence ungrammatical.

(60) a. The boy who ate haggis was happy

b. *[The boy ate haggis] was happy

There are quite a few varieties, though, where it is possible to leave out a subject relative pronoun in existential constructions with an expletive *there* subject. Here there is no other potential interpretation or misanalysis of the relative clause, as the NP has already been established as a complement of the *be* verb at the point where the relative clause is introduced.

(61) %There was a boy ate haggis

We can therefore conclude that there is a PF requirement for a [*u*REL] subject pronoun to be pronounced because of the problems in parsing that arise if it is not. For most speakers this applies globally, but for some speakers it is possible to omit this pronoun where these processing difficulties do not apply.

The example here is the most common type of this phenomenon, sometimes called **subject contact relatives**, but there are others, such as those that apply to objects. Like the existential forms, these are typically unambiguous, but there are exceptions to this generalisation where omission of a subject pronoun occurs despite a potential garden path interpretation.

(62) I know a boy has never worked

Colloquial speech allows not only the omission of relative pronouns, but also in some instance the repetition of a pronoun in a relative clause where there would otherwise be a 'gap'. **Resumptive pronouns** of this type are Non-Standard in that they are almost never encountered in writing or very formal speech.

(63) a. There's the boy who I gave him haggis
          (cf. There's the boy who I gave haggis)
      b. Maisie ate the haggis that it was in the fridge
          (cf. Maisie ate the haggis that was in the fridge)

When asked directly, speakers often claim these forms are ungrammatical, but they are nevertheless not uncommon. They give us another data point to confirm the idea of syntactic Movement as Remerge, with realisations of the pronoun pronounced in both its initial and Moved position.

5.4 Conclusion

In this chapter we have introduced the CP, a functional projection that allows us to account for a wide range of data in terms of embedded clauses and questions. In looking at these structures we have refined our view of Movement as resulting from Attract by the probe, the projection in which the 'Moved' element Remerges, rather than requirements of the Moved element, the goal, itself.

We have also looked at several instances in which an overtly pronounced lexical item alternates with a null form, forcing us to reconsider whether all ungrammaticality/unacceptability can be attributed to failures at a syntactic level, or must in some cases be accounted for at PF. In several instances we have shown that parameterisation of a single feature leads to differences between varieties.

Finally, we introduced the idea of the phase, a section of the syntax that goes to Spell Out before the next part of the derivation, with implications for the distances over which Movement can apply.

5.5 Further reading

For discussion of a number of phenomena related to question formation see Pesetsky and Torrego (2001). McCloskey (2000) looks at quantifier/ float stranding in Irish English questions, and Henry (2012) talks about this phenomenon for different varieties of Irish English.

For description and discussion of 'bare' *got* see Tyler (2016). To learn more about subject contact relatives see Henry (1995), Haegeman et al. (2015) and McCoy (2016). For discussion of the grammaticality/ acceptability of resumptive pronouns see McDaniel and Cowart (1999), as well as Cann et al. (2005).

5.6 Exercises

1. Trees
   Draw trees for the following sentences. You don't have to include features, but you should think about what they are.
   a. Who has spilled the milk?
   b. Should Billy clean up the mess?
   c. Martha knows that the pancakes will be nice
   d. Is she happy that there are eggs?
   e. That the breakfast was delicious was surprising
   f. What might she have cooked?
   g. Alastair asked if Flora had poached the eggs
   h. What do you think that Maisie would like?

2. Further analysis
   In §5.1 we represented embedded finite clauses as complements of VP within the split verb phrase. This contrasts with our analysis for direct objects, which were Merged as specifiers of VP. Consider the following data with particle verbs. Should CPs be analysed differently?
   a. She figured out that he lied
   b. *She figured that he lied out
   c. She figured out the answer
   d. She figured the answer out
   e. She put forth that lied
   f. *She put that he lied forth
   g. She put forth an answer
   h. She put an answer forth
   i. She made up that he lied
   j. *She made that he lied up

k. She made up the answer
l. She made the answer up

For Answers see edinburghuniversitypress.com/englishsyntax.

6 Negation

So-called **Double Negation**, embodied in a well-known Rolling Stones' lyric, is arguably one of the most derided English syntactic constructions of all time.

(1)   I can't get no satisfaction

Prescriptivist sticklers argue that use of two negative forms to denote a single negation is not just wrong, but downright illogical: the two negatives must cancel each other out to form a positive. Yet not only is such **Negative Concord** possible crosslinguistically, but even in English its meaning is almost always unmistakeable. Mick Jagger is not claiming in the line in (1) to be satisfied.

Moreover, while forms such as (1) are highly stigmatised, and certainly Non-Standard, they are also widespread throughout the English-speaking world. 'Double Negation' is not exclusive to any particular region or variety. It therefore cannot be dismissed as a minor morphosyntactic idiosyncrasy but must be accounted for alongside Standard negative constructions.

In this Chapter we will begin by exploring Standard negation, typically expressed by either *not* or *-n't*. We will then extend our analysis to a number of other negation-related phenomena, and make a comparison with Non-Standard negative forms specific to Scotland. In the last part of the chapter we will return to the construction above to see how it fits into a larger picture of English negatives.

6.1 *Not* and *-n't*

Standard English has two seemingly equivalent means of expressing negation: the independent word *not* and the affix *-n't*.

(2)   a.   Charlie is not eating haggis
      b.   Charlie isn't eating haggis

In sentences such as (2)a and (2)b *not* and *-n't* make identical semantic contributions. Their apparent synonymy, and surface similarity, suggests that *-n't* is simply a phonologically reduced form of *not*, tacked on to a preceding word as a **clitic**, a morpheme that cannot stand independently as a word but is not integrated into its host in the same manner as an affix. Examples of clitics include the shortened forms of *is* and *have*, *-'s* and *-'ve*, which must be preceded by some element on which to cliticise.

(3) a. Flora is eating haggis
    b. Flora's eating haggis
    c. Is Flora eating haggis?
    d. *'s Flora eating haggis?

(4) a. I have eaten haggis
    b. I've eaten haggis
    c. Have you eaten haggis?
    d. *'ve you eaten haggis?

Like *-n't* these contracted verb forms are identical in interpretation to their longer equivalents. But *-n't* differs in its syntactic distribution from *not* in ways other than might be expected only from the limitations imposed by the requirements of cliticisation.

The word *not* typically follows the highest auxiliary in a clause. It can occur anywhere in the auxiliary 'range' however, although many speakers find it decreasingly acceptable the more auxiliaries it follows. It is ungrammatical for *not* to follow a lexical verb.

(5) a. Alastair might not have been eating haggis
    b. Alastair might have not been eating haggis
    c. Alastair might have been not eating haggis
    d. *Alastair might have been eating not haggis

The ungrammaticality of negation after a lexical verb is in line with the proposal, already discussed in Chapter 5, that lexical verbs in English do not undergo Head Movement to T. If negation must Merge to *v*P or some higher projection, it follows that auxiliary verbs will precede *not*.

Not is not only possible in a range of positions within the clause, but also may modify an adjective. In these instances it is typically used with an adjective that does not have a form with a negative prefix such as *un-*. *Not* may also be employed with a negative adjective. Here the two negatives, one syntactic and the other morphological, do together have a positive interpretation, unlike the prescriptively scorned 'Double Negatives' discussed in the introduction.

(6)   a. Billy had some not nice haggis (cf. *unnice)
      b. His not inconsiderable expertise impressed me
          =His potentially considerable expertise impressed me

These uses, in which *not* applies to a particular lexical item or phrase, are termed **constituent negation**. In applying to both verbal and adjectival constituents *not* shows characteristics of an adverbial. We can see the similarity to adverbs as well in examples such as (7)a, where *is* precedes negation in the same way as did *soon* in (7)b (repeated from Chapter 4), or another adverb.

(7)   a. He was not happy
      b. He was soon happy
      c. Haggis is frequently delicious

The form -*n't* has a far more restricted distribution that *not*. It may only be realised on the highest auxiliary in a series, even for auxiliary forms that can otherwise be used with -*n't*.

(8)   a. They haven't eaten haggis
      b. They won't have eaten haggis
      c. They will have not eaten haggis
      d. *They will haven't eaten haggis

In essence, -*n't* is restricted to the finite (tensed) form of auxiliaries. *Have* in (8)c and (8)d is a non-finite form which happens to be syncretic with third person plural form in (8)a and (8)b.

The limited distribution of -*n't* differentiates it not just from *not*, but also clitics such as -'s and -'ve, which have an essentially identical distribution to uncontracted forms of *is*, and *have*, with the exception of the clause-initial examples such as (3)d and (4)d, which lack a host for the clitic.

(9)   a. They have eaten haggis
      b. They've eaten haggis
      c. They will have eaten haggis
      d. They will've eaten haggis
      e. They will not have eaten haggis
      f. They will not've eaten haggis

These clitics are also indifferent to what kinds of constituents they attach to: in (9)b -'ve cliticises to a pronoun, in (9)d it cliticises to a modal auxiliary verb, and in (9)f to the negation *not*.

Clitics also have no effect on the phonological or morphological realisation of their 'hosts'. On the other hand, -*n't* produces idiosyncratic irregular verb forms such as *won't* and *shan't*, akin to, for example, irregular past tense inflections (e.g. *wrote* rather than **writed*). Its restriction to particular verb types, in this instance auxiliaries, also suggests a similarity to other types of inflectional morphology. Recall, for example, that past tense *-ed* (or irregular equivalent) is not available for modal verbs.

The observations that *-n't* appears in only a single syntactic position of the many available to *not*, and exhibits other characteristics not shared with contractions such as *-'ve*, indicates that it is neither a reduced form of *not* nor a clitic. Its behaviour is much more like that of an inflectional affix, and as such we might expect it to constitute part of the functional structure of the clause, akin to Tense.

That said, while *not* and *-n't* have distinct (morpho)syntactic behaviour, it would also be incorrect to designate them as wholly separate, given that they make apparently identical semantic contributions, and are so clearly related in form. We can instead account for them as expressions of a negation feature, which may be instantiated as one or the other depending on its position in the syntax.

Considering the range of positions in which we get constituent negation, it appears that any verbal head (i.e. the *v*P itself, or a functional auxiliary head) may enter the derivation with an uninterpretable negation feature [*u*NEG]. This feature can also be present in an adjectival head. *Not* has an interpretable negation feature [*i*NEG], and thereby checks its uninterpretable counterpart by Merge with any phrase having a [*u*NEG]. This checking represents a type of **Agree** operation, a matching of feature values between a head and a constituent Merged within the phrase it projects.

(10)

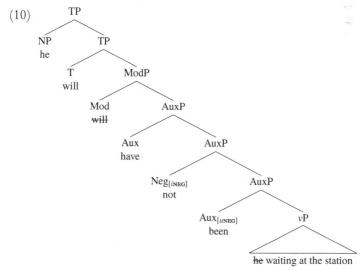

Of course, *-n't* does not express constituent negation. Rather, it gives us **sentential negation**, applying to a whole clause rather than a single constituent. *Not* appearing directly after the first auxiliary verb has a similar interpretation. In many instances, the contrast in meaning between constituent and sentential negation is subtle, or essentially non-existent, but we must still differentiate these syntactically.

(11) a. He will be not happy (constituent negation)
          'He will be unhappy'
      b. He {won't/will not} be happy (sentential negation)
          'It is not the case that he will be happy'

We can also demonstrate the difference between constituent and sentential negation by using both simultaneously in a single clause. This is another example in which two negatives do cancel each other out.

(12) He won't have not eaten the haggis
      =He will have eaten the haggis

The limitation of the affix *-n't* to tensed auxiliaries suggests that T has a special relationship with negation. It is also notable that although *not* can appear in a wide range of positions with respect to auxiliaries, as shown in (5), it cannot precede the highest auxiliary verb.

(13) *He not might have been eating haggis

As a preliminary proposal, then, we will posit that negation may be realised on T as on other functional heads, but only as an interpretable feature. This [*i*NEG] feature results in sentential negation, which is realised as *-n't* in tandem with tense morphology. Merge of *not* in TP is ruled out, because there is no [*u*NEG] feature that must be checked.

(14)

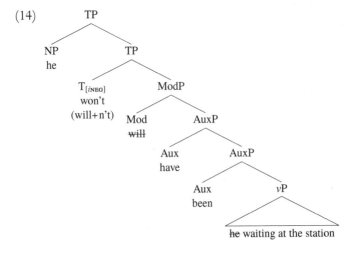

6.1.1 Negation and modality

The position of *not* within the sequence of auxiliaries brings us once more to the question raised in Chapters 4 and 5 regarding the position of the highest auxiliary in relation to T. You may have noticed that in trees (10) and (14) above the highest auxiliary begins in its own projection and Moves to T. Justification for this separation of the highest auxiliary from T can be found in variation in the interpretation of modal verbs in relation to negation.

Recall that modal auxiliaries can be divided into two categories: epistemic modals, which denote possibility or necessity, and deontic modals, which denote permission or obligation. Modal verbs can also be divided according to the dimension of negative **scope**, a term which describes the semantic interpretation of one element being nested in the interpretation of another.

(15) He may not eat haggis

In its deontic reading, denoting permission, *may* tends to have **inverse scope** with respect to *not*, such that its meaning falls within the meaning of the negation, contrary to the surface word order. With emphasis on *not* it can also have **surface scope** in which the negation is interpreted as falling within the permission denoted by *may*, in line with the modal-negation word order.

(16) a. 'He does not have permission to eat haggis' (inverse scope)
      b. 'He has permission to not eat haggis' (surface scope)

We can explain the mismatch between word order and the interpretation in instances of inverse scope such as (16)a through Head Movement, which we have already suggested may occur for modal auxiliaries. If *may* Merges initially as the head of a Mod(al)P projection, below negation, and then Remerges in T, above negation, an inverse scope reading will arise when it is interpreted at LF in its original Merge position, despite being pronounced at PF in its higher position.

(17)

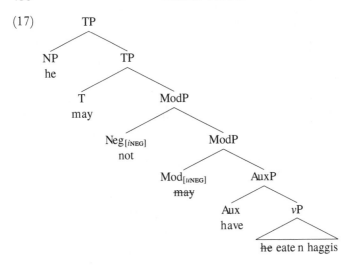

Not all modal auxiliaries allow both interpretations. In its epistemic reading, denoting possibility, *may* has a surface scope reading; an inverse scope reading is impossible.

(18)   He may not be eating haggis
     ≠'It is not possible that he is eating haggis' (inverse scope)
     'It is possible that he is not eating haggis' (surface scope)

The availability of inverse scope readings is not, though, as simple as a difference between epistemic and deontic interpretations. *Should* and *must* have only a surface scope reading, regardless of whether they are epistemic or deontic.

(19)   a.   He should not eat haggis (deontic)
        ≠He is not required to eat haggis (inverse scope)
        =He is required not to eat haggis (surface scope)
    b.   He must not have eaten haggis (epistemic)
        ≠It is not the case that he probably has eaten haggis (inverse scope)
        =It is probably the case that he has not eaten haggis (surface scope)
    c.   He cannot eat haggis
        ='He is not allowed to eat haggis (inverse scope)
        ≠He is allowed to not eat haggis (surface scope)

Like *may*, *might* favours inverse scope when deontic, but permits only surface scope when epistemic.

(20) He might not have eaten haggis
       ≠It is not possible for him to have eaten haggis (inverse scope)
       =It is possible for him to have not eaten haggis (surface scope)

It is also not the case that the availability of inverse scope with modal
verbs is tied to their strength on the scale of possibility/permission
versus necessity/obligation. Epistemic *can* is similar to epistemic *may*
in only allowing surface scope if *not* is stressed prosodically.[1] Unlike for
deontic *may*, however, the same distinction is made for deontic *can*. In
other words, while deontic *may* cannot have inverse scope, for deontic
can it is preferred.

(21) a. He cannot eat the haggis (deontic)
          =He is not allowed to eat haggis (inverse scope)
          ≠He is allowed to not eat haggis (surface scope)
       b. He cannot be eating haggis (epistemic)
          It is not possible that he is eating haggis (inverse scope)
          ≠It is possible that he is not eating haggis (surface scope)
          (cf. He can not be eating haggis)

The surface scope alternatives to these sentences give us another
indication that there is distinction between constituent and sentential
negation.

(22) a. He can not eat the haggis
          'He is allowed to not eat the haggis'
       b. He can not be eating haggis
          'It is possible that he is not eating haggis'

Where *not* is stressed following *can* it appears to have Merged with the
projection immediately below it: there is no inverse scope because *can*
has not Moved over it. Where *not* is unstressed it acts as a sentential
negative affix in T akin to -*n't*. The atypical lack of space in the orthog-
raphy of *cannot* apparently indicates that it functions as a single word.
Therefore, while the only surface difference between these is prosodic,
they have distinct underlying syntactic structures.

---

[1] The epistemic use of *can* is a common prescriptivist bugbear. Many children have
     it drilled into them that *can* can only represent the ability to do something, but in
     practice it is often synonymous with *may* in indicating permission.

(23)   SENTENTIAL NEGATION

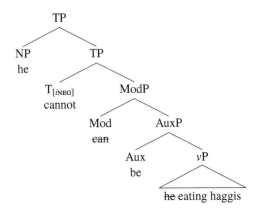

(24)   CONSTITUENT NEGATION

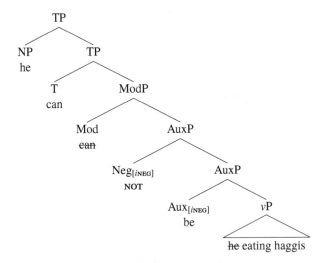

Inverse scope readings are no longer possible if *not* follows multiple auxiliaries. Contrasts such as that in (25) lend further support to the argument that inverse scope reflects the initial position of a modal verb preceding negation: if only the highest in a string of auxiliaries Moves to T, then there cannot have been Movement over *not* in (25)b.

(25) a. He may not be eating haggis (when she arrives)
   =He is not allowed to be eating haggis
   =He is allowed to no be eating haggis

   b. He may be not eating haggis (when she arrives)
   ≠He is not allowed to be eating haggis
   =He is allowed to not be eating haggis

If inverse scope is the result of Head Movement over negation, then surface scope means either that some modal verbs are interpreted at LF in their Moved positions, or that they Merge above negation. The latter explanation is appealing, in that it accounts for why some modals never have inverse scope readings, but it requires that there be two positions in which modals can Merge initially. The lower of these would be some Modal head, and the higher one T. As described above, which modals Merge in which position would be somewhat idiosyncratic. We will revisit this hypothesis in the next section.

Ideally we would be able to tie these facts about scope with respect to negation to our observations about the order of double modals in Chapter 4. Unfortunately, the lack of correspondence to any other grouping of this set of auxiliaries, especially the epistemic/deontic distinction so clearly relevant for double modals, rules out an analysis that unites the two.

6.2 *Do*-support with negation

Up to this point we have depicted *not* as Merged in some functional projection, with negation alternatively realised as *-n't* where a negative feature is present in T. However, while negation can follow the highest auxiliary in a clause (in the form of *not*), or be realised on it (in the form of *-n't*), in the absence of any auxiliary verb the presence of negation requires a 'dummy' auxiliary *do* akin to that we have seen in questions.

(26) a. *I not like haggis
   b. *I like not haggis
   c. I do not like haggis

In Chapter 5 we argued that *do*-support was a Last Resort PF operation, which occurred because an uninterpretable tense feature, Moved to Remerge in C, was too distant from the interpretable tense feature in the lexical verb at the point of Spell Out for feature-checking to occur. *Do* was therefore inserted in order to host overt expression of tense features and prevent the derivation from crashing.

In the case of negation, *not* also blocks the realisation of tense inflection on the verb, thereby triggering insertion of *do*. There are two possible explanations for this situation. The first is that intervention by *not* Merged in *v*P is sufficient to block realisation of tense morphology at PF. In this analysis, we would assume that tense inflection applies post-syntactically, and is dependent on the linear relationship of immediate precedence. But this approach ignores the feature-checking that is likely to occur during the derivation. Regardless of what else is Merged in *v*P, if it is selected by T it should be in a local enough relationship with that head to check its [*u*T] feature.

The second explanation involves the intervention of an additional functional head, Neg, which has a [*u*NEG] feature that is checked by Merge of *not*, as already proposed. This Neg head appears between T and *v*P, so that, as with questions, they are no longer in a local enough relationship for feature-checking to occur. *Do* is then inserted at the point of Spell Out to prevent the unchecked [*u*T] feature from causing the derivation to crash.

(27)

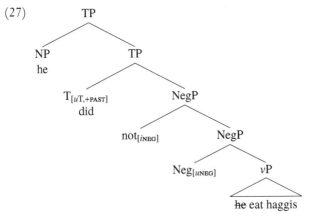

This approach forces a re-evaluation of our analysis of negation. A Neg head must always be present where there is no auxiliary, as otherwise *do*-support would not be required. We therefore have to assume that all instances of negation involve an independent NegP projection, which may be selected by T or any auxiliary projection. Where Neg appears between T and Aux the auxiliary verb will pass through the Neg head in undergoing Movement to T.

(28)

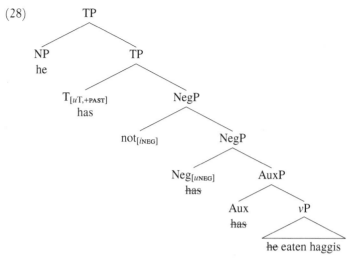

Although this analysis requires significant freedom in terms of where Neg can Merge, placement of this head is straightforward if lexical verbs and auxiliaries share some categorial [+V] feature that can be selected by Neg. Presumably this is the same feature that is selected by T. If Neg not only requires a [+V] complement, but has this categorial classification itself, we can also explain how it is selected by a range of auxiliaries and T. A potential problem arises under this approach in terms of the rest of the auxiliary range. If a NegP projection can have as its complement any verbal or auxiliary projection, and in turn be the complement of any verbal or auxiliary projection, how do these projections maintain their strict order with respect to each other in the presence of an intervening NegP? The simplest solution is the proposal, already made in Chapter 4, that these functional projections are ordered semantically, rather than by c-selection. The presence of a negative projection will therefore have no effect on their order, which is not constrained by the syntax.

The introduction of an independent NegP projection also necessitates an amendment to our analysis of -n't. The features of Neg may Move to T along with an auxiliary passing through this position. If Neg consistently has an uninterpretable negation feature, then this allows two possibilities for it to be checked. An interpretable negation feature on *not* will check this [uNEG] feature where it Merges in NegP. As proposed before, however, T may have in its head this [iNEG] feature, which will check the uninterpretable feature Moved from Neg with the auxiliary. The confluence of the auxiliary, tense and negation will result in realisation of an -n't affix.

(29)

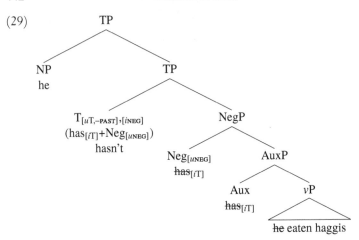

Here the notion that words are bundles of features comes to the fore. Sometimes these feature bundles are inserted into the derivation en masse as complete lexical items. In other instances, as above, features come together as part of the derivation. Either way these bundles are only converted to pronounceable units after Spell Out, when phonological (and morphological) rules may be applied. They do not, during the derivation, have the form of words as we say them.

Even in the absence of an auxiliary, the inflectional affix -n't is still possible preceding a lexical verb. In this scenario the features of Neg undergo Head Movement to T independently. As in any instance where an uninterpretable tense feature is unchecked, *do*-support applies as a Last Resort operation.

(30)

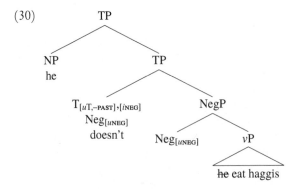

The independent Movement of the Neg head (or, rather, its features) to T allows us as well to maintain the hypothesis that some modal verbs originate in T, and others Move to T from a separate modal auxiliary head. A 'Moved' modal (one that has an inverse scope interpretation) will pass through Neg, thereby 'collecting' an uninterpretable negation feature. Where a modal originates in T, and therefore has surface scope, this [uNEG] feature will Move to T independently, combining with the modal to be expressed as an -n't affix.

(31)

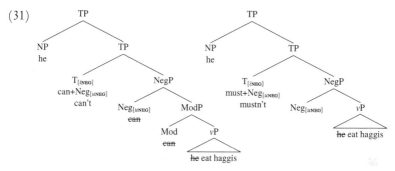

As with questions, *be* is an exception among lexical verbs, and does not have *do*-support with negation.

(32) a. *He {does not/doesn't} be happy
       b. He {is not/isn't} happy

Lexical *have* may also pattern this way, depending on the variety of the speaker.

(33) a. %I {have not/haven't} (any) wool
       b. %I do not have wool
       c. %I have not got wool
       d. %I {do not/don't} got wool

Reviewing the evidence discussed so far, we can see that verbs which require *do*-support in questions also require *do*-support with negation. Those verbs that do not have *do*-support in questions (auxiliaries, lexical *be* and, for some speakers, lexical *have*) also lack this operation with negation. This correlation falls out from (un)availability of Head Movement for these classes, which itself can be boiled down to checking of a single feature. Recall the argument that this Head Movement depends on the strength of [iT]. If this feature is strong, as it is for auxiliaries and lexical *be*, the verb (and its concomitant features) will Move to T; if this feature is weak, as it is for other lexical verbs, no Movement is triggered, but its interpretable tense feature may still be checked by selection.

To summarise, speakers who have a strong interpretable feature on lexical *have* allow it to undergo subject-auxiliary inversion in questions and precede *not*; speakers who do not require *do*-support in these instances. Particular constructions such as these thus can be argued to cluster together because they reflect a single underlying syntactic feature parameterised for strength, rather than existing as independent, unrelated rules.

6.3 Negation in questions

The behaviour of negation in questions gives further support to the distinction we have made between *not* and *-n't*. The former cannot precede the subject in questions, but the latter may.

(34)   a.   *Do not you like haggis?
        b.   Do you not like haggis?
        c.   Don't you like haggis?

In the (34) examples there are two possible reasons for *do*-support: question formation and the presence of negation. In both (34)b and (34)c the features of T have Remerged in C, as in any main clause question. Insertion of auxiliary *do* as a Last Resort PF operation should therefore apply at PF regardless of the presence of a negation feature. *Do* will not be inserted in T, as is typical where a NegP blocks realisation of negation features on a verb, because at the point of Spell Out tense features will have already undergone Head Movement. In the case of (34)c the negation feature Moved to T will undergo Movement along with the other features of that head, leading to realisation of the affix *-n't* in the C position. This carrying along of negation features applies for auxiliaries other than *do* as well.

(35)

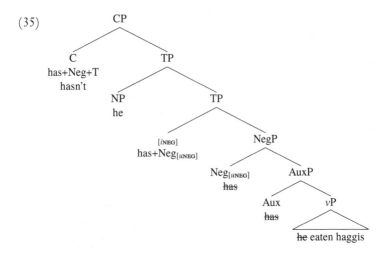

Negative questions introduce another example that underscores the notion that the pronunciation of lexical items is only determined at PF. For most Standard English speakers first person singular *aren't* is possible in questions, including **tag questions** appended at the ends of declarative clauses, but not declarative sentences.

(36) a. *I aren't invited
     b. Aren't I invited?
     c. I'm invited, aren't I?

This discrepancy can be explained if *aren't* as a lexical item represents a confluence of tense, person/number, negation, and question features. In the absence of a question feature, a bundle of auxiliary *be*, present tense, first person singular and negative features will not be realised as *aren't* at PF. We cannot say, therefore, that the word *aren't* Moves in any syntactic sense from a position in Aux or T, as not all of the requisite features for *aren't* have been Merged at earlier points in the derivation.

In some varieties, including Scottish and Northern English ones, speakers allow first person singular *be* with a negative inflection to be realised as *amn't*. This form is permitted in both declarative and interrogative contexts.

(37) a. %I amn't invited
     b. %Amn't I invited?
     c. %I'm invited, amn't I?

While it is Non-Standard, *amn't* is exactly the regular form we might expect from a combination of present tense, first person singular *be* and a negative inflection. As such, it gives lie to any claims that Standard morphosyntax is intrinsically more logical or consistent. For speakers who do not fill the ***amn't* gap** there is simply no PF representation corresponding to a *be* with present tense, first person singular, and negative features.

The reasons behind the absence of *amn't* in Standard English are unclear. It is possible it has arisen because of the unusual consonant cluster of proximate nasals, but the existence of this form in other varieties shows it is not impossible, or even particularly difficult, for English speakers to articulate. There are similar arbitrary gaps elsewhere, such as the ungrammaticality of *mayn't* for speakers of many varieties. Where a particular feature grouping has no single representation at Spell Out, the availability of alternatives (e.g. *I am not, I may not*) means that there is no strong linguistic pressure to have a substitute to express these features as a single word.

On the opposite end of the spectrum, the highly stigmatised *ain't*, present in a number of Non-Standard varieties, represents a smaller bundle of features. It can be used as a form of negated present tense *be* for any person or number, and for some speakers stands in for other auxiliaries as well.

(38) a. {I/you/she/they, etc.} ain't invited
     b. She ain't seen him (=have not)

In these examples 'Movement' is not necessarily just Remerge of a lexical item that has already been Merged at some point in the syntactic derivation, but can also involve features rather than words or lexical items per se. Therefore, while a constituent may Merge multiple times in the syntax, Movement, in the sense of audible displacement of a word to a different point in a sentence, is not strictly a syntactic process, and we cannot say that a word exists in its pronounceable form at any point during the derivation prior to Spell Out. Moreover, we can say that syntactic derivation is not just lexically-driven, as we have already claimed, but more precisely feature-driven.

6.4 Negation in Scottish English

Our discussion so far has given us several sources of variation with respect to negation: syntactic differences, pertaining to where particular features are Merged and checked, and realisational differences, pertaining to the pronunciation of particular groups of features after Spell Out. Scottish English has *no* and *-nae* instead of the *not* and *-n't* used in other varieties. The question here is whether these negative forms are distinct on a syntactic level, or whether they are simply alternative pronunciations of the same morphemes.

(39) a. He's no eating haggis
     b. He isnae eating haggis

Although they are undoubtedly related to their Standard counterparts in terms of etymology, these Scottish negators do not exhibit identical behaviour. Unlike *-n't*, which alternates freely with *not*, *-nae* must be used in the presence of an auxiliary. The only exceptions to this requirement are constrastive negation, with emphasis on *no*, or instances where the auxiliary itself has been contracted.

(40) a. %He isnae eating haggis
     b.   *He is no eating haggis
     c. %He is NO eating haggis
     d. %He's no eating haggis

In questions, the *-nae* form, unlike *-n't*, cannot Move with an auxiliary that undergoes Movement to C. Instead, akin to *not*, Scottish negation remains in situ in the presence of subject-auxiliary inversion, and is pronounced as *no* rather than *-nae*.

(41) a. Isn't he eating haggis?
     b. Is he not eating haggis?
     c. *Isnae he eating haggis?
     d. %Is he no eating haggis?

Taken together these restrictions indicate that both forms of Scottish negation are equivalent to English *not* that Merges in NegP in order to check an uninterpretable negation feature. The difference between them is one of pronunciation rather than syntactic position or behaviour. If an appropriate 'host' auxiliary is available negation will be realised as a clitic *-nae* after Spell Out. Otherwise, it will be realised as *no*. In instances of contrastive negation the emphasis in pronunciation must be at PF, a further indication that the *-nae/no* contrast is determined post-syntactically.

Unlike the *-n't* affix, the *-nae* clitic rarely leads to deformation of the root to which it attaches. For example, *won't* and *shan't* are *willnae* and *shallnae*. An exception to this is the change in vowel from [e] in *dae* 'do' to [ə] in *dinnae* 'do not', but this can be explained as either an articulartory dissimilation of repetitive vowel sounds that otherwise occur in *dae* and *nae*, or reduction of the vowel sound in line with a general tendency, across varieties, to weaken unstressed vowels.[2] The lack of change in other forms again highlights that, unlike the inflection *-n't*, *-nae* is not an integrated part of the word to which it attaches.

A consequence of this analysis is an apparent limitation on where an interpretable negation feature may be Merged in Scottish English. Unlike in Standard English, it is impossible for the T head to have a [*i*NEG] feature, as this would result in a negative affix that would be 'carried' to C by Head Movement when the features of T are Remerged in this position. The Standard/Scottish English difference in negation therefore represents another instance of a difference arising from the behaviour of a single feature, here in terms of where it may occur with respect to particular functional heads, rather than its strength.

---

[2] For some Scottish speakers in the northeast *dinnae* can further be reduced to *da*.
   (i) %I da ken
       'I don't know'

6.5 Negative Polarity Items

Our current picture of negation encompasses only forms expressed by checking of features present in the functional structure of the clause, either in a functional head, or through Merge of a negator (*not* or *no/-nae*) in a phrase projected by that head. There are other types of 'negative' words, including a set of so-called **Negative Polarity Items** (NPIs), which do not denote negation in themselves but may only appear in negative or interrogative contexts. Many English NPIs contain the morpheme *any*.[3]

(42) a. *I saw anybody
      b. I didn't see anybody
      c. Did you see anybody
      d. *I have any money
      e. I don't have any money
      f. Do you have any money?

There are also a number of idiomatic expressions that function as NPIs.

(43) a. */#He lifted a finger to help
      b.   He didn't lift a finger to help
      c. */#I have seen him in donkey's years
      d.   I haven't seen him in donkey's years

The negative element that permits the NPI need not be *not*, or *-n't*. 'Negative' adverbs such as *never*, *rarely* and *scarcely* can also create a context in which an NPI can appear.

(44) a. I never had any money
          (cf.*I always had any money)
      b. I rarely had any money
          (cf.*I often had any money)

The array of possible NPI **licensors**, as well as their potential distance from the NPI, indicates that this is not an agreement relationship mediated by feature-checking. Instead, the NPI is **licensed** at LF.

We have already introduced the concept of scope, an element falling within the interpretation of another, when discussing the interaction between modal verbs and negation. Here the NPI must be

---

[3] Another set of elements, called **Positive Polarity Items** (PPIs), are resistant to negative contexts. Many of these correspond directly to NPIs.
   (i)   I saw somebody
   (ii) I have some money

within the scope of its licensor, and while scope is essentially semantic, it is nevertheless constrained by the syntax, specifically c-command. An NPI Merged in a low position in the tree cannot 'look' upwards in order to check for a c-commanding licensor. At Spell Out, however, the LF component can translate the c-command relationship as one of scope, thereby ensuring that the NPI is licensed. Evidence that this licensing occurs at LF rather than before Spell Out comes from the ungrammaticality of an NPI moving to precede its licensor, even if it initially Merges in a position where it would be licensed. For instance, an NPI which acts as an object in an active sentence cannot be Moved to function as a subject in an equivalent passive sentence.

(45) a. I didn't break anything

　　 b. *Anything wasn't broken by me
　　　　 (cf. Nothing was broken by me)

Similarly, an NPI object cannot be fronted past the position of negation.

(46) a. I don't have any money
　　 b. *Any money, I don't have
　　　　 (cf. Money, I don't have)

In these passivation and topicalisation examples the NPI begins in a position that is c-commanded by negation, which should be sufficient for it to be licensed. By Spell Out this configuration has been disrupted by Remerge of the NPI in a higher position. It is thus the final syntactic position of the NPI that matters rather than any other place it Merges during the derivation.

　　 Licensing of NPIs can also occur across clause boundaries. Whether it is permitted in an embedded clause where negation is in the main clause depends on the main verb or other predicate.

(47) a. He did not {know/realise/say} that she had any money
　　 b. *He did not {explain/like} that she had any money
　　 c. *He was not {pleased/disappointed} that she had any money

The sensitivity of this NPI licensing over multiple clauses to specific matrix verbs again points to a semantic explanation rather than a purely syntactic one, as otherwise we might expect the CP to consistently intervene (or not) between the negation of the matrix verb and the NPI. That said, as we will see in the next section, embedded clauses under negation are not all interpreted in equivalent ways, and it is possible that these should be distinguished syntactically.

6.6 Neg-Raising

The relative freedom of negation applies not just within the range of auxiliaries or to adverbs/adjectives but can also extend beyond the clause. In **Neg(ative)-Raising** constructions a verb which takes a finite CP clause as a complement is negated, but the negation is interpreted as applying to the verb within the embedded complement.

(48)   Charlie doesn't {think/believe} that Nancy likes haggis
      =Charlie {thinks/believes} that Nancy doesn't like haggis

Only specific verbs can act as Neg-Raisers. Unlike *think* and *believe*, *know* and *remember* have only surface interpretations with respect to negation.

(49)   Charlie didn't {know/remember} that Nancy liked haggis
      ≠Charlie {knew/remembered} that Nancy didn't like haggis

Older proposals regarding Neg-Raising dubbed it **Not-Transportation**, based on the notion that *not* was moving from the lower clause to the higher one. Our Minimalist reconception of Movement brings up a number of questions regarding this sort of analysis. In our Chapter 5 discussion of questions we argued that the Movement of *wh*-words does not occur across arbitrarily long distances. Where a question word of this type begins in an embedded clause it must Merge first in the embedded CP before Remerging in the CP of the matrix (main) clause. Otherwise, when the rest of the CP phase containing the *wh*-word is sent to Spell Out, it will no longer be available as part of the syntactic derivation for further Movement. The embedded CP therefore acts as an escape hatch, and must have a [uQ,uWH] feature to motivate Remerge of the *wh*-word before its subsequent Remerge in the higher CP.

The phase-based cycle of Spell Out means that in order for a negation *not* to Move out of an embedded clause it would also need to 'stop' in the embedded CP; C would require some negative feature [uNEG] to motivate this Movement. An additional negation feature (indeed, a NegP) would have to be present in the matrix clause to motivate Remerge of negation in its final position.

Can we be sure that the negation in a Neg-Raising sentence actually begins in the embedded clause? Neg-Raising sentences license NPIs in an embedded clause. Non-durative *until*, which gives a single point in time when something will happen, is another example of an element that requires a negative or interrogative context.

(50) a. Lucy won't arrive until tomorrow
  b. *Lucy will arrive until tomorrow

It can be licensed in a Neg-Raising context.

(51) I didn't {think/believe} Lucy would arrive until tomorrow

As we saw in the previous section, though, a number of matrix verbs allow licensing of NPIs across clause boundaries. Not all of these are necessarily Neg-Raisers.

(52) I didn't {know/remember} that Lucy would arrive until tomorrow

An NPI can also be licensed by a matrix verb with an intrinsically negative meaning in the absence of any overt negator such as *not*.

(53) I doubt she'll arrive until tomorrow

NPIs therefore do not offer a reliable indication that negation is present in the embedded clause.

Another argument that negation begins in the embedded clause comes from tag questions, which reverse the polarity of the declarative clause to which they are appended.

(54) a. Billy will arrive on time, won't he?
  b. Billy won't arrive on time, will he?

A tag question matching the embedded verb in a Neg-Raising sentence will be positive, possibly indicating that there must be some negative feature in the embedded clause that requires this reversed polarity.

(55) a. I don't think he'll arrive on time, will he?
  b. *I don't think he'll arrive on time, won't he?

This argument is again weak, as the polarity reversal in tag questions is not an absolute requirement. For some speakers they may echo the polarity form of the declarative sentence to which they are appended.

(56) a. %He will arrive on time, will he?
  b. %He won't arrive on time, won't he?
  c. %He is a good boy, is he?

Unlike with *wh*-Movement, where we could see the quantifiers stranded by Movement in at least one variety of English, there is no overt indication of negative Movement. It is also possible to have negation in both the main clause and the embedded clause, such that they cancel each other out. This configuration raises a question about why an uninterpretable negation feature in the main clause would prompt Remerge of the lower *not* in some cases, resulting in a single negative interpretation, but in other instances prompt Merge of an additional *not*, resulting in two negative interpretations.

(57) I don't think he does not like haggis
      =I think that he likes haggis

Overall, there is no knock-down evidence from English that *not* Moves out of the embedded clause in Neg-Raising contexts, but also no solid evidence to rule out that it does. One remaining point of interest is the observation that speakers vary with respect to which verbs are Neg-Raisers. Some southern US speakers, for example, have a Neg-Raising reading with *guess*. For other speakers, sentences such as (58) have only a surface interpretation.

(58) I don't guess that he'll be late
      %=I guess he won't be late

Many British speakers also use the verb *imagine* to mean something like *suppose*, an interpretation unavailable to speakers of American English varieties. In this reading *imagine* is a Neg-Raiser. Where it means 'fantasise' it is not.

(59) I didn't imagine he would be late
      %='I supposed he wouldn't be late'
      ≠'I fantasised he wouldn't be late'

One way to explain the apparently idiosyncratic specificity of which verbs can and cannot be Neg-Raisers is to frame this as a selectional requirement: Neg-Raising verbs select for a CP with a [NEG] feature, and non-Neg-Raising verbs do not. This hypothesis is compatible with an analysis in which *not* Moves from the embedded clause. As we have said already, it would have to Remerge with the CP in order to do so.

This explanation is also compatible with an analysis in which *not* does not Merge in the lower clause initially, but instead Merges only in a NegP in the matrix clause. If so, the negation feature in C would act as an NPI, licensed by the matrix negation. Some partial evidence for this approach comes from the observation that verbs such as *think* can allow Neg-Raising with negative elements other than *not*.

(60) He {never/rarely} thought that she ate haggis
      ?=He thought that she {never/rarely} ate haggis

I leave open the exact analysis of Neg-Raising, except to say that it almost certainly involves a negative feature on the CP selected by the matrix verb, which cannot be selected by non-Neg-Raising verbs.

6.7 Negative Concord

We started this chapter with examples of 'Double Negation', where a clause has two elements syntactically which amount to a single negation semantically. Alongside our Rolling Stones example we can add lyrics from the soul singer Nina Simone and 1990s' R&B artist Aaliyah.

(61) a. I can't get no satisfaction
      b. I ain't got no home, ain't got no shoes ...
      c. Age ain't nothing but a number

Given that the negation here is not doubled, in the sense of the two negatives adding up to express a positive, this phenomenon is better termed Negative Concord (NC). Double negation (DN) does exist where independent negatives cancel each other out. Often this requires emphasis on one of the negators.

(62) I haven't got NO shoes
      'I have got some shoes'

It is tempting to argue that negative concord is really just NPI licensing, with negative forms replacing Standard NPIs. The (61) examples can be 'translated' into Standard English equivalents using *any* without altering their meaning (although they do lose some of their flair).

(63) a. I can't get any satisfaction
      b. I don't have any home, I don't have any shoes ...
      c. Age isn't anything but a number

Unlike an NPI, though, a negator in an NPI can precede the main sentential negation as a subject. In this sense they are not directly comparable.

(64) a. *Anybody didn't know that
          (cf. Nobody knew that)
      b. Nobody didn't know that

This difference indicates that Negative Concord is licensed not just at a semantic but also at a syntactic level. The concord between the two negatives also points to their having, at some point in the derivation, a single source. In the presence of two negative features we would expect true Double Negation.

   Recall our hypothesis that *not* within the auxiliary range is Merged in a NegP to check an [uNEG] feature in its head. We can extend this idea to encompass all negative structures: any element expressing negation contains a NegP. Recall as well that Movement is triggered by feature-checking, and that to the syntax a lexical item or word is really just a bundle of features.

Under our composite view of negation we can propose that Negative Concord involves an [*i*NEG] feature moving from its initial Merge position in the lower negative element (*no, nothing,* etc.) to Remerge in order to check an uninterpretable feature in a higher NegP. The interpretable feature is pronounced resumptively in both positions resulting in the morphologically 'Double' Negation. Because they are checked by the same interpretable feature, the two NegPs are understood as a unitary negation, even though each has its own uninterpretable negation feature. Where there is a negative subject, the same process applies, followed by subsequent Movement of the subject to Merge in TP.

Given the surface similarity to NC constructions, *any*-NPIs might be explained in the same way, with the PF component simply instantiating a particular bundle of features as e.g. *nothing* or *anything,* depending on whether the speaker is using a NC variety. This analysis is appealing in reducing this variation to a relatively trivial surface difference, especially considering that there are speakers who use both NC and NPIs, and that speakers who do not use NC themselves still typically understand it as intended, rather than as Double Negation. If this is so, an additional LF licensing restriction would still need to apply for NPIs, both to explain the ungrammaticality of sentences such as (64)a and to account for other contexts, such as questions, in which NPIs are licensed.

6.8 Conclusion

This chapter has investigated negation in Standard and Non-Standard contexts. Our analysis shows that a variety of negation-related phenomena can be accounted for through the introduction of a NegP projection, requiring checking of an uninterpretable negation feature in its head by an [*i*NEG] feature in various configurations. While different forms of negation within varieties (e.g. *not* and *-n't*) and across them (e.g. *-n't* and *-nae,* or NPI *any* and NC *no*) may appear to be surface forms of the same underlying structure, often they are syntactically distinct.

6.9 Further reading

For arguments that *-n't* is a negative affix rather than a clitic see Zwicky and Pullum (1983). Cormack and Smith (2002) look at the interaction between negation and modal verbs. Zanuttini (2001) discusses sentential negation.

For consideration of Negative Concord and related phenomena see Blanchette (2013, 2015), as well as Blanchette et al. (2018). See Weir (2013) for discussion of Scottish English negation. Collins and Postal (2014, 2017) offer recent analyses of Neg-Raising. Horn (1989) and Haegeman (1995) are classic overviews of phenomena related to negation, with the latter focused in particular on syntax.

6.10 Exercises

1. Trees

   Draw trees for the following sentences. You don't have to include features, but you should think about what they are.

   a. Maisie hasn't met Martha
   b. Lucy does not want any pancakes
   c. I will not be having any sausages
   d. Doesn't Billy like eggs?
   e. Must Martha not poach the eggs?
   f. Oscar will have not brought anything

2. Further analysis

   English has a phenomenon of Negative Inversion, in which an auxiliary Moves to precede a subject in the presence of a sentence-initial negative form. This inversion also involves *do*-support where relevant. It can occur with a variety of negative elements, but not *not*.

   i. Never have I seen such a thing
   ii. *Never I have seen such a thing
   iii. Only once did Hazel speak to Jack
   iv. Rarely does Julian visit Alec
   v. *Not have I seen such a thing

   What kind of structure could be proposed for these constructions? How do they fit with the proposals about negative features we have outlined in this chapter?

For Answers see edinburghuniversitypress.com/englishsyntax.

7 Non-finite complements

Visiting the Scottish side of my family as a child, I often encountered utterances such as (1).

(1)   The cat needs fed

Having lived in Scotland for many years now, I hear these forms, a verb such as *need* followed directly by a passive participle, at least once a week. Yet even though such constructions are widespread across Scotland and parts of the United States, to non-users they sound incomplete, as noted in an observation quoted in the *Boston Globe* (Freeman 2007), from a non-native Pittsburgher commenting on 'Pittsburghese'.

> The words to be are eliminated from phrases on a regular basis ... The sink needs fixed. The lawn needs cut. Just last week, we got a notice from our son's school, saying that the kids' homework 'needs reviewed' by parents.

While many speakers prefer the alternative with *to be*, as in (2)a, others may employ a progressive participle, as in (2)b. The latter is sometimes called a **concealed passive**, because it has a passive meaning without typical passive morphology.

(2)   a. The cat needs to be fed
       b. The cat needs feeding

All of these forms can also be used with an object preceding the embedded participle. Both the bare participle and *to be* versions are widely used and completely Standard with an object. Many speakers who do not use sentences such as (1) find ones such as (3)a unremarkable. Use of the progressive form is more regionally restricted, mainly confined to speakers in certain parts of England, and correlates with use of the progressive form without an object, as in (2)b.

(3) a. I need the car washed
     b. I need the car to be washed
     c. %I need the car washing

As seen in Chapters 2, 3 and 5, verbs can have NPs and CPs Merged within the split VP. The variation shown above indicates the need to expand our view of the shape of these 'objects' and how they are selected. In this chapter we will begin by looking at the structure of Standard non-finite complements, before considering these special cases.

7.1 Non-finite complements

Recall the difference between finite and non-finite verbs, outlined in Chapter 3. Finite verbs are tensed. Non-finite verbs may have all manner of other verbal morphology, but lack tense specifically. A clause with a finite verb can stand on its own, whereas a non-finite clause cannot be independent, indicating that tense is central to sentencehood.

(4) Dashing for the bus, he fell in a puddle

In (4) the non-finite clause headed by *dashing* functions as an adjunct: it is optional and unnecessary, not selected by the any other constituent. There is a subclass of verbs, however, that select for non-finite *to-infinitives*, verbs preceded by *to*. Not to be confused with the homophonous preposition, this *to* is an infinitival marker, indicating that the verb is tenseless. Non-finite verbs with *to* also lack any other verbal morphology.

(5) a. He needs to dash
     b. *He needs to dashing
     c. *He needs to dashed

As in many other instances we have seen throughout this text, the complementary distribution of non-finite *to* with tense suggests that they are the 'same thing', or, in this instance, alternative values of that thing. We therefore assume that *to* occurs in T and selects for a bare form of the verb. This non-finite T is in turn selected by a **matrix verb**.

7.1.1 Raising verbs

Some verbs such as *seem* can select for both finite and non-finite clauses.

(6) a. It seems [that he likes haggis] (finite)
     b. He seems [to like haggis] (non-finite)

Seem also happens to be a linking verb, comparable to copular *be*, which can have as its complement an adjective denoting a property of the subject. This adjective can be accompanied by a non-finite *to* form or progressive participle.

(7) a. He seems happy
     b. He seems happy eating haggis
     c. He seems happy to have eaten haggis

Not all verbs which take non-finite complements allow the range of other complement types given in (6) and (7). These other sentences can give us insight into the semantics of *seem* that will inform our analysis of sentences with non-finite complements such as (6)b. Where *seem* has a finite CP as a complement it also has an expletive *it* as its subject.

Recall that expletive subjects of this type are not semantically contentful, and are not Merged in theta-positions. Because these 'dummy' pronouns — inserted as a Last Resort to prevent derivations crashing due to the absence of a subject — have no meaning, they are not true arguments, and are not subject to the theta-criterion. A number of other verbs with finite complements can have expletive subjects of this type. Unlike instances where the verb has an additional object, the finite CP cannot Move to the subject position.

(8) a. It {seems/appears/happens} that he likes haggis
     b. *That he likes haggis {seems/appears/happens}
     c. It surprises me that he likes haggis
     d. That he likes haggis surprises me

Where *seem* has an adjectival complement it still does not assign a theta role to its subject. Rather, as with copular *be*, the theta role comes from the complement adjective. *Seem* and related linking verbs are more semantically contentful than *be*, but nevertheless essentially incompatible with an adverb such as *intentionally*, indicating agentivity. Forms such as (9) are possible, but only in a specialised sense where the subject is feigning happiness, as with these verbs the subject is an experiencer or theme, regardless of what they might do to try to induce this state in themselves.

(9) #He intentionally {was/became/seemed/appeared} happy

The incompatibility of *intentionally* with *seem* also applies in contexts with non-finite complements. Here the adverb is interpreted as modifying the embedded rather than the matrix verb, regardless of its position preceding *seem*.

(10) He intentionally seemed to miss the bus
= He seemed to intentionally miss the bus

Seem with non-finite *to* has other properties that indicate it does not assign an external (agentive/causative) theta role to its subject. It is possible to use this verb with weather verbs such as *rain* and *snow* which have expletive subjects. This *it* can be identified as an expletive because it cannot be replaced with any full NP, even among obvious candidates.

(11) a. {It/*The sky/*The clouds/*The weather} is raining
b. It {seems/appears/happens} to be raining today

Verbs such as *seem* are also compatible with expletive *there*. This expletive is distinguishable from *there* expressing location, as it can be used alongside locational *there* or *here* without being redundant or contradictory.

(12) a. There are three children {there/here}
b. There {seem/appear/happen} to be three children here.

Seem is possible as well with idiomatic subjects. Like expletives, the NPs in idioms are semantically vacuous. They have meaning in the context of the idiomatic expressions of which they form a part, but not independently: an idiom is a complete lexical item which cannot be semantically decomposed. Thus in English *headway* can be made, but uses of this word outside this expression are rare. When we speak of *grabbing a bull by the horns* we are almost exclusively referring to taking direct action in a difficult situation, rather than literally getting hold of a dangerous male bovine. Likewise, *letting the cat out of the bag* usually means revealing a secret rather than releasing some abused feline from captivity. These idiomatic meanings are maintained when these expressions combine with non-finite *seem*.

(13) a. Headway seems to have been made
'It seems that progress has been made'
b. The bull seems to have been grabbed by the horns
'It seems that direct action has been taken'
c. The cat seems to have been let out of the bag
'It seems that the secret has been revealed'

Another indication that *seem* does not assign an external theta role to its subject is the consistency of meaning with passivisation where it takes a non-finite complement. In (14)a the agent of *phone* is *Alastair*. In (14)b, where the non-finite clause is passivised, Alastair remains the agent (rather than *Jack*). If *seem* assigned a theta role to its subject we would expect a change to meaning here. As it stands, only the verb *phone* is assigning a theta role to the subject, and as with any instance of passivisation the alteration of information structure does not affect the fundamental semantics of the argument-predicate relationships.

(14) a. Alastair seems to have phoned Jack
　　　b. Jack seems to have been phoned by Alastair

Taking all this evidence together, we have a strong indication that *seem* assigns no external theta role to it subject. At the same time, the subject of a sentence such as (15) must be assigned a theta role by the embedded verb because it is an argument of this predicate, and more generally because a semantically contentful argument such as this requires a theta role to satisfy the theta-criterion.

(15) Nancy seems to be reading a book

As with any argument, the subject will therefore be Merged initially with a phrase projected by a theta role assigner, i.e. in a theta-position, in this instance the *v*P of the embedded verb.

(16)

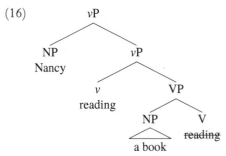

The subject will then Remerge with the embedded TP.

(17)

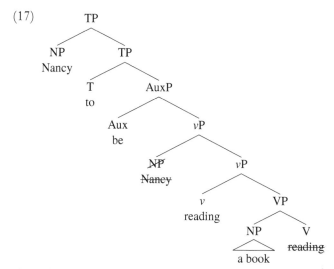

Non-finite T does not, unlike finite T, assign Nominative Case, which means that this Movement cannot be motivated by Case assignment. There is evidence from floating quantifiers, though, that the subject Merges in this position, as seen in (18). We will therefore assume, as we did in Chapter 5, that this Remerge is motivated by an Extended Projection Principle (EPP) feature, essentially a requirement that TPs have a subject in English.

(18) The children seem all to have read the book

The non-finite TP will then be selected by the matrix verb. Because it assigns no external theta role, *seem*, like unaccusative and passive verbs, is a bare VP, lacking *v*P and AgrOP projections. The lack of theta role assignment by *seem* means that the subject need not be in a local relationship with this verb. Instead, finite T Attracts the subject of the lower verb as the closest NP/argument which may check its uninterpretable features. This subject therefore Remerges directly with the matrix TP, where it is assigned Case, and undergoes subject-verb agreement.

(19)

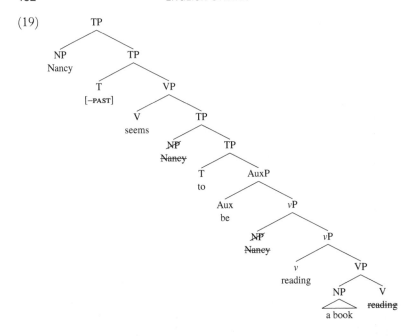

Because the subject 'raises' from the embedded clause to the subject position of the matrix clause, verbs such as *seem* are called **Subject-to-Subject Raising** verbs, or more typically just Raising verbs. A number of predicates which take non-finite complements and do not assign theta roles to their subjects fit into this category, among them *appear, happen* and *tend*. There are also a set of adjectives that act as Raising predicates in copular constructions, such as *likely*.

(20) Charlie is likely to read the book too

Not all verbs that take non-finite complements have the same characteristics as *seem*. In the next section we look at so-called **Control** verbs, which also take non-finite complements, but are semantically and syntactically distinct from Raising verbs.

7.1.2 Control verbs

On the surface, sentences such as (21) appear identical apart from the difference in matrix predicate.

(21) a. Nancy seemed to be happy
     b. Nancy tried to be happy

Closer inspection reveals that *try* passes all the diagnostics, which *seem* fails, that indicate external theta role assignment. First, it may be used with *intentionally*. In a sentence such as (22) the adverb is interpreted as modifying the matrix rather than the embedded predicate.

(22) a. Alastair intentionally tried to break the window
=Alastair's effort to break the window was intentional
(cf. Alastair intentionally seemed to break the window)

Try is marginal with expletive weather *it*. Speakers do make utterances such as (23), but only in a specialised sense of personifying atmospheric conditions.

(23) */#It is trying to rain

Expletive *there* is categorically ungrammatical with *try*.

(24) *There tried to be three children here

Idiomatic subjects are also impossible, or at least dubious, with *try*. Example (25)a is unacceptable because inanimate *headway* cannot make an effort to do something, while (25)b appears only to have a non-idiomatic interpretation where an actual steer is making an effort to have its horns taken hold of.

(25) a. */#Headway tried to be made
b. The bull tried to be grabbed by the horns

Some speakers report that there is ambiguity in (26). It is likely to have a non-idiomatic meaning, in which an actual cat attempts an escape from confinement, but might also have an idiomatic reading if its meaning is extended so that there is a one-to-one metaphorical mapping between the cat and the secret it represents. Here again we are personifying some essentially inanimate entity.

(26) a. The cat tried to be let out of the bag
?=The secret was trying to be revealed

Try with a non-finite complement shows a very clear shift in meaning when it comes to passivisation. In (27)a Jack is making an effort to phone Alastair, while in (27)b Alastair is making an effort to get Jack to phone him (perhaps by texting, leaving voicemail messages, etc.).

(27) a. Jack tried to phone Alastair
b. Alastair tried to be phoned by Jack

The change of meaning corresponding to elevation of *Alastair* to the subject position in (27)b shows that *try*, in contrast to *seem*, does assign a theta role to its subject. That said, in a sentence such as (28), the embedded verb also apparently assigns a theta role to the subject: it is *Nancy* who is doing the reading.

(28) Nancy tried to read the book

Sentences such as (28) create problems for the view of theta role assignment we have adopted. In this example there are two potential theta role assigning predicates, the verbs *try* and *read*, but only a single argument, the subject *Nancy*. If we require a one-to-one relationship between available theta-positions and arguments, as specified by the theta-criterion, example (28) represents a mismatch.

The solution to this conundrum has been the introduction of an **empty category**, an unpronounced syntactic element, **PRO**, a silent pronoun which functions as the subject of the lower non-finite verb (in this instance *read*). Like other subjects we have seen, PRO Merges in *v*P, where it is assigned a(n external) theta role.

(29)

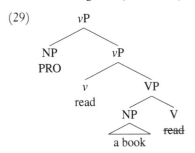

PRO Remerges with TP to satisfy its EPP subject requirement. As a silent NP PRO is not subject to the Visibility Condition, and it is therefore unproblematic that it is not assigned Nominative Case in this (or any) position.

(30)

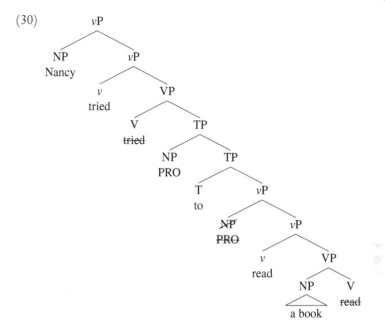

The higher subject, in this instance *Nancy*, is then Merged with the projection of *try*, where it is assigned its own external theta role. Note here that *try*, unlike *seem*, has a *v*P projection, reflective of its assignment of external theta roles.

(31)

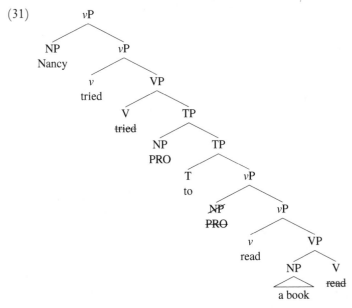

The subject then Remerges in the matrix TP, where it satisfies the subject requirement of the clause, and is assigned Nominative Case.

(32)

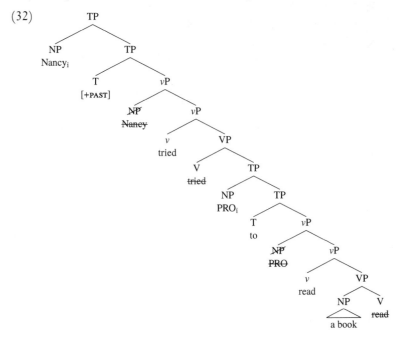

The overt subject controls PRO, determining its meaning. We represent the relationship between Controller and Controllee through co-indexing, the subscript *i* letters on *Nancy* and PRO.[1] These indices are a notational convention, and do not stand in for actual cognitive objects that we assume to exist in our model. Verbs such as *try* are called (**Subject**) **Control** verbs. These also include *want, attempt* and *yearn*. Certain adjectives can also act as Control predicates, such as *pleased*.

(33)   Charlie was pleased to read the book

Besides the differences in theta role assignment, along with the concomitant absence/presence of *to be* and PRO, there is another structural distinction between Raising and Control verbs that in English is not immediately apparent in most varieties. In Belfast English an infinitive under a Subject Control verb may be introduced by *for*, but not an infinitive under a Subject Raising verb.

(34)   a.   %He {tried/wanted} for to leave
         b.   *He {seemed/happened} for to leave

This distinction indicates that complements of Subject Control verbs are 'bigger' than those of Subject Raising verbs. If we take *for* in this instance to be a complementiser, we can argue that these Control verbs select for CPs, whereas Raising verbs select only for TPs. Even though an overt instantiation of C only shows up in some varieties of English, this is consistent with a wide array of crosslinguistic evidence. We will see as well in Chapter 9 that there is other indirect evidence for a difference in complement size. For the moment we will accept that this distinction is consistent regardless of the variety in question, and amend our Control tree accordingly.

---

[1]   By tradition the first index letter used is *i*, standing for 'index', followed alphabetically by *j, k*, etc. These letters are not in themselves meaningful, so as long as the same one is used to match up co-indexed elements it does not matter what the index letter is.

(35)

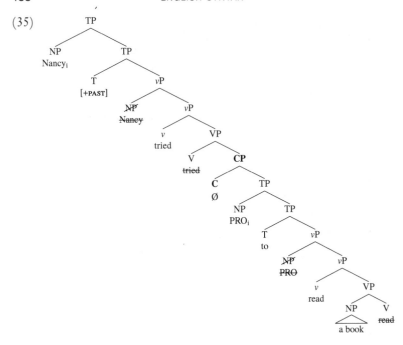

7.1.3 Accusativus cum Infinitivo

The Raising and Control constructions we have looked at in the preceding sections involve a single overt NP subject. Some verbs with finite complements additionally have objects which function as the subject of the finite complement clause.

(36) a. I persuaded him to read the book
     b. I expected him to read the book

These forms may be referred to as **Accusativus cum Infinitivo** (ACI), Latin for 'accusative with infinitive'. ACI constructions divide along similar lines to the Raising/Control distinction we have already seen, this time according to whether the matrix verb assigns an external theta role to the object/non-finite subject. Here we can apply similar diagnostics as were applied for (Subject) Control and (Subject-to-Subject) Raising verbs. Verbs such as *persuade* assign a theta role to the lower NP, while verbs such as *expect* do not. *Persuade* is therefore incompatible with expletive *it* and *there* in the embedded clause. These are grammatical with *expect* in ACI contexts.

(37) a. */#I persuaded it to rain
    b. I expected it to rain
    c. */#I persuaded there to be three people there
    d. I expected there to be three people there

Idioms are similarly unacceptable with *persuade*, or require a literal interpretation, but maintain their idiomatic reading under ACI *expect*.

(38) a. */#I persuaded headway to be made
    b. I expected headway to be made
    c. I persuaded the bull to be grabbed by the horns
       =I convinced the bull that he should be taken hold of
    d. I expected the bull to be grabbed by the horns
       =I expected someone to take direct action to deal with the situation

Passivisation of the verb embedded under *persuade* results in a change in meaning; passivisation under ACI *expect* does not.

(39) a. I persuaded Alastair to be phoned by Jack
     ≠I persuaded Jack to phone Alastair
    b. I expected Alastair to be phoned by Jack
     =I expected Jack to phone Alastair

We can therefore conclude that *persuade* assigns a theta role to its object; that object is also an argument of the embedded verb. Once more we are faced with a potential violation of the theta-criterion resulting from a single argument being assigned two theta roles (or appearing in two theta-positions). Again we can resolve this issue by having a PRO as the subject of the embedded clause.

(40)

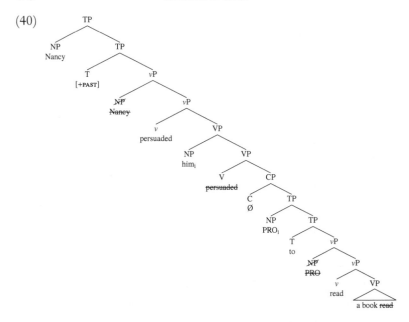

Here the embedded PRO subject is controlled by the Object of the matrix verb, as indicated by their matching indices. *Persuade* is therefore classed as an **Object Control** verb. PRO is assigned a theta role by the lower verb, with the Object assigned a theta role by the higher one, as well as the Accusative Case we would expect with any object in this position.

Because the object of ACI *expect* receives a theta role only from the embedded verb, its dual object/subject function does not have the potential to violate the theta-criterion. As such, this NP is only a single syntactic entity, Raising from a subject position in the embedded non-finite clause to an object position in the matrix VP.

(41)

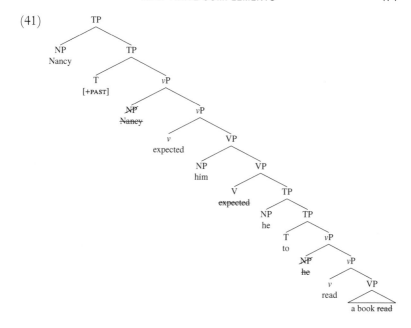

Although **Raising-to-Object** (RtO) verbs such as *expect* do not
assign theta roles to their objects, the *v*P still assigns Accusative Case.
Case on the subject of the embedded clause is checked by its Remerge
as an object in the VP, as it cannot be assigned Case by non-finite
T. Because Movement is always motivated by the requirements of
the probe rather than goal (recall Greed), there seems to be some more
fundamental subcategorisation requirement here that an object be
Merged in the matrix VP

Again, then, while Object Control and Raising-to-Object constructions appear similar on a surface level, we assume a different cognitive computation, and accordingly a different model, to account for
the distinction in theta role assignment. In the next section we will take
a closer look at PRO, which has proved controversial in the Minimalist
framework.

7.2 Is PRO (un-)Minimalist?

PRO was introduced in pre-Minimalist approaches to generative
grammar in order to maintain the theta-criterion. With the elimination
of other empty categories such as *t* (trace) has come the question of
whether PRO, too, should be done away with as an artefact of the model
rather than an element that represents some real cognitive object or

lexical item. PRO is problematic in several respects: it is always silent, and is not subject to many of the requirements on other NPs, such as the Visibility Condition, or must be assigned its own special 'Null Case' which does not apply elsewhere.

Elimination of PRO would necessitate a rethinking of theta role assignment. Some Minimalist syntacticians view this as a positive outcome, inasmuch as it unifies the treatment of properties assigned to NPs, collapsing together the treatment of theta roles and **phi-features**, grammatical features such as gender, number, person, etc. Without PRO there can be no one-to-one match between theta roles/-positions and arguments. Instead, theta roles would undergo feature-checking operations.

In our model this PRO-less approach means that a Control verb would Attract the subject of the embedded verb, which would already have checked a theta-feature lower down, to check a theta-feature in the vP of the main verb. Under this view Control is identical to Raising in terms of Movement/Remerge. The only difference between them is whether the subject (or object, as the case may be) is assigned a theta role in multiple positions.

We would therefore revise our Subject Control tree in (35) to look like (42). Here an interpretable theta-feature on [NP *Nancy*] checks an uninterpretable theta-feature on the embedded v (*read*), and then Moves to check an uninterpretable theta-feature on the matrix v (*tried*). As with the examples we have seen already the NP would Merge in the embedded TP in order to satisfy its subject requirement. It would also have to 'stop' in the CP phase edge in order to allow it to Move out of the embedded clause at all. Presumably Merge in this position would be motivated by some feature of C akin to that which motivates Movement of the subject to Merge with TP.

(42)

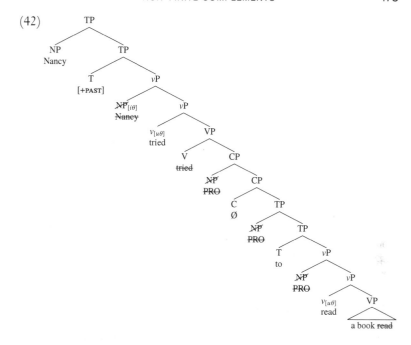

There is nothing inherently un-Minimalist about eliminating the theta-criterion. It would require a slight reworking of our view of feature-checking, inasmuch as the interpretable theta-feature on NP arguments would check uninterpretable theta-features in more than one position. We have in fact made a proposal not dissimilar from this one for Negative Concord in Chapter 6, although in that instance checking by the same interpretable feature meant that the two positions of negation were interpreted as a single unit semantically; here we have a single argument NP, but the theta roles assigned to it are distinct.

Whether Control should be re-envisioned as a specialised form of Raising therefore depends on how similar they are in terms of other syntactic properties, and particularly how the Controller of PRO is construed. If Control is equivalent to Raising, the Minimal Link Condition, which specifies a preference for the shortest possible Movement 'chains', would mean that the closest possible antecedent to the embedded subject should be its Controller.

We can see this relationship between the understood embedded subject and its antecedent in Raising-to-Object constructions, where it is the object, rather than the matrix subject, with which the embedded subject is construed. In (43) it is Alastair doing the leaving rather than Jack.

(43) Jack expected Alastair to leave

Most Object Control verbs, such as *persuade* exhibit the same pattern. *Promise* is an exception to this. In (44)a it is the closer antecedent, *Alastair*, that is the Controller, as we would expect if Control, like Raising-to-Object, involves Movement of the embedded subject to an object position. In (44)b, however, it is *Jack* that is the Controller. This construal of the embedded subject with the matrix subject is unexpected if Control is Movement, as it would involve it moving over the closer object (*Alastair*), in violation of the Minimal Link Condition.

(44) a. Jack persuaded Alastair to leave
       b. Jack promised Alastair to leave

The counterargument to this example is that *promise* is a one-off, with the object actually embedded under a silent preposition that renders it invisible to the higher *v*P when it triggers Movement. Indeed, for many speakers it is at least marginally possible to have an overt preposition with *promise*.

(45) ??Jack promised to Alastair to leave

In this sense *promise* is similar to semantically related verbs such as *vow* and *commit*. Where a preposition is present the subject is the Controller; where it is absent the object is the Controller.

(46) a. Jack committed Alastair to leave (Object Control)
       b. Jack committed to Alastair to leave (Subject Control)
       c. *Jack vowed Alastair to leave
       d. Jack vowed to Alastair to leave (Subject Control)

There are a number of other verbs that have **Control Shift**, in which whether it is the Subject or Object that is Controller largely depends on context. Among these are *ask*, *beg* and *plead*. In a sentence such as (47)a which person is the Controller is ambiguous, but in both (47)b and (47)c *the pupils* seems the most likely Controller, regardless of subject/object status, based on our pragmatic knowledge of teacher-pupil relationships.

(47) a. Jack asked Alastair to leave early
       b. The teacher asked the pupils to leave early
           (likely Object Control)
       c. The pupils asked the teacher to leave early
           (likely Subject Control)

A very clear 'in the wild' example of Subject Control in a possible Control Shift context comes from an aeroplane-safety video, in which passengers who were unhappy sitting in an exit row were advised as in (48).

(48)   Please ask a flight attendant to be reseated

If Control is a special form of Raising we would also expect the Controller and Controllee, as the same syntactic object Remerged, to be identical entities. But there are actually a couple of possible Control configurations where Controller and Controllee do not exactly match up. In **Partial Control** constructions the Controller is singular, but the embedded predicate requires a plural subject. Not all Control verbs permit Partial Control.

(49)   a.   {*Hazel/The children} met at the park
       b.   Hazel {wanted/*tried} to meet at the park

Split Control, where both a subject and object are Controller, is also possible for some Control verbs. There is once more a lack of one-to-one equivalence that we would expect if Control is the result of Movement.

(50)   Hazel suggested to Flora to meet at the park

Taken together, the availability of Subject Control in the presence of a potential Object Controller, Control Shift, Partial Control and Split Control all suggest that the Controller is determined semantically rather than by syntactic Movement. There are still syntactic constraints on this construal. For instance, where a verb with a non-finite complement is itself in an embedded finite clause the PRO cannot be controlled by the higher subject. In (51), for instance, *Flora* must be the subject rather than *Hazel*.

(51)   Hazel suggested that Flora try to read the book
       ≠Hazel suggested to Flora that Hazel try to read the book

For the moment, then, we will conclude that PRO is a necessary component of our model for explaining the Control/Raising distinction, while acknowledging that in a Minimalist model the introduction of a specialised category of this type is an imperfect solution.

7.2.1 Raising and floating quantifiers

In several places in this text we have noted that the presence of floating quantifiers such as *all* may be 'stranded' by a Moved NP, indicating positions in which it has Merged prior to Spell Out. Since we have argued that Control is not the result of Movement, we would expect floating quantifiers to be acceptable in positions with Raising verbs for which they are not in otherwise similar Control constructions.

(52) a. The children seem all to have enough cake
      b. ?*The children want all to have enough cake

As a native speaker I find (52)b, if not downright ungrammatical, significantly degraded compared to (52)c. A quantifier in a lower position, however, reads as equivalently acceptable with both the Raising verb *seem* and the Control verb *want*.

(53) a. The children seem to all have enough cake
      b. The children want to all have enough cake

It is possible, of course, that silent PRO may have its own quantifier, but this would not account for the low acceptability of (52). What these examples tell us therefore remains an open question.

7.3 Other verbal complements

We have so far limited our discussion of Raising and Control to non-finite *to* complements. Having established the distinction between these in terms of theta role assignment and structure, we are now in a position to consider other types of non-finite complements, and other verbal complements more generally.

Standard embedded passives, in which a passive clause is the complement of a non-finite selecting verb, offer no surprises in terms of structure. They differ only inasmuch as the passive subject may undergo Raising, or be replaced by a PRO.

(54) a. The car seemed to be washed (quickly)
      b. The cat wanted to be fed

Where there is an additional subject in the embedded clause, these function as Raising-to-Object and Object Control constructions.

(55) a. I expect the car to be washed
      b. I persuaded the cat to be washed

Omission of the non-finite *to be* produces apparently identical readings for Raising-to-Object verbs, although this configuration is less acceptable for some verbs in this category.

(56) a. I {need/want/would like} the car washed
      b. ?I {expected/believed} the car washed (by the time I returned)

The embedded passive auxiliary *to be* cannot be omitted for Object Control verbs.

(57) *I {persuaded/convinced/asked} the cat washed

This contrast suggests that RtO verbs may select directly for a VP instead of a non-finite TP, but that Object Control verbs may select only for a full clausal complement, presumably a CP. This notion is in line with the proposal we have already made that Control verbs in general have 'larger' complements than Raising verbs. The restrictions on which main verbs can select for them means that the difference between these structures with and without *to be* is not just a matter of the non-finite passive auxiliary being unpronounced. A sentence such as (56)a would therefore have the structure in (58).

(58)

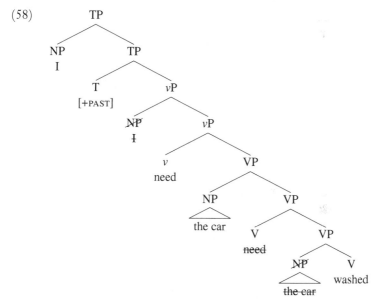

Similar constructions with adjectives are also possible for verbs such as *want* and *need*.

(59) a. I need the car shining
     b. I want the children happy

As with other passive forms, it is conceivable that any participle in these constructions might actually be adjectival. These verbs also in fact allow non-participial adjectives. Where there is a related parti-ciple, it is possible to differentiate between a **resultative** reading, in which the adjective describes an endstate, and an **eventive** reading, where the participle describes not just the endstate but the process leading up to it.

(60) a. I need the car {clean/cleaned}
     b. I want the door {open/opened}

These adjectival forms bear a resemblance to other resultative constructions with adjectives, such as those in (61).

(61) a. He wiped the table clean
     b. He hammered the metal flat

Such forms are lexically restricted, suggesting a specific selectional relationship between the verb and complement adjective.

(62) He wiped the table {dry/*wet/*dirty}

These constructions also look somewhat like the verb-particle constructions we discussed in Chapter 3, in that they consist of a verb in collusion with another element denoting an endpoint. As with particle verb constructions, the object may follow the word denoting an endpoint but these forms are marginal in a way that particle-object orders are not.

(63) a. He wiped up the spill
     b. ??*He wiped dry the table
     c. ??*He hammered flat the metal

This dispreference suggests that while the adjective is in a close relationship with the verb, it is not part of the verb in the same way as a particle. Where the object does precede an object Merged to its left, as above, it must undergo some special Movement operation in order to do so. This adjective Movement will be to Merge with some projection within the split VP, probably motivated by topicalisation, as we have seen for other instances of Remerge within the split VP. The adjective-object order for these examples is indeed better if the object is emphasised prosodically, as in (64). This intonational stress indicates that the object is focused, making the adjective a topic.

(64) He hammered the plastic flat
     No, he hammered flat THE METAL

7.3.1 Concealed and alternative embedded passives

So-called concealed passives consist of a verb such as *need* or *want* followed by an -*ing* participle.

(65) a. The car needs washing
b. The dog wants walking
c. The naughty children deserve scolding
d. Those windows require cleaning

Whether these forms should be labelled 'Non-Standard' is debatable. Equivalent embedded passives with *to be* (e.g. *the dog needs to be walked*) are certainly Standard, but concealed passives are not particularly regionally restricted or stigmatised. They are not possible with all verbs that can take non-finite *to* complements. For some verbs it is simply ungrammatical to have an *-ing* participle as a complement.

(66) *The dog {seems/appears} walking
(cf. The dog seems to be walking/being walked)

For other verbs the embedded participle is interpreted as a progressive, active form rather than a passive.

(67) The dog tried walking
≠'The dog tried to be walked'

Some verbs may also be ambiguous between the active and passive interpretations.

(68) The dog {likes/enjoys} walking
= The dog likes/enjoys taking a walk
OR The dog likes/enjoys being walked

Many of the matrix verbs which permit concealed passives can also have a nominal object, as in the examples in (69), which correspond fairly directly to the sentences in (65).

(69) a. The car needs a wash
b. The dog wants a walk
c. The naughty children deserve a scolding
d. Those windows require a clean

This similarity suggests that there is an ambiguity regarding whether the embedded participles in these constructions are really progressive verbs or **gerunds**, nouns derived from verbs. Modification by adjectives indicates instances where they are unambiguously nominal.

(70) The car needs careful washing

The Non-Standard version of these constructions with an overt object appears to have a verbal participle.

(71) a. %He needs the car washing
    b. %I want it doing
      (cf. I want it done)

It is likely that their structure is identical to that of Standard constructions of this type (*He needs the car washed*), as shown in (58), with the only difference consisting in the type of participle selected for by the main verb. It is arguable that this contrast is determined at PF rather than LF, since nothing other than overt morphology changes.

Similar to concealed passives, but much less widely used, are the **alternative embedded passives** (AEPs) mentioned in the introduction to this chapter, in which the embedded participle is a passive *-en* (or *-ed*) form rather than an *-ing* one. The AEP is most commonly used with the matrix verb *need*, somewhat less commonly with *want*, and least commonly with *like*.

(72) a. The cat needs fed
    b. The dog wants walked
    c. Babies like cuddled

This order of preference applies not just globally, but also for individual speakers: those who accept *like* AEPs also accept AEPs with *want*, and those who accept AEPs with *want* also accept them with *need*. Other possible matrix verbs, such as *love, hate, deserve, require, wish* and *could use* have been attested in this construction, but they are extremely rare compared to the three exemplified in (72). In this respect AEPs are much more restricted than Standard embedded passives and concealed passives.

These AEPs are comparable not only to concealed passives, but also to copular and linking constructions with adjectival complements.

(73) a. The cat seems (well-)fed
    b. The bicycle looks polished

However, a variety of tests indicate that the embedded participle is verbal rather than adjectival. The embedded verb can be modified by an adverb.

(74) The car needs washed carefully

AEPs may also be used with a *by*-phrase, in line with traditional verbal passives, and with a purpose clause, which is only possible with eventive (verbal) participles, rather than stative (adjectival) ones.

(75) a. The car needs checked by a mechanic
    b. The car needs washed (in order) to keep it looking nice

The AEP is permitted with participles beginning with verbal *un-*, denoting the reversal of the process represented by the root verb, but incompatible with participles beginning with adjectival *un-*, which may occur with adjectival participles that denote a state of not having undergone a particular process (these are distinguishable in that the process denoted by the root is not something that can be undone once it is completed).

(76) a. The door needs unlocked
     b. *The biscuits need unbaked
        (cf. The biscuits are unbaked, because the oven wasn't on)

Where a participle has a clearly stative reading it is not possible in the AEP.

(77) a. You need refreshed by a good sleep
     b. *You need refreshed if you're going to enjoy your holiday
        (cf. You need to be refreshed ...)

We can therefore take the AEP to have a verbal rather than adjectival participle, making it similar to the Standard object forms lacking *to be*, although these also allow a non-participial adjective where the AEP does not (see (60)).

(78) The windows need {*clean/cleaned}

The constraints on the AEP that do not apply to related Standard constructions, both in terms of possible matrix verbs and types of embedded participle, suggest that it is syntactically distinct from these forms, rather than representing a phonological ellipsis of *to be*. There is another apparent difference in terms of theta role assignment that confirms this hypothesis.

In Standard English *need* is ambiguous between (Subject) Control and Raising readings. It can have a subject which appears to be agentive (or at least volitional) but which also passes all of the diagnostics for Raising verbs.

(79) a. She needs to leave now
     b. It needs to rain
     c. There need to be more people
     d. Headway needs to be made
     e. The bull needs to be taken by the horns

The one contradictory diagnostic for *need* as a Raising verb is passivisation, where a change in who is interpreted as having a need points to Control.

(80) a. Jack needs to phone Alastair
     b. Alastair needs to be phoned by Jack

Want fails most of the tests for Subject Raising (although, as we have seen, it is a Raising-to-Object verb), indicating that it is a Subject Control verb.

(81) a. She wants to leave now
     b. ??It wants to rain
     c. *There want to be more people
     d. *Headway wants to be made
     e. The bull wants to be taken by the horns (non-idiomatic reading)

There is also a clear meaning shift with (Standard) passivisation under *want*.

(82) a. Jack wants to phone Alastair
     b. Alastair wants to be phoned by Jack

That said, there are uses of *want* that have a non-volitional flavour, meaning something like 'be without', 'lack' or 'need'.

(83) Those walls want a coat of paint

An example of this type of *want* with the concealed passive can also be found in the story *Alice's Adventures in Wonderland*, where the Mad Hatter uses *want* with an inanimate (and clearly non-volitional) subject.

(84) Your hair wants cutting

Like, the least used of the AEP matrix verbs, also most clearly falls into the Subject Control category

(85) a. She likes to leave early
     b. ??It likes to rain every day
     c. *There like to be more people
     d. *Headway likes to be made
     e. The bull likes to be taken by the horns
         (non-idiomatic reading)

It also exhibits a meaning shift with passivisation.

(86) a. Jack likes to phone Alastair
     b. Alastair likes to be phoned by Jack

In the AEP, though, many speakers produce inanimate subjects with *need* and *want* much more readily than for Standard embedded passives.

(87) a. Those dirty dishes want washed
 b. The grass wants mowed
 c. My hair likes cut once a month
 d. That plant likes watered every day

From this evidence we might argue that the AEP is always a Raising construction, such that *want* and *like*, which are typically Subject Control verbs, behave as Raising verbs in AEP contexts (as evidenced by the *Alice* example, concealed passive *want* may also fall into this category). Where the subject does seem to have some volition, this can be explained as a contextually-directed interpretation rather than resulting from assignment of a theta role. The same can be said for Standard, *need* and modal verbs such as *must*. While the sense of obligation typically appears to apply to the matrix subject, it need not.

(88) She {needs to/must} leave now
 ... to catch her train
 ... because I have to lock up the house

In many respects, therefore, AEP and Standard embedded passive forms are not interchangeable. One final piece of evidence that the AEP is not simply the Standard form with *to be* unpronounced is that not all speakers who use the AEP can produce equivalent Standard constructions. While quite a lot of speakers allow both, it is reported that some unselfconsciously reject Standard *to be* embedded passives as overly wordy or markedly formal.

The optional pronunciation of the complementiser *that*, by comparison, appears to apply for all English speakers, with no restrictions on, for example, what matrix verbs it may be used with. Speakers may also find overt pronunciation of *that* more formal, but, as far as I am aware, there are no speakers who deem it ungrammatical.

According to our analysis, the structure for a sentence such as *the cat wants fed* would be as in (89)a, while the structure for *the cat wants to be fed* would be as in (89)b.

(89) a.

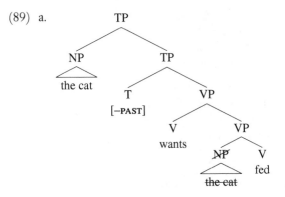

b.

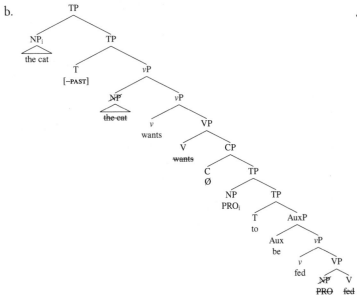

We see here another instance of distinction between varieties by means of selection, as well as a continuation of the trend for external theta role assigning verbs to select for larger complements than ones that do not.

One last observation to be made here, which you may have already noticed yourself, is the similarity between AEPs and *get*-passives, and their corresponding object forms.

(90) a. My neighbour needs arrested
     b. I need my neighbour arrested
     c. My neighbour got arrested
     d. I got my neighbour arrested

The structure we have given for these is also quite similar, although *get* was proposed to be instantiated in a *v* head that is defective in *get*-passives. It is plausible that AEPs are essentially the same as *get*-passives in having a semi-lexical matrix verb, and that the sense of agency for *get*-passives is contextually directed in the same way as the sense of volition in AEPs.

7.4 Conclusion

In this chapter we have introduced the distinction between Raising and Control constructions with embedded non-finite clauses. We then looked at a number of other forms of embedded non-finite construction, including Standard embedded passives, embedded resultative constructions, concealed passives and alternative embedded passives. We concluded that these different forms vary not only according to whether the matrix verb assigns an external theta role (and therefore whether it has a *v*P projection), but also according to the structure of the complement clause it selects for.

7.5 Further reading

Most of the diagnostics to distinguish between Raising and Control predicates were proposed in Postal (1974). For extensive debate for and against PRO see Hornstein (1999, 2000, 2003), Culicover and Jackendoff (2001, 2006) and Landau (2003, 2006, 2007).

For discussion of alternative embedded passives as used by Pittsburgh speakers see Tenny (1998), Edelstein (2014) and Duncan (2019)

7.6 Exercises

1. Decide whether the following sentences have a Subject Control predicate, Subject Raising predicate, an Object Control predicate or a Raising-to-Object predicate.
   a. Billy asked to leave
   b. Billy asked Martha to leave
   c. Oscar happens to like syntax
   d. Lucy demanded an answer
   e. Maisie wants us to be on time
   f. Julian told me to fill out the form
   g. Alec threatened to reveal the truth
   h. I am eager to talk to Lucy

    i. Oscar appeared to be tired
    j. Lucy showed Oscar to be lying

2. Trees
   Draw trees for the sentences in the previous exercise. You do not
   have to include features, but you should think about what they are.

3. Further analysis
   At the end of the chapter we observed that AEPs may be similar
   to *get*-passives. What other parallels can we draw between these
   constructions. Are there ways in which they are not comparable?

For Answers see edinburghuniversitypress.com/englishsyntax.

8 Nouns and determiners

Watching a political debate in a room full of people several years ago, I heard someone behind me exclaim 'and I!' in reaction to the sentence in (1).

(1)   And that's the difference between the President and me

Even though particular Cases are, in theory, assigned in particular syntactic positions, as claimed in Chapters 3 and 4, the limited overt case marking that does exist in English does not entirely bear out the expectation that subjects have a Nominative form and objects an Accusative one. For first person singular pronouns this holds especially true: the *I/me* distinction is a shibboleth of prescriptive grammar. Coordinated forms such as those in (61) are particularly subject to forms of **hypercorrection**, in which, following a (perceived) prescriptive norm, a speaker produces a form that deviates from what we would otherwise predict from their grammar.

The distribution of reflexive *-self* is subject to similar hypercorrections. Many speakers employ these as a marker of politeness where they would otherwise be unacceptable. Some Scottish speakers also use such reflexives in existential constructions, possibly as a result of Gaelic influence (although the speakers who do this are not necessarily Gaelic speakers themselves). In both instances these are distinct from Standard use, in that there is no preceding noun corresponding to the *-self* pronoun.

(2)   a.   %Myself and Alastair will meet you
           (cf. *Myself will meet you)
      b.   %It is herself!
           (cf. It is {she/her})

Some speakers from parts of the northern, Midwest United States also allow **long-distance reflexives**, in which a *-self* pronoun appears at a

187

greater distance than it would in Standard English from the noun to which it corresponds.

(3)   %The boy said that the girl spoke to himself

While pronouns are specifically restricted, in terms of syntactic distribution within the clause and with respect to each other, full nouns show a number of interesting restrictions in terms of their relationship to **determiners**, such as *a(n)*/*the* and other articles. This chapter will begin by looking at this relationship, before moving beyond the internal structure of NPs to their behaviour within a larger syntactic context.

8.1 The DP hypothesis

Up to this point in the text we have largely ignored the internal structure of nominals, as the question of how these are structured is tangential to the structure of the verbal/clausal domain, and so has been irrelevant to our analysis thus far. In the development of GB/Minimalist generative grammar there have been two approaches to the relationship between the noun and the determiner. The difference between them boils down to which of these categories selects the other.

In the more traditional NP hypothesis, which we have been implicitly assuming, the noun is the head of the NP, a constituent formed by Merge of a noun and determiner. In Bare Phrase Structure this means that a noun without a determiner or other dependents may function as both a head and a maximal projection.

(4)

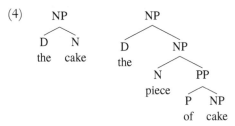

In the newer but nevertheless well-established DP hypothesis, the determiner is the head of a constituent formed with a noun.

(5)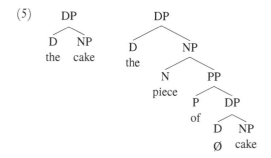

One of the primary motivations behind the proposal of the DP hypothesis was the requirement that every phrase conform to the X-bar structure schema. This could be accomplished in a trivial way with a DP in the specifier of an NP, but branching within the DP phrase will always be unary in this representation: it would select for no complements, and could have no adjuncts.

(6)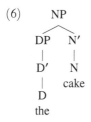

If the determiner takes an NP as its complement we have a structure that more consistently conforms to X-bar requirements. This structure can in fact be seen as parallel to what we have proposed for the clause, with a lexical projection (the noun) dominated by a functional one (the DP, and possibly others), in a similar fashion to the (split) VP and Aux, T, C, etc.

(7)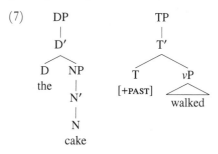

This parallel becomes even more striking with possessive forms. The genitive clitic -'s cannot co-occur with any articles on the second NP in a genitive construction (roughly, the 'possessee'). The complementary distribution of the possessive clitic and determiner indicates that these occupy the same position in the syntax and fulfil the same function, i.e. genitive -'s is a type of determiner.[1]

(8)   a.   the girl's book
      b.   *the girl's the book

If -'s is in D, taking the 'possessee' NP as its complement, the 'possessor' may be Merged in its specifier, akin to the subject of a clause Merged in TP.

(9)

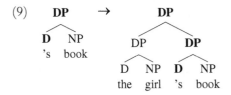

This parallel can be extended to instances of **deverbal nouns**, nouns derived from verbs. The possessor DP will initially Merge within the possessee NP, representing that it is assigned a theta role in this position, before Remerging in the 'subject' position of the 's DP.

(10)

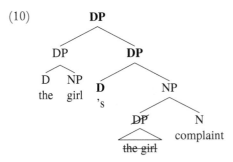

This proposal is akin to the VP-internal subject hypothesis presented in Chapter 4, in which the two positions of Merge represented the dual function of the subject as a subject of the clause and argument of the verb. Here we have the possessor DP as a 'subject' of the -'s clitic, as well as an argument of the deverbal noun.

---

[1]   As illustrated in (8), it is possible for the first element of a genitive construction (the 'possessor') to have a determiner. This determiner is not in complementary distribution with the -s clitic because it is the head of a separate DP projection

(11)

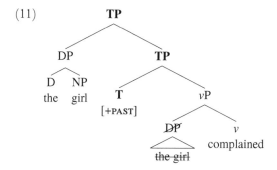

Analysing genitives in this way not only gives us an elegant parallel between verbal and nominal structures but helps to explain why -'s cliticises to phrases rather than acting as a nominal inflection: a DP of any size or complexity, including ones containing relative clauses and other dependents following the head, can still Merge in the 'subject' position of the -'s DP.

(12) a. the girl with a red coat's book
    b. the girl who arrived early's complaint
    c. the girl I went to the cinema with's jacket

Recall our discussion of clitics in Chapter 6. Unlike affixes, it was argued, clitics are not restrictive in the category they attach to, and do not alter the form of the words to which they attach. These criteria allowed us to distinguish contracted auxiliaries such as -'ve, and the negative inflection -n't.

On the first count, -'s behaves as a clitic. As demonstrated in (12), -'s can attach to phrases as well as single words. This cliticisation is categorially restricted, but only because other selectional restrictions mean that the -'s must have an NP Merged to its left. The word to which the NP attaches – in our examples a noun, an adverb and a preposition – may be of any category as long as it is contained within an NP.

On the second count, -'s fails our diagnostic for cliticisation when it comes to possessive pronouns. It does not change the phonological shape of full NPs, but with pronouns it produces *my*, *your*, *his*, etc., instead of *me's*, *you's*, *he's*, etc. Nevertheless, consistency in our model demands that these have the same structure as any other clitic (we will return to the status of pronouns as DPs in the next section).

(13)   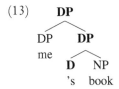

The answer here lies again in the relationship between -'s and the possessor DP. Unlike a contracted auxiliary, the -'s clitic is in agreement relationship with the element it cliticises to. Where that element is pronominal, it will be read at Spell Out as a single bundle of phi-features with an additional [*i*POSS] feature, and realised as a possessive pronoun accordingly. In this sense the representation in (13), like any tree that gives each terminal node as a word or piece of morphology, is misleading. It is a possessive feature that is the head of the DP, rather than the clitic -'s per se.

What is the alternative to the DP representation of possessives? English has one other specific way to connect closely related NPs, through use of a preposition, usually *of*. This structure gives us an alternative to genitive -'s structures, with the 'possessee' preceding the 'possessor'.

(14)   a.   a cup of tea
       b.   a book of poetry[2]

To make the possessor NP a complement of the possessee NP in -'s-genitives, however, would introduce complications in terms of selection, namely in instances where the noun already has dependents that are closer to the head than the -'s clitic, as in (12). We could maintain the apparent selectional relationship between the possessive head and the possessor through a sort of hybrid NP/DP hypothesis analysis, in which the -'s occupied a determiner position within the possessee NP, and the possessor NP still Merged within the DP projected by -'s.

(15)   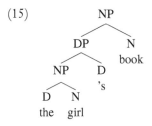

---

[2]   *Of*-genitives and -'s-genitives are of course not interchangeable. Which is used depends on a variety of factors largely external to the syntax, such as animacy, whether a possessee is (in)alienable, etc. Discussion of this choice is beyond the scope of this book.

This approach is potentially tenable, but it lacks the parallel with clause structure that characterises the full DP approach.

8.1.1 Re-evaluating the DP hypothesis

While the DP hypothesis is undoubtedly an elegant solution for X-bar structure, much of the reason for this approach is obviated by the development of Minimalism. The elimination of X-bar structure reduces the pressure to have uniformity of different types of phrases, although there is nothing that precludes the inclusion of DPs in Bare Phrase Structure.

The strongest argument against the DP hypothesis comes from selectional restrictions. Recall in Chapter 2 that we introduced the idea of both categorial (syntactic) and semantic selection. If c-selection requirements are not met, a sentence will be ungrammatical; if c-selection requirements are met, but s-selection requirements are not, it will be semantically anomalous.

(16) a. *I drank shoogly
     b. #I drank the haggis

If selection of both types occurs in a local relationship, it becomes problematic for the head of a constituent such as *the haggis* to be the determiner *the* rather than the noun *haggis*. The verb *drink* requires an object that is drinkable (which *haggis* is generally not), making the second sentence semantically anomalous. The determiner is also irrelevant to the selecting verb: the sentence would be equally nonsensical with the object *a haggis*, *that haggis* or *some haggis*.

Where the determiner *the* is coupled with a potable substance, the sentence is grammatical and semantically sound. Equally, it is grammatical if that entity is used with a different determiner or none at all.

(17) a. I drank the whisky
     b. I drank a glass of whisky
     c. I drank whisky

There are no instances where a particular determiner, rather than a noun, is selected by another constituent. As such, it would be surprising for the determiner to be the head of a nominal constituent. We could address this issue by arguing that the features of a noun **percolate** up, or are copied, through the DP, making this a sort of dual-headed phrase and thus allowing a verb or other predicate to select an NP embedded within a DP.

(18)   DP$_{[+N]}$

      D   NP
    the cake

We can also counter this claim with the observation that semantic selection is to some extent external to the syntax. According to our model theta roles must be assigned in order for an utterance to be grammatical, but they need not be assigned appropriately: hence, semantic anomaly. Furthermore, not all instances of semantic anomaly result from assignment of theta roles to incompatible arguments. They may instead be dictated by real-world knowledge rather than thematic relationships between specific constituents, as in (19).

(19)   #I am my own Grandpa
      (cf. I am my own advocate)

To address the selectional argument against the DP hypothesis, we must therefore be careful to tease apart c-selection and s-selection. Verbs and other predicates may c-select for DPs. They may also s-select for DPs in terms of assignment of theta roles, but the outcome of this theta role assignment does not apply till after Spell Out, at LF.

Setting aside s-selection, there is still the question of why, if another head c-selects for DP, it should not syntactically require a specific determiner. We have certainly seen instances where there is selection for a specific type of head, such as in embedded clauses: some verbs can select for C heads with a question feature (*if/whether*), while others select only for C heads that do not have such a feature (*that/Ø*).

On the other hand, some verbs allow c-selection of pretty much any element of a given category. For instance, the linking verb *look* can be followed by pretty much any predicative adjective. Any unacceptability comes down to semantic anomaly.

(20)   He looks {happy/squashed/outspoken/#computable/#invisible}

We can therefore propose that the DP can be c-selected by an element such as a verb with no requirements of the particular type of determiner that is the head of that phrase.

This analysis comes with the caveat that in terms of c-selection the DP hypothesis may force us to introduce a null or silent determiner in order to account for instances in which no overt determiner is present. In English **mass nouns**, denoting uncountable or amorphous substances, and plural countable nouns do not require determiners.

(21) a. (The) porridge is delicious
      b. (The) oatcakes are also nice

As we argued for CP complements with and without *that*, representing these as DPs when the determiner is present and NPs when it was absent would create essentially redundant selectional requirement: every verb (or preposition, etc.) that could select for a DP would also have to select for an NP. If every NP is the complement of D we can reduce this requirement to selection of DPs, representing nominal constituents such as those in (21) as in (22) (you may have spotted that we already did this for *cake* in (5)).

(22)
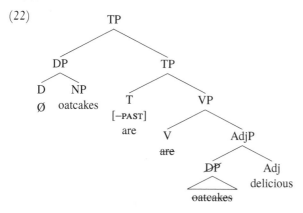

The introduction of a null determiner, an unpronounced element that apparently exists with the sole purpose of ironing out selectional inconsistencies, appears costly. However, while the null determiner was the only possible solution in X-bar theory, the Minimalist view of feature-checking gives us an alternative.

Throughout the text we have argued that the position of nominals is determined by the Visibility Condition: a nominal must be Merged in a Case position at some point in the derivation in order to be licensed. This idea can be recast in terms of an interpretable Case feature on the nominal which checks an interpretable Case feature on particular heads. It is therefore not the general category DP or NP which a verb or other predicate selects for, but rather [*i*CASE].

We can argue, furthermore, that this phi-feature may be present on both DPs and NPs, and that where a determiner selects for an NP this Case feature will have the same value. Neither determiners nor full NPs have overt case marking in English, but they can clearly share other phi-features such as plurality.

(23) a. Billy likes {*this/those} dogs
      b. Billy likes {this/*those} dog

Historically and crosslinguistically it is also the case that a determiner and noun in the same phrase will share Case features if they are overtly marked (e.g. you will not get a nominative determiner with an accusative noun).

Checking of an interpretable Case feature therefore eliminates the need for a null determiner, as any head that selects for [*i*CASE] on a DP can equally select for [*i*CASE] on an NP. This applies even where a selecting head such as V has no [*u*CASE] feature, with [*i*CASE] functioning as a stand-in for a broader categorial feature such as [+N(oun)] or [+D(eterminer)].

8.1.2 Subcategorisation

A further consideration when comparing the DP and NP hypotheses is whether one provides an advantage in terms of subcategorisation. In this respect it appears that these approaches are equivalently economical.

English nouns can be divided into a number of subcategories relevant to determiners. Most broadly we categorise them as **proper**, pertaining to names, and **common**. Proper nouns in English typically do not have determiners unless it is part of the name (e.g. *The Empire State Building*), but can do under specific, often emphatic conditions.

(24) a. (That) Alastair is a crazy guy
      b. I mean THE Adele (not someone else with the same name)
      c. Alec is a Baldwin (a member of this specific family)
      d. The September I started school ...

Common nouns may be divided according to whether they are mass nouns or countable ones. Mass nouns do not require a determiner, but may have a definite article if they refer to a specific entity.

(25) I drank (the) water

Singular common nouns require a determiner, which will be indefinite if the noun is specific, and indefinite if it is not.

(26) a. I broke a window
      b. I broke the window

Plural common nouns have a definite determiner if specific, and no determiner if not.

(27) a. Windows are fragile
     b. The windows were fragile

We could equally group the same information by determiner rather than type of noun. In this approach definite *the* can select any common noun and, in specific circumstances, proper nouns. The indefinite *a* can elect only singular ([–PLURAL]) count nouns. In an account with a null determiner (although, as we have argued above, this may be superfluous), [_D Ø] can select proper and common mass nouns.

From either perspective, the Merge of D(P) and N(P) depends on the checking of shared features between these two heads. As such, whether the noun or the determiner is the head of the phrase is irrelevant to subsequent selection, as a number of phi-features such as [±SPECIFIC], [±COUNTABLE] and [±PLURAL] will be present regardless of which projects.

Some linguists have argued that the functional structure of nominals should be extended to encompass heads pertaining to these phi-features, so that an NP is selected by a Num(ber)P (pertaining to plurality), and so on. We will revisit this idea when looking at adjectives in Chapter 9.

Again, though, these features do not appear to be relevant to c-selection: where a verb requires a countable or plural nominal as an object, the use of a mass or singular noun renders the sentence semantically anomalous rather than ungrammatical. We can therefore still argue that it is the [*i*CASE] feature on NPs and DPs alone that is responsible for their selection.

(28) #I counted {the air/dog}

An additional point that weighs in favour of the DP hypothesis is the behaviour of **pronouns**. These function as determiners, as evidenced by complementary distribution with, e.g., *the* and *a*.

(29) a. *The he likes haggis
     b. *I saw the them yesterday

The pronouns *you* and *we/us* can also form a constituent with a noun, indicating a determiner-like function.

(30) a. You readers love syntax
     b. Life can be confusing for [us syntacticians]

Given that pronouns stand in for a constituent formed by Merge of a determiner and noun, that they themselves are determiners suggests that we should accept the DP hypothesis, as it would otherwise be problematic to replace an NP with a constituent of a different category. Pronouns in this respect might better be classed as pro-determiners.

Demonstratives such as *this* and *that* also function as determiners, and in some contexts can stand on their own, fulfilling a pronominal function.

(31) Did you read *Anne of Green Gables?*
      Yes, I read that (book)

Contextual ellipsis of this type tends to target dependent constituents. For instance, a PP complement within an NP can be elided, or a main verb following an auxiliary.

(32) a. Would you like a cup of tea?
          Yes, I'll have a cup ~~of tea~~
      b. Have you had your tea?
          Yes, I have ~~had my tea~~

Without going into the details of ellipsis, it is notable that it is impossible for a determiner to be omitted without its accompanying NP, where it is a type of NP that requires a determiner, but acceptable the other way around.

(33) a. I'm going to read this next
      b. *I'm going to read book next

Demonstratives therefore also indicate that the determiner is the head of the nominal rather than N.

Regarding the DP hypothesis, our conclusion must therefore be that while in a Minimalist approach it does not confer the advantages of structural consistency required for X-bar structure, it is nevertheless plausible. Considering the potential for semantic anomaly, and the implications thereof for the minimal role that any kind of semantic selection plays in syntactic derivations, whether it is a DP or NP that is syntactically c-selected may be immaterial to the success of our model. Moreover, the DP hypothesis provides a particularly good way to account for the distribution of genitive -'s, and so in this respect might be deemed superior. We will look more at the shape of nominals in Chapter 9.

8.2 Reflexive pronouns

Recall that in Chapter 3 we proposed that *each other* must be c-commanded by its antecedent, another element in the discourse to which it refers. This requirement gave us evidence that in a ditranstivie construction the direct object c-commands the indirect object, but not vice versa.

(34) a. I gave Alastair and Flora each other's toys
     b. *I gave each other Alastair and Flora's toys

Each other can more generally be classed as an **anaphor**, a lexical item that gets its reference from that of some other lexical item. Traditionally, reflexive *-self* pronouns have also been described as anaphors, requiring an antecedent to determine their reference.

In the introduction to this text I mentioned that Minimalism is an outgrowth of the Government and Binding approach to syntax. **Binding** is a concept particularly applicable to the behaviour of anaphors, and indeed other nominal elements, within the clause. In the GB approach these are subject to three Principles or conditions. Binding Principle A, which applies to anaphors, is as follows:

Principle A
An anaphor must be bound in its binding domain.

Within the scope of this definition, an element is **bound** if it is c-commanded by its antecedent, and also co-indexed with that antecedent. We have seen this co-indexing already with PRO in Control constructions; it specifies that two elements refer to the same entity. As we said in Chapter 7, the indices used for co-indexing are notational rather than part of any syntactic computation, but co-indexing does stand for a computational reality, inasmuch as it represents that co-indexed elements share the same phi-features. The **binding domain** of an anaphor is essentially the CP that minimally contains it.

This requirement therefore rules out binding of reflexive *-self* pronouns across clause boundaries. For this reason although (35)a is possible, in (35)b *herself* in an embedded clause is too distant from the subject of the main clause, *Lucy*, to be bound by it, rendering the sentence ungrammatical.

(35) a. Lucy$_i$ surprised herself$_i$
     b. *Lucy$_i$ said that you surprised herself$_i$

We have already looked at a number of other anaphoric elements besides *-self* reflexives, including NPIs, and PRO. In both instances we argued that the antecedent was determined or at least restricted at LF, rather than purely on a syntactic level. In instances of Negative Concord, however, we proposed that the second negative element and its negator were related by Movement, thereby accounting for the two syntactic elements functioning as a single semantic negation.

We therefore broadly have two options to explain reflexive -*self* anaphors: one in which the antecedent-anaphor relationship is determined by Movement, on a syntactic level, and one in which it is construed post-syntactically.

A Movement explanation can itself broadly be construed in two ways. The first is that the anaphor and its antecedent are the same element Remerged, realised at PF as separate words. This idea requires the same elimination of the theta-criterion as the Movement Theory of Control, necessitating that theta roles be reimagined as features, such that an element in a chain can Remerge in multiple theta-positions. Hence *Lucy* and *herself* in (35)a would be copies of the same argument, even though *Lucy* is a cause/agent, and *herself* an experiencer.

We could also argue for an approach similar to that which we took for Negative Concord, in which the antecedent and the anaphor are not the same syntactic object, but enter into a checking relationship accomplished by Remerge in a local configuration. In this analysis the anaphor, despite having Remerged with its antecedent, is realised in its original position. This operation is a kind of **covert Movement**, a Remerge that applies at LF after Spell Out rather than during the syntactic derivation, so that it is invisible to PF.

One point in favour of these Movement analyses is that they give us a straightforward explanation for the domain restrictions on antecedent-anaphor relationships. Given that Movement is restricted to phases, we might argue that a -*self* pronoun cannot be bound by an element outside it minimally containing CP because it cannot Move out of that CP. That an anaphor must be c-commanded by its antecedent arises naturally in a Movement analysis from the idea that an element may only be Attracted by, and therefore Remerge with, an element that c-commands it.

A Movement analysis, however, is potentially subject to some of the same criticisms as the Movement Theory of Control. Partial binding of a -*self* anaphor in English is impossible, but a sort of split binding, in which the anaphor has multiple antecedents that do not form a constituent, and binding shift, in which there is more than one potential antecedent, are possible.

(36) a. *Lucy_i surprised themselves_i
      b. Lucy_i showed Maisie_j themselves_{i+j} in the mirror
      c. Lucy_i showed Maisie_j $\text{herself}_{i/j}$ in the mirror

One other consideration that comes into play is the acceptability of -*self* anaphors in contexts where Movement places them in a position in which they are no longer c-commanded by an antecedent. In examples such as (37)b, a *wh*-phrase containing the reflexive *himself* has been Moved to CP with no apparent effect on the licensing of the anaphor.

(37) a. Alec$_i$ liked the picture of himself$_i$
b. Which picture of himself$_i$ did Alec$_i$ like?

This preservation of the anaphor licensing indicates that construal of the anaphor occurs before topicalisation, unlike NPI licensing, which was unacceptable under any configuration in which the NPI preceded the licensing negation.

(38) a. I don't have any money
b. *Any money, I don't have

In attempting to establish an analysis for anaphors, it is helpful to compare their distribution to that of non-reflexive pronouns, which in GB were described as subject to Binding Principle B.

Principle B
A pronominal must be free [not bound] in its binding domain.

Here the same definitions of binding and binding domain apply. Thus a pronoun can be c-commanded and co-indexed with its antecedent, but not within the clause that minimally contains it. This restriction puts anaphors and pronominals in complementary distribution.

(39) a. *Lucy$_i$ surprised her$_i$
b. Lucy$_i$ said that you surprised her$_i$

As with anaphors, Principle B applies even when the pronominal has been Remerged in a position where it is no longer c-commanded by its antecedent, as in questions.

(40) a. *Alec$_i$ liked the picture of him$_i$
b. *Which picture of himi did Alec$_i$ like?

We can also define the distribution of **Referring expressions**, lexical items that do not get their referent from an antecedent, in terms of binding and binding domain. These R-expressions are essentially full DP/NPs.

Principle C
An R-expression must be free [not bound] everywhere.

This means that no matter the number of intervening CPs between them, an R-expression will be ungrammatical if co-indexed with a c-commanding antecedent.

(41) a. *She$_i$ surprised Lucy$_i$
      b. *She$_i$ said that he explained that the news surprised Lucy$_i$

Again, Remerge of the R-expression in a position where it is no longer c-commanded by a potential antecedent has no effect on its grammaticality.

(42) a. *He$_i$ liked the picture of Alec$_i$
      b. *Which picture of Alec$_i$ did he$_i$ like?

The related facts on anaphors, pronominals and R-expressions indicate that they should all be accounted for in the same way, inasmuch as binding is a single operation that occurs at the same point in the syntax. Our constraints in terms of the binding domain indicate that the CP is relevant for this operation, but the preservation of binding relationships in the context of Remerge within CP indicates that binding must occur prior to completion of the CP, i.e. before it is sent to Spell Out.

Recall that vP also constitutes a phase, as evidenced by the position of floating quantifiers in at least one variety of Irish English. If we assume the true binding domain for -*self* reflexives is the vP phase we can explain the data we have seen so far. In each instance we have seen these anaphors licensed either by another object within a split VP or a subject that originates in vP. The locality of this relationship also applies in Object Control and Raising-to-Object constructions, where the anaphor will be in the same vP as VP-internal subject, either by virtue of this being initial Merge position (OC), or Remerge in this position (RtO). In Subject Control constructions the -*self* pronoun in an embedded clause will be bound by PRO in the lower vP, which in turn will be construed with the matrix subject. In Subject Raising constructions it will be construed with the subject that begins in the embedded vP.

(43) a. Julian persuaded himself to enter the race (Object Control)
      b. Julian expects himself to win the race (Raising-to-Object)
      c. Julian tried to see himself in the mirror (Subject Control)
      d. Julian seems to have seen himself in the mirror (Subject Raising)

Where there are two potential antecedents, or a combined antecedent (see examples (36)a and (36)b), both antecedents must be in the vP at the point when its complement is sent to Spell Out.

Because binding is restricted to a single phase, it is tempting to argue that it is a syntax-based operation. If so, we would expect it to be mediated by feature-checking. As we have seen, though, there are a number of reasons to suppose that the relationship between an anaphor and its antecedent is not one determined by Movement, either by way of identity or feature-checking. Moreover, construal of a pronominal and its antecedent, which occurs at a distance, cannot be achieved this way, as the Movement required would either be at too great a distance or ruled out by the Minimal Link Condition if there are intervening potential referents, as in (44).

(44) Lucy$_i$ said that Maisie$_j$ surprised her$_{i/j}$

It instead appears that construal of anaphors, pronominals and R-expressions occurs at LF, mediated by the verb. It is restricted to vP because this is the domain of a single predicate. In other instances, as in the licensing of NPIs, LF can 'see' outside this phase, but here it cannot.

8.2.1 Unbound and long-distance reflexives

It has long been observed that, contrary to Principle A, there are several situations in which -*self* pronouns are either not bound at all or apparently bound at a distance. In many of these instances the anaphor is emphasised prosodically and can alternate with a pronominal.

(45) a. Julian$_i$ thought Alec saw {him$_i$/himself$_i$}, not Maisie
    b. Julian$_i$ thinks that Alec won't talk even to {him$_i$/himself$_i$}
    c. Julian$_i$ thinks that boys such as {him$_i$/himself$_i$} should be given sweets

Although these occur in relatively Standard English, a number of Non-Standard uses of -*self* pronouns can be explained as resulting from instantiation of an emphatic feature at PF.

(46) a. %It is herself!
    b. Maisie and myself are going out
    c. And how about yourselves?

As such these **logophoric** uses are not subject to Principle A, because -*self* here is not an instantiation of an anaphoric feature, but rather is subject to other requirements, such as salience of the referent.

More problematic are the long-distance reflexives used by certain speakers in an area of northern Minnesota known as the Iron Range. In these sentences an antecedent may bind a reflexive pronoun in an embedded clause despite the intervention of a CP boundary.

(47) %Julian$_i$ knew that Maisie saw himself$_i$

Examples such as this appear to be in direct violation of Principle A, and cannot be explained simply as an instance of emphasis because they are limited to cases in which the apparently intervening subject matches in person with the anaphor and its antecedent (but not necessarily in gender and number).

(48)　*Julian$_i$ knew that I saw himself$_i$

Here it is likely that there is covert Movement which puts the anaphor in a sufficiently local configuration with its antecedent in order to allow for co-reference. An intervening element that does not agree in person may block this Movement by creating an unacceptable mismatch of features.

8.3 Coordinated pronouns

The use of pronouns coordinated by *and* is almost certainly something that you have been corrected on by a well-meaning parent or teacher at some point in your life, regardless of whether you are a native speaker of English or not. All of the following forms are considered incorrect, or at best informal, even by people who are fairly relaxed about prescriptive grammar rules. All of them are also produced quite naturally by native speakers.

(49)　a.　%Me and Alastair left early
　　　b.　%Him and me left early
　　　c.　%She and him left early

Prescriptivists would argue that these sentences should be recast as (50).

(50)　a.　Alastair and I left early
　　　b.　He and I left early
　　　c.　She and he left early

Throughout this text we have argued that nouns have an interpretable Case feature, and are subject to the Visibility Condition, a requirement that every noun be Merged in a Case position at some point in the derivation in order to be licensed for theta role assignment. Yet with the exception of pronouns Case is not expressed overtly in English, a reality we acknowledge with the capitalisation of this term to indicate that it is abstract. Where we do see Case in pronominal morphology it does not necessarily match up to what would be expected from a one-to-one correspondence between the value of a particular Case and its expression.

　　English has essentially two Cases: Nominative, which applies to subjects (we have said this is assigned by T) and potentially the complements of copular/linking verbs, and Accusative, which applies to nouns everywhere else.[3]

The prescriptivist complaint about the sentences in (49) is largely based on the fact that while they are subjects, these pronouns are marked with Accusative Case. The argument here is that the pronouns should have the same case expression as they would when not coordinated. Certainly the sentences in (51) are ungrammatical, although perhaps not unexpected for small children (another piece of evidence that they do not acquire language by repeating exactly what they hear).

(51) a. *Me left early
     b. *Him left early
     c. *Her left early

One other aspect of these sentences that might be judged 'wrong' is the placement of the first person pronoun as the first element in (49)a. This is not a strictly grammatical issue, even though it may be lumped in as such, but rather is a politeness convention. It is probably natural to mention yourself first, in that we are all most salient to ourselves compared to other people, but it is considered bad form in the same way as barging to the front of a queue before it is your turn. We will set this issue aside as irrelevant to our discussion.

While prescriptivism demands that the case (lower-case c) on coordinated pronouns be the same as that for uncoordinated ones, there seem to be a number of possible rules that actually determine this. For some speakers any coordinated elements are assigned Accusative Case, as in (49)a and (49)b. For other speakers it is only the second element assigned Accusative Case, as in (49)c. While these options diverge from the Case assignment for subjects, this Accusative Case assignment is consistent with what we expect for non-subject nominals, such that for objects or complements of prepositions what speakers actually produce typically matches up with what would be considered 'correct' in prescriptive terms.

(52) a. Alastair spoke to him and her
     b. *Alastair spoke to he and she

---

[3] For English this 'elsewhere' Case is often referred to as 'Objective' in acknowledgement that it covers a number of contexts that in other languages would be categorised as Dative, Prepositional, Instrumental, etc. as well as Accusative Case. I employ the term 'Accusative' in the understanding that this covers more ground than it might outside of English.

This case realisation is not strictly syntactic, inasmuch as it is a morphological property. As we said in the introductory chapters, the syntax does not 'care' how a word is pronounced, including the instantiation of phi-features. In syntactic terms *sneaked* and *snuck* are equivalent: both represent the verb *sneak*, and all the associated features of this lexical item, combined with a tense feature valued [+PAST]. At the same time, the particular morphological differences for coordinated pronouns indicate that post-syntactic case assignment is sensitive to the structure introduced by the coordinating conjunction *and*.

In traditional representations coordinated elements might be modelled using ternary branching, in which each coordinate is its own phrase, with the composite forming a phrase of the same type.

(53)

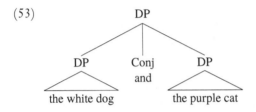

Given the Minimalist prohibition against ternary branching, we are forced to revise this structure. One possibility is that *and* Merges initially with the second conjunct nominal, before Merging with the first.

(54)

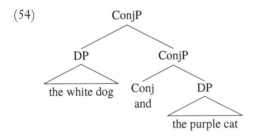

This structure gives a straightforward explanation for discrepancies in case for coordinated subjects. For some speakers the Conj head *and* has a [*u*CASE] feature valued as [+ACC], which is eliminated when checked by Merge with the complement DP. The DP Merged in its specifier has its Case valued as [+NOM] through Merge of the coordinated subject with TP, as is typical for uncoordinated subjects, resulting in forms such as *she and him*. For other speakers the [*u*CASE +ACC] feature remains active after Merge with the complement DP, so that there is subsequent valuation of the case on the DP Merged in its specifier as accusative, resulting in forms such as *me and him*.

Of course, the coordinate structure in (54) is problematic because it creates a phrase of a different type than would typically appear in the same positions as DPs. We can solve this problem by assuming a special property of Merge in coordinate structures in which both heads project their features, so that the maximal projection has the features of the DP as well

(55)

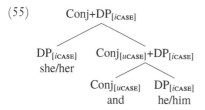

This represents a digression from our typical Merge operations, but it can be reduced to a property of the particular lexical item *and* (and perhaps other coordinators such as *or* more generally). We might in fact argue that, having had all of its features checked by Merge of each coordinate, the ConjP does not project, making the maximal projection simply a DP. There must, though, be some reflex of the coordination present in the maximal projection, as coordinated DPs are not identical to the highest Merged DP. If nothing else, they are realised as plural rather than singular.

(56)   a.   {The boy/The girl} {is/*are} happy
        b.   The boy and the girl {*is/are} happy

That this percolation of a feature or features from a dependent occurs specifically for the lexical item *and* is not to say that such an operation is unique to this context. We have already suggested a similar possibility within DPs/NPs. In questions English also has pied-piping operations, in which a preposition is carried along by Movement of a *wh*-word in its complement.

(57)   Hazel cut the cake with a knife
        a.   What did Hazel cut the cake with? (Preposition Stranding)
        b.   With what did Hazel cut the cake? (Pied-piping of Preposition)

Here, too, we can assume that the interpretable question/*wh*-features of the complement optionally percolate up into the PP in order to enable the preposition to be Attracted to Remerge in the CP along with the question word.

The presence of the [iCASE] feature in the maximal projection for the coordinated phrase means that it can check the [uCASE] feature on the TP. Where one or both interpretable Case features on each of the coordinated DPs have not already been valued by *and* they will be assigned Nominative Case, resulting in Standard pronominal forms, as in (50). Where one or both DPs have already been valued with Accusative Case by *and*, this will supersede any Case assignment by TP.

One drawback to this analysis is that it requires a particular type of *and* that differs from the *and* that coordinates other lexical or phrasal categories such as adjectives or Verb Phrases.

(58) a. Nancy is tired and cross
 b. Charlie will eat dinner and wash the dishes

Complicating matters further, coordination may also occur with words or phrases from different lexical categories.

(59) a. She likes piña coladas and getting caught in the rain
 b. The boy was in trouble and very upset about it
 c. ??I want a cup of tea and to read a book

Arguably the -*ing* participle in (59) is acting as a nominal in coordination with the DP *piña coladas*, although the fact that this is a *get*-passive appears to indicate otherwise. One might also argue that while (59)b represents coordination of a PP and and AdjP, they fill similar functions. Least acceptable of the three is (59)c, which represents coordination of an NP and a non-finite complement.

Such coordinations are nevertheless relatively amenable to the analysis we have proposed, in that we may assume the relevant selectional features of both coordinates, regardless of their lexical category, are present in the maximal projection of the coordinate structure. If either is incompatible with a selecting head (e.g. the verb *like*, *be*, or *want*), it will be ruled out.

That there should be different types of *and*, with the one coordinating DPs assigning Case, is not particularly problematic if we consider that there are a number of heads which may select for different types of complement. Looking to the examples in *want*, we see that it can have either a DP or a non-finite clause complement. Within the complex of the split VP this means that sometimes it assigns (Accusative) Case to an object, and sometimes it does not.

The asymmetric structure proposed here for coordinated elements is also somewhat problematic because it seems to obviate an apparent difference between coordination and subordination. A subordinating conjunction such as *because* seems significantly more asymmetric than a coordinating one such as *and*. In a sentence such as (60)a we would assume that only the embedded clause is within the phrase headed *because*, with the whole subordinate phrase acting as an adjunct elsewhere. It is notable that *because* is much more limited than coordinators such as *and* or *or*, allowing only finite clause complements, the preposition *of*, or, if you speak Internetese, nominals.

(60) a. I arrived late because there was lots of traffic
      b. I arrived late because of the traffic
      c. %I arrived late because traffic

There are a couple of things to note here. First, the elements in coordinated structures are not always semantically equivalent. For instance, in (58)a the first conjunct might be interpreted as leading to the second ('Nancy was tired, and therefore she was cross'), while in (58)b coordination of the VPs indicates temporal progression ('Charlie will eat dinner, and then he will wash the dishes').

Second, the asymmetry we have argued for coordinated structures is only a partial one. The structure is symmetric inasmuch as the coordinator *and* selects for each conjunct, and the features of each conjunct are present in the maximal projection of the coordinated phrase. In contrast, a subordinating conjunction selects only for a complement, and in turn is either selected by, or adjoined to, some other phrase.

On a final note, we can return to the example from the introduction, where a speaker suggested the following form for a first person singular pronoun in object position.

(61) And that's the difference between the President and I

This correction is somewhat puzzling, as the Nominative form contradicts the Accusative Case we would expect from Case assignment in an object position, or following a coordinator for speakers who have *and* with a Case-assigning feature. As suggested at the beginning of the chapter, this example appears to be a hypercorrection. Because many people are particularly corrected on *me and X*-type subjects, both in terms of putting the first person singular pronoun second and using the Nominative Case, the perception that *and I* is (always) correct has become a particularly salient one for many speakers. Thus this overrides any other Case assignment that would occur in the grammar of that speaker.

That this hypercorrection is essentially a surface-based rule rather than a syntactic one is evidenced by its limitations to first person forms.

It can be layered over a coordination where both coordinators are assigned Accusative Case. For no other persons/numbers do we get an accusative pronoun preceding a nominative one in a coordination.

(62) a. %Him and I left early
b. *Him and she left early

Likewise, this type of pronoun case asymmetry does not occur for objects in any other person/number.

(63) a. %Flora looked at him and I
b. *Flora looked at him and she

Thus, while at least some Non-Standard Case use can be traced back to syntactic feature-checking operations, here we appear to have a genuine surface requirement.

8.4 Conclusion

This chapter has explored the internal structure of nominals and external factors that influence their distribution. In particular, we have looked at the arguments for, and possible drawbacks to, the DP hypothesis. We have also considered the behaviour of anaphors and pronominals, and how this is influenced by requirements in relation to their antecedents. Finally, we considered how the overt realisation of case on pronouns may in some instances be influenced by underlying Case features, but in others reflect rules that apply only post-syntactically. In the next chapter we will return to the internal structure of DPs in our discussion of adjectives.

8.5 Further reading

Abney (1987) is usually identified as the origin of the DP hypothesis (although other authors had made similar arguments). For more recent discussion of and arguments against the DP hypothesis see Bruening (2009).

Zribi-Hertz (1989) outlines a number of instances of binding that do not conform to the traditional binding Principles. For discussion of anaphor and pronoun binding in a Minimalist context see Reuland (2001). Antonenko (2012) also provides a wide-ranging look at binding. To learn more specifically about long-distance reflexives see Loss (2011, 2014).

For discussion of coordinated pronouns in genitive constructions see Payne (2011).

8.6 Exercises

1. Trees
   Draw trees for the following sentences, assuming the DP hypothesis. You don't have to include features, but you should think about what they are.
   a. My sister is not very happy
   b. I observed the statue's destruction
   c. The pieces of cake were all eaten by her
   d. His teacher disliked his explanation of the answer
   e. Jack's friend does not think he is tired
   f. Which book of poems did Martha say she believes Maisie likes?

For Answers see edinburghuniversitypress.com/englishsyntax.

9 Adjectives and adverbs

In 1997 Apple computers introduced an advertising slogan which, like the 'Got milk?' campaign launched across America earlier in the same decade, relied on a catchy two-word phrase that grammatical purists deemed incorrect.

(1)   Think different

While some prescriptivists insist that the slogan should be *Think differently*, use of an adjective without an *-ly* ending to give an adverbial reading is common across varieties of English.[1] Some adverbials are even identical to their adjectival equivalents, or have no corresponding adjective.

(2)   a. Hold on {tight/²tightly}!
      b. He thought {long/*longly} and {hard/*hardly}
      c. He runs {fast/*fastly}
      d. He eats haggis {often/*oftenly}

Where an adverb does have a potential *-ly* ending, the non-*ly* form can only be used post-verbally.

(3)   a. He {*quick/quickly} ate up the haggis
      b. He ate the haggis up {%quick/quickly}

Besides variation in the use of *-ly*, the examples in (3) indicate another important aspect of adverb behaviour: despite the relatively strict rules of English word order, adverbs can appear in a number of positions within a clause. At the same time, the order in which multiple adverbs can occur is relatively restricted. For instance, *probably* can precede *never* within a clause, but the reverse is generally not possible.

---

[1]   In contrast, when running for office, US President Donald Trump added an unexpected *-ly*, asserting 'I'm going to cut taxes bigly.'

(4) a. He probably will never eat haggis again
     b. *He never will probably eat haggis again

Adjectives have similar ordering restrictions. An observation to this effect from the book *The Elements of Eloquence* (Forsyth 2013) went viral as a Tweet in 2016: the author noted that (5)a is ungrammatical. In contrast, *great* may precede *green*.

(5) a. *green great dragons
     b. great green dragons

As well as restrictions on their placement and order, adverbs and adjectives pose a number of challenges to the Minimalist model of syntax we have been developing throughout the text. This chapter will explore these questions of structure before returning to the data above.

9.1 Rethinking structure

9.1.1 Specifiers and adjuncts

Recall that in Chapter 2 we noted that the advent of Bare Phrase Structure (BPS) means it is no longer possible to differentiate between adjuncts and specifiers purely in terms of structural descriptions. We can still argue that complements are unique, in that they are sisters to, and must be selected by, the head of the phrase. Subsequent Merge operations muddy the picture. Without an X' level, any constituent Merged with a projection other than the head of a phrase itself is potentially indistinguishable from any other constituent Merged in this way. We can see this lack of distinction by comparing a classic X-bar schema with the equivalent BPS form.

(6)   X-BAR STRUCTURE   BARE PHRASE STRUCTURE

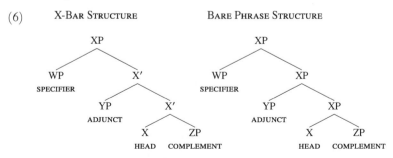

In the BPS tree both the adjunct and specifier are sister of XP and daughter of XP. Some linguists have taken this similarity to mean that it is impossible for a phrase to have more than one adjunct/specifier because the syntax would have to specify the order they are Merged in, which seems to be a stipulation on the order of Merge that does not come directly from any lexical item.

There is also a problem with a multi-specifier/-adjunct configuration in terms of c-command. In Chapter 2 we argued that this relationship is the result of Merge in a bottom-up derivation, such that an element can see another syntactic element that it is Merged with, and anything contained within that syntactic element that has come into the derivation previously. Some syntacticians have argued for an alternative to c-command, called **m-command**, in which it is not first branching node that counts for an element to be able to 'see' other constituents lower down in the tree, but the first maximal projection. As a result, multiple specifiers/adjuncts in the same phrase would symmetrically m-command each other, again calling into question how they could be ordered within the phrase.

This order in which elements are Merged has potential consequences in terms of linear precedence. Where multiple dependents (whether they be complements, adjuncts or specifiers) are Merged to the right of a head, the lowest will come first linearly; where they are Merged to the left of a head, the highest will be first in terms of precedence.

In Chapter 2 we suggested direction of linearisation for any given syntactic element with respect to the phrase with which it is Merged may be determined post-syntactically by a head-directionality parameter that is not part of the syntax proper. If this is true then the mirror image trees in (7) are actually identical up to the point of Spell Out, with the directionality parameters instantiated at this point determining their mirrored linear orders.

(7)

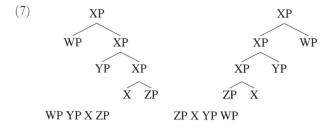

There is another school of thought, the **Linear Correspondence Axiom** (LCA), that says c-command (or, really, m-command) maps to precedence: one element will precede another in the syntax if it m-commands it. One consequence of this proposal is that trees such as the second one in (7) are ruled out. There can be no Merge of dependents following a head (right-adjunction), because this would result in incorrect linear order. This hypothesis is directly contradictory to the notion of head-directionality we have outlined so far in assuming that precedence is determined syntactically at the point of Merge, making this an operation that creates ordered pairs.

Another consequence of the LCA is that a phrase may have only a single specifier/adjunct because otherwise they would symmetrically m-command each other, so that not only would it be impossible to determine their order of Merge but also their linear order. As a result the first tree in (7) would also be ruled out at the point where WP Merges.

The idea that a phrase may have only a single specifier position has significant consequences for how we view the structure of clauses and nominals. It has particularly shaped proposals regarding the inclusion of optional elements such as adverbs and adjectives. We will ultimately reject these proposals, and consequently the LCA, but it cannot be ignored in evaluating approaches to adjective and adverb distribution.

9.1.2 Selection of dependents

In introductions to syntax the distinction often made between adjuncts and complements is that the former are optional and the latter are obligatory. This classification is only partially accurate. Consider the sentence in (8). The adjective *happy* is obligatory, and the adverb *frequently* is not.

(8)   Alastair seems happy frequently

Here the obligatory/optional dichotomy applies. Ignoring for the moment the possibility that right-adjunction is impossible, we can represent the structure for (8) in (9), in which the complement adjective *happy* is a sister of the V head *seem*, and the adjunct adverb *frequently* is sister to the VP formed by Merge of *look* and *happy*.

(9)

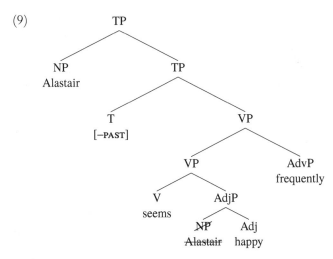

Recall, though, that some lexical items fit into more than one subcategory. In Chapter 3 we cited *eat* as an example of this, allowing an object or not.

(10) a. When he arrived, I was eating [intransitive]
b. When he arrived, I was eating haggis [transitive]

Given the expanded structure we have proposed for Verb Phrases this difference is actually more than straightforward selection for an object complement or not, but rests on whether the structure has both *v*P and VP projections.

In other instances we see that the same verb can have different kinds of complement or object. *Know*, for instance, can select for a nominal, a PP or various types of CP. With the PP especially we can see that it is an adjunct rather than a complement, because only specific prepositions are permitted, indicating selection by *know*.

(11) a. I know Alastair
b. I know {about/of/*in/*through} the answer
c. I know {that/Ø/if/whether} it will rain

We can also see optional complements in the nominal domain. A noun such as *cup* can happily occur on its own without dependents. Where it is accompanied by Prepositional Phrases, however, these are not all equivalent, even though they can all be left out.

(12) a. a cup
b. a cup with a blue handle
c. a cup of tea
d. a cup of tea with a blue handle

The preposition *of* is in almost all instances essentially meaningless, serving as a functional connector in the syntax within NPs. PPs with *of* are almost always complements. Another indication that, while optional, [$_{PP}$ *of tea*] is a complement here is that leaving it out in certain contexts creates a sense of something missing. This is not so for [$_{PP}$ *with a blue handle*].

(13) a. I bought a cup (with a blue handle)
      b. I drank a cup #(of tea)

Finally, if we accept the DP hypothesis, the complements of determiners such as *that* are also optional, again depending on context.

(14) He read that (article)

The line between complements and adjuncts, as between adjuncts and specifiers, is therefore possibly somewhat less clear than traditionally supposed. Reconsideration of these structural descriptions becomes particularly pertinent in analysis of adjectives and adverbs.

9.2 Adjectives

Adjectives can be divided into two categories by their syntactic distribution. We have already seen predicative adjectives, those that follow a copular or linking verb. Only one predicative adjective is permitted per linking verb, presumably because they are selected by the verb, occupying a unique complement position.

(15) The boy looked cheerful (*pleased)

Attributive adjectives precede a noun, and may be unlimited in number.

(16) The lovely friendly big brown dog barked

Some adjectives are limited to predicative uses, such as *awake* and *aghast*.

(17) a.   The children were {aghast/awake}
      b. *The {aghast/awake} children left

Others adjectives, such as *alleged* and *former*, are limited to attributive uses.

(18) a.   My {former/alleged} friend left
      b. *My friend is {former/alleged}

Some adjectives vary in meaning according to whether they are being used predicatively or attributively. *Poor*, for example, can mean either

'unfortunate' or 'impecunious' when modifying a noun, but only 'impecunious' following a linking verb.

(19) a. The poor girl had no shoes
        =The {unfortunate/impecunious} girl had not shoes
     b. The girl with no shoes was poor
        =The girl with no shoes was impecunious
        ≠'The girl with no shoes was unfortunate'

Semantics may play some role in restricting which adjectives can
be attributive or predicative, but the different distribution of synonymous adjectives such as *poor* and *unfortunate* suggests this cannot be the
only determinant. There is also at least a small amount of variation in
this respect. For example, some speakers may use *quality* predicatively,
while others use it only attributively, or as part of a compound such as
high quality.

(20) a. Their quality service impressed me
     b. %Their service was quality

We will revisit adjectival complements in later sections, giving further
consideration to how these are Merged with verbs.

9.2.1 Attributive adjective order

Multiple attributive adjectives used with a single noun often only have
one 'correct' order. Reversing or reordering them is possible, but only in
contexts where particular emphasis is placed on one adjective.

(21) a. the big red car
     b. the RED big car
     c. a nice old house
     d. an OLD nice house

In other instances it is possible to change adjective order. The different
options often introduce subtle shifts in interpretation, and in that sense
may be context dependent.

(22) a. a small cute dog
     b. a cute small dog

As with alternations between predicative and attributive uses, switching
the placement of an attributive adjective with respect to another may
have an effect on its meaning.

(23) a. a delicious cool drink
        =a drink that is tasty and cold

b. a cool delicious drink
= a drink that is excellent and tasty

Incarnations of the so-called 'royal order' of adjectives often crop up in writing and grammar instruction texts. While there are some variations in how it is presented, the version given in *The Elements of Eloquence* (Forsyth 2013) provides a fairly representative example.

(24) opinion > size > age > shape > colour > origin > material > purpose

Various explanations have been suggested, both by laypeople and linguists, to account for what underlies the order. Some people argue that the less separable a characteristic is from the noun, the closer it is to the noun. For example, material is an intrinsic and often unchangeable property of a thing, whereas size is relative to other things of that type, and opinion is dependent on the speaker rather than being inherent to the thing being described.

(25) an amazing large steel building

It has also been argued on a more technical level that some adjective ordering can be attributed to the distinction between intersective and subsective adjectives. **Intersective adjectives** identify the nouns that they modify as belonging to a set of things with a property which overlaps with the set of things denoted by the noun. A *happy child*, for example, represents the intersection of the set 'happy things' and the set 'children'.

A **subsective adjective** gives a property that denotes a smaller group of things within the set of things denoted by the noun. A *young child*, for instance, refers to a child who is young with respect to the set of children. By comparison, a *young adult* is significantly older than a *young child*, and within the set of people, all children are *young*.

As a general principle, subsective adjectives precede intersective ones.

(26) a. a happy young child
     b. *a young happy child

This generalisation applies as well to the examples in (21), where *big* and *old* are subsective, and *red* and *nice* are intersective. At the same time it predicts that *nice* and *red* should be interchangeable in order, which does not seem to be the case.

(27) a. a nice red house
     b. ?*a red nice house

From a syntactic perspective the potential for multiple attributive adjectives raises two interrelated questions. First, is their order determined only by semantic factors, or does it in fact reflect constraints on syntactic selection? And, second, how are adjectives incorporated into the syntax of a nominal constituent?

Traditional accounts of adjective order place them as adjuncts stacked within the NP. This approach is compatible with both the DP and NP hypotheses, as the structure would differ only in whether the determiner is Merged in the NP after all of the adjectives, although based on the arguments from Chapter 8 we will assume the former.

(28)

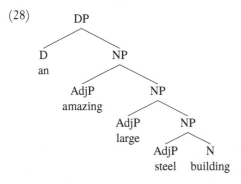

In a structure of this type the ordering of adjectives must be a purely semantic operation. In adjoining this way the adjectives are entirely optional, and do not check features of the N head. The adjectives themselves nevertheless appear to impose some sort of categorial selectional requirement, as they cannot be adjoined to elements of other categories, such as verbs or determiners.

(29) a. Alastair did a beautiful dance
      b. *Alastair beautiful danced
      c. Maisie read that lovely book
      d. *Maisie read lovely that

In this sense the relationship between heads and adjuncts must be an asymmetric one.

An alternative view is that adjectives are not adjoined within the NP, but Merge in functional projections external to the main NP projection. As with the addition of the DP hypothesis, and other possible nominal functional projections (e.g. NumP) mentioned in Chapter 8, the syntax proposed mirrors the architecture of the clausal domain, where we have expanded the structure within and outside of lexical verbs.

In this approach an adjective is Merged with a silent functional projection between the noun and determiner, with each adjective checking a feature on the appropriate projection.[2]

(30)

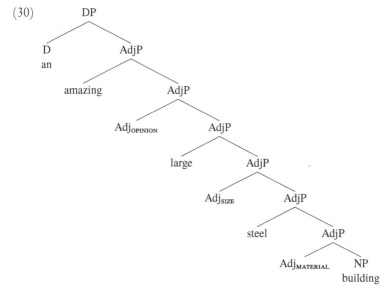

This structure corresponds to the LCA, eliminating the multiple adjunction within the NP that is otherwise required. Sequencing of these AdjP functional projections remains a problem. Considering the potential multiplicity of projections required, they cannot be ordered straightforwardly through c-selection, as each projection would have to select for all projections it may precede.

One solution is to argue that the functional structure within the DP is fixed and invariant, so that all adjectival heads are available in all nominals, even when not all (types of) adjectives are expressed. In the respect that it reduces mental computation, since there is essentially a predetermined structure rather than one that must be built up for every nominal, this is a relatively Minimalist approach. It also requires, however, a great deal of unpronounced structure, raising questions about how the features of these functional heads are checked in the absence of particular adjectives. Do they revert to some kind of default? Is checking of features in this instance optional?

As an alternative we could propose that a functional head within the nominal domain can c-select for any other functional head (or NP), and

---

[2] The tree here is intended as an exemplar, rather than a comprehensive representation of what the structure of an expanded DP might look like.

that restrictions on their order are strictly semantic, based on some of the reasons already discussed. This proposal is similar to what we have argued for the clausal domain in Chapter 4, and we will return to this issue again in our discussion of adverb order.

A more difficult obstacle for this kind of proposal, regardless of how the intervening functional projections are ordered, is the distance it creates between the NP and determiner. We argued in Chapter 8 that if we accept the DP hypothesis a determiner must select for nouns with specific features. We have considered as well the possibility that some of these features are encoded in functional heads external to the core, lexical NP. Regardless of the exact position of such features, the potential presence of other functional adjective-hosting projections would mean that they would have to percolate up through the structure in order to allow for selection of the NP by the determiner.

For English, then, other than conforming to the LCA, the placement of adjectives in functional projections offers no definitive advantage, but it is not necessarily ruled out either. We will consider a related proposal for adverbs, and conclude that their order cannot be determined purely by syntactic means.

9.3 Adverb order

As with adjectives, adverbs cannot occur in any order, but have a relatively specific sequence in relation to each other. For example, there is a strong preference for an adverb such as *possibly* to precede one such as *often*, or for *fortunately* to precede *quickly*.

(31) a. He possibly often eats haggis
      b. *He often possibly eats haggis
      c. He fortunately has quickly eaten the haggis
      d. *He quickly has fortunately eaten the haggis

For adverbs, unlike adjectives, there is a great deal of variation with respect to where they may appear within the clausal domain. *Maybe*, for example, can occur in any pre-verbal position, and post-verbally with an **intonational break**, a small pause between constituents in speech (represented orthographically by a comma in our examples). It is ruled out only between a verb and its object, a position that is generally ungrammatical for adverbs (and other elements) in English. The position of *maybe* does not affect its interpretation.

(32) a. Maybe Alastair will have been taking photos
      b. Alastair maybe will have been taking photos
      c. Alastair will maybe have been taking photos
      d. Alastair will have maybe been taking photos
      e. Alastair will have been maybe taking photos
      f. *Alastair will have been taking maybe photos
      g. Alastair will have been taking photos, maybe

For other adverbs a change in position results in a change of meaning.
Happily can have a speaker-oriented reading, expressing the speaker's
opinion, a subject-oriented meaning, expressing some disposition of the
subject, or a manner reading, expressing how a particular activity was
undertaken. Which of these readings is available depends on where in
the sentence the adverb appears.

(33) a. Happily, he will have arrived on time (speaker-oriented)
          =It is fortunate that he will have arrived on time
      b. He will happily have arrived on time (subject-oriented)
          =He will have been happy to have arrived on time
      c. He will have arrived on time happily (manner)
          =He will have arrived on time in a happy way (e.g. whistling,
          skipping, etc.)

The contrast between different available readings can be seen in the
employment of multiple adverbs with potentially contradictory meanings. *Cleverly* and *stupidly* both have subject-oriented and manner readings. They can be used in conjunction to show the difference between
these interpretations.

(34) a. He cleverly has answered the questions stupidly
          =It was clever of him to answer the questions in a stupid way
          (perhaps because he has reason to conceal his intelligence)
      b. He stupidly has answered the questions cleverly
          =It was stupid of him to answer the questions in a clever way

There is also a set of adverbs that occur only following the main verb of
a sentence. Many of these are the 'flat' adverbs mentioned in the introduction, such as *well, fast* and *hard*, which lack an -*ly* affix. Other non-*ly*
adverbs, such as *still* and *just*, have broader distributions, so it would
be wrong to identify lack of -*ly* as the only determinant of obligatory
post-verbal distribution.

(35) a. Flora has spoken well
      b. *Flora has well spoken
      c. Hazel will walk fast
      d. *Hazel will fast walk

   e. Nancy has been trying hard
   f. *Nancy has been hard trying

Adverbs therefore present a complex puzzle of interacting factors pertaining to order, interpretation and placement, which cannot be addressed wholly in isolation from each other.

As with other instances of particular sequencing requirements, namely of auxiliaries and adjectives, the question with respect to adverb order is whether it is determined semantically, and therefore not within the syntactic derivation, or by means of syntactic operations such as c-selection and feature-checking. In Chapter 4 we considered whether the sequence of auxiliaries in the functional range of the clause is determined by syntactic or semantic constraints. We argued that this order cannot be determined by syntactic selection, as it would mean that each auxiliary must select for each other type of auxiliary that can follow it. Reducing the order to c-selection risks replicating the order requirements for each individual lexical item in such a way as to miss what appears to be an overarching hierarchy.

   There is another approach that takes the series of functional projections as present in every clause, having a fixed invariant order, in the style of (36).[3]

(36)

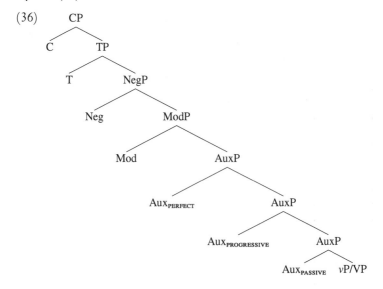

---

[3] This tree is representative of the available auxiliaries in English but gives only a small approximation of the structure required for a crosslinguistic account. Therefore, as with the tree in (30), it is not meant as a comprehensive representation of what this analysis would require.

It has also been noted that there is correspondence between the ordering of auxiliaries and of adverbs, given that they often match up in the kind of semantic contribution they make. For example, *maybe*, denoting epistemic possibility, tends to precede *already*, denoting the completion of an action, in the same way that epistemic *might* precedes perfective *have*. The sentences in (37) are in essence semantically equivalent

(37) a. He maybe already ate the cake
     b. He might have eaten the cake

One theory of adverb distribution takes the similarity between adverb and auxiliary order (for which there is much crosslinguistic evidence beyond the small example here) as an indication that they are manifestations of the same syntactic features. This **functional specifier approach** is similar to the one described for adjectives: an adverb Merges in a functional projection, checking its features by means of an Agree operation. Depending on the language, the same notion may also be expressed by an auxiliary in the head of that function projection, e.g. an epistemic Modal projection might have *might* in its head, or an adverb such as *possibly* Merged in its specifier. This is similar to the analysis we gave for negation in Chapter 6, and indeed it is possible to have **modal concord**, where a modal auxiliary and adverb are used together to express a single modal meaning, which looks not dissimilar from Negative Concord.

(38) He might possibly like some cake

The functional specifier approach also conforms to the LCA and, if we take the structure given to be invariant across clauses, cuts down on required selectional restrictions within the syntax. But it also potentially places intervening structure between auxiliaries and their corresponding participle forms (e.g. *have* and V-*en*), making it unclear how these dependencies can be determined at a distance.

9.4 Adverb placement: evidence from Adverb Climbing

Because the functional specifier approach requires adverbs to be in fixed positions, it means that any variation in adverb position must result from other elements moving around adverbs. Recall the example of *maybe*, which can appear in at least five positions in relation to a string of auxiliaries, not including the final, intonationally marked position.

(39) (maybe) Alastair (maybe) will (maybe) have (maybe) been (maybe) taking a photo

The tie between position and Merge is proposed to be interpretation-specific rather than adverb-specific per se, so that an adverb such as *cleverly* has two possible Merge positions, depending on whether it has a subject-oriented or manner reading. For *maybe*, though, there is no apparent variation in interpretation, which means that it would have only a single Merge position. Taking the highest position of *maybe* as its base position, each lower instance of this adverb would have to represent Movement of other elements around it. These optional Movements become highly problematic in terms of motivation and position of Merge.

Another serious challenge to the functional specifier of adverb distribution comes from adverbs that appear higher in the syntactic structure than they are interpreted. **Adverb Climbing** (AC) refers to a configuration in which an adverb preceding a verb which takes an infinitival complement modifies an embedded verb. AC is most obvious in instances where a Raising verb is used with an **agent-oriented adverb**, one that requires an argument with an agent theta role, making interpretation of the adverb with the main verb impossible. In (40), for example, *intentionally* modifies *pushed* rather than *seem*.

(40) Flora intentionally appears to have pushed Alastair
      =Flora appears to have intentionally pushed Alastair

AC is also possible with temporal adverbs, although these may be ambiguous between a matrix clause or embedded clause reading.

(41) Flora always seems to say the right thing
      =It always seems that Flora says the right thing or
      =It seems that Flora always says the right thing

These AC constructions are particularly problematic for a functional specifier account of adverb distribution because they would require the adverb to Move from its initial Merge position in the embedded clause. It is possibly difficult to motivate such Movement, but we will argue below that Remerge of adverbs occurs for reasons related to focus.

There is also a correlation between AC and particular types of non-finite complement. Where an agent-oriented adverb is used with a Control verb such as *try* or *neglect*, it has only a surface reading.

(42) a. Flora intentionally neglected to tell Alastair
          ≠Flora neglected to intentionally tell Alastair
      b. Flora knowingly tried to break the vase
          ≠Flora tried to knowingly break the vase

Recall that in Chapter 7 we argued that Raising verbs select for smaller complements than Control verbs, i.e. TPs instead of CPs. CPs are also phases, whereas TPs are not.

The availability of AC seems therefore to be sensitive to phase boundaries: an adverb may be interpreted as modifying an embedded verb if they are in the same phase, as occurs for Raising verbs, but not if the embedded verb is in a separate CP phase, as occurs for Control verbs. Notably, AC interpretations are available as well with both epistemic and deontic modal verbs, which would follow if these are part of the functional structure of the clause.

(43) a. I unknowingly must have bumped my head (epistemic)
=I must have unknowingly bumped my head
b. He voluntarily should resign from the party (deontic)
=He should voluntarily resign from the party

These examples contrast with combinations of modal verbs and negation, where a negation below the modal verb often takes scope over it. Here a modal takes scope over the adverb that precedes it.

The one instance where AC interpretations are possible with Control verbs is with temporal adverbs. The most famous example of this comes from a poem by American poet Gelett Burgess, written in the late nineteenth century.

(44) I never saw a Purple Cow
I never hope to see one
(=I hope never to see a purple cow)

These AC Control constructions also occur with adverbs such as *always* and *soon*. They are typically ambiguous between surface and AC readings.

(45) a. I always want to be with you
=I want to be with you always
b. I soon expect to see him
=I expect to see him soon

Not all Control verbs allow AC with temporal adverbs, however.

(46) a. I always forget to turn off the lights
≠I forget to always turn off the lights
b. I never tried to phone her
≠I tried to never phone her

The group of Control verbs that do allow AC with temporal adverbs (e.g. *hope, want, expect*) differ in another dimension from those that do not (e.g. *neglect, forget, try, manage*): they have **temporally independent infinitives**. This means that even though both sets of verbs take non-finite complements, for the first set the complement can be interpreted on a different timescale from the main verb, while for the second set it cannot be. We can see the difference through the (un)acceptability of contradictory temporal adverbs.

(47) a. Today I expected to leave tomorrow
      b. #Today I neglected to leave tomorrow

It has been suggested that this temporal independence of the non-finite complement is accomplished by T-to-C Movement, whereby certain Control verbs only select for CPs that have T features. This Head Movement would mean that T is available at the phase edge under certain Control verbs, and therefore 'available' in a higher phase.

We can thus propose a theory of adverb placement which says that certain functional projections are relevant to particular adverbs, but variation in adverb placement results not from the Movement of other elements, but rather from relative freedom with respect to where an adverb can Merge. Each adverb has a functional projection relevant to its interpretation(s) but does not enter into a feature-checking relationship with that projection. The relationship between them is instead asymmetric, with the adverb selecting for a particular functional projection. The relationship is not dissimilar from one of predication, in which a predicate must fill a 'hole' with an argument.

In practice this analysis means that an adverb will Merge initially with the relevant functional projection, but then may Move to a higher position within the same phase (or the next phase, if it is Merged at a phase edge). For AC with Raising this means that the adverb Merges in the embedded non-finite complement and may then Move out of the TP to position preceding the matrix verb; for Control verbs this is impossible, because the embedded clause is a CP, from which the adverb cannot escape. However, if features of T are present in C, as in temporally independent infinitives, then this is sufficient for a T-modifying temporal adverb to Merge in this position at the phase edge, and then Move to precede the matrix verb higher in the next phase.

As we have noted before, all Movements must be motivated. In the case of adverbs which do not change their interpretation in different positions, we will argue tentatively that there is a difference in information structure, the way elements of the clause are packaged and presented. We have seen this already with the active/passive distinction and topicalisation, among others, where the use of a particular argument as a subject, or moving it to the beginning of the sentence, seems to change what the sentence is 'about'. For adverbs, the higher the position the more emphasis there seems to be. In (48), for example, the AC version gives particular attention to *knowingly*.

(48)   a.   He knowingly seems to have insulted her
        b.   He seems to have knowingly insulted her

Remerge of the adverb in the pre-matrix verb position would therefore result from a focus feature in a position in the matrix clause that is checked by the adverb.

9.5 Sentence-final adverbs

Having argued that variation in adverb placement is a result of (Re) Merge of adverbs in different positions within a phase, we can largely reject the notion that other elements Move around adverbs. One remaining question is what determines the position of post-verbal adverbs, especially those that are obligatorily so.

We have already argued that particular adverbs select for particular functional heads. We can extend this idea to post-verbal adverbs, arguing in this instance that they select for V. Considering our proposal that the verb is typically not pronounced in this position (but instead in *v*), we could claim that the adverb is still Merged to the left of the head, as we have seen elsewhere. Given that such adverbs also must follow unaccusative verbs, which lack a *v*P projection, it seems that the adverb must be Merged to the right.

(49)   a.   *Martha late arrived
        b.   Martha arrived late

Because they are on different sides of the V head, the order in which the adverb and any objects Merge with the VP is actually of no consequence in terms of word order. An adverb could therefore be Merged in what would traditionally be a 'complement' position.

(50)

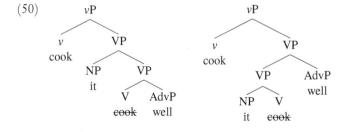

The first tree in (50) avoids right-adjunction. If we add an indirect object in a PP, though, we end up again with a structure that does not conform to the LCA.

(51)

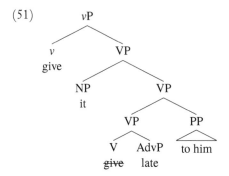

Alternatively, the adverb may Merge after the indirect object PP, reversing their order.

(52)

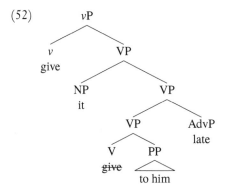

The most straightforward way to treat post-verbal adverbs thus seems to be to place them in a position Merged with V that is always linearised to the right. This directionality may be a general requirement on V in English, which means that we do not have to specify for each adverb whether it Merges to the right or left, but only what projection it Merges to. Indeed, it appears that only objects Merge to the left of the V head.

A further piece of evidence that adverbs sometimes function as 'complements' comes from **middles**, so termed because these constructions function halfway between active and passive constructions. A middle has what would typically be an object acting as the subject, in the same way as in a passive sentence, but without typical passive morphosyntax.

(53) a. This book reads well
    b. That bread slices easily

Middles are relevant to the discussion here because without adverbs they are ungrammatical. In this respect, then, adverbs sometimes have an obligatory, complement-like function.

(54) a. *This book reads
    b. *That bread slices

In the next section we return to 'flat' adverbs, and suggest that these and other necessarily post-verbal adverbs may have implications for how we categorise adverbs and adjectives.

9.6 Post-verbal adverbs

Adverbs that can appear post-verbally without an intonational break fall into a few categories.[4] Agent-oriented and manner adverbs can appear in this position, as can frequentative adverbs. All of these adverbs can also be pre-verbal

(55) a. Billy (intentionally) tore the paper intentionally
    b. Billy (carefully) folded the paper carefully
    c. Billy (frequently) writes letters frequently

Adverbs such as *late*, *well*, *tight*, *hard* and *fast* fall into the manner category. They not only share the characteristics of monosyllabicity and lack of *-ly* form, but can also all function as adjectives.

(56) a. The late train got in at 3
    b. Dolly was not well
    c. The tight knot couldn't be untied

Other adverbs lack *-ly* endings but are not obligatorily (or even optionally) post-verbal.

(57) a. Billy will soon see Martha (soon)
    b. Martha just spoke to Billy (*just)
    c. Billy still likes Martha (?still)

These adverbs do not function as adjectives in other contexts, or have entirely distinct meanings if they do.

---

[4] Almost all adverbs can appear in this position if separated from the rest of the clause by 'comma intonation'. The status of such prosodically separated elements is a large question, which it is beyond the scope of this text to answer.

(i) Billy likes the bookcase, {unfortunately/probably/unexpectedly}

(58) a. *The soon train got in at 3
      b. #The just passenger got off quickly
          (just≠recent/only)
      c. #That still knot is annoying me
          (still≠remaining)

Another set of adverbs that do end in -*ly* has been argued to occur
after the verb obligatorily. *Beautifully, poorly* and *terribly*, denoting how
well something is done, are sometimes called **degree of perfection
adverbs**.

(59) Martha explained the answer {poorly/beautifully/terribly}

These adverbs are most naturally post-verbal, but there are contexts in
which they can precede the verb.

(60) a. Martha's explanation beautifully captured the answer
      b. Billy poorly understood what she was saying

We can therefore conclude that truly obligatorily post-verbal adverbs
are those that not only lack -*ly* but do not differ significantly from their
adjectival counterparts in interpretation. Given our proposal above that
adverbs Merged with VP are obligatorily to the right of the head, and
that at least in some instances they are in what would traditionally be
classed as complement positions, this correlation further suggests that
there is a special relationship between the V head and adverbs adjoined
to it. These adverbs in fact appear actually to be adjectives, entering
into a special selectional relationship with the head. Specifically, we
can argue that the *late* group of adjectives/adverbs can select for a
V head.

This selection is possible as well for other 'flat' adverbs, which in this
analysis are adjectives. Thus *quick* or *bright* can select for V, and like any
non-object Merging with V(P) they must be linearised to the right.

(61) a. The lights {*quick/quickly} flashed {%quick/quickly} in the
          dark
      b. The lights {*bright/brightly} shone {%bright/brightly} thro-
          ugh the darkness

Adverbs that are not obligatorily post-verbal may also be joined higher
up, but still linearised to the right. Where there are two post-verbal
adverbs, it is typical for the second to take scope over the first. The
same scope facts generally apply when that second adverb is pre-verbal.
If scope is the result of c-command, this suggests that regardless of
what projection the scope-taking adverb adjoins to, it must be structur-

ally higher. For the two post-verbal adverbs, scope therefore implies right-adjunction.

(62) a. Alastair intentionally stirred the batter fast
          =It was intentional that Alastair stirred the batter fast
      b. Alastair stirred the batter fast intentionally

Thus, while adverbs Merged with V are obligatorily Merged to the left of the head, adverbs Merged to at least some other projections may be directionally unrestricted.

(63)

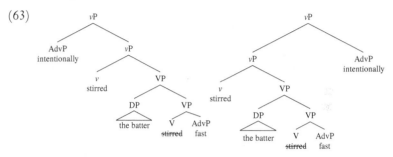

9.6.1 Are adjectives and adverbs the same thing?

We have argued here that 'flat' adverbs are actually adjectives, even though they have an adverbial function. This analysis suggests that the line between these categories is not as clear-cut as traditional lexical category grouping might suggest. There is in fact good reason to argue that adverbs and adjectives are a single category, and that the *-ly* affix is an inflectional one, contributing grammatical information, rather than a category-changing derivational one.

From a distributional perspective the *-ly* affix is relevant to the syntax because it allows adjectives to appear in places that they normally would not, as is already apparent from our discussion of adverbs that have both *-ly* and non-*ly* counterparts. Adjectives and adverbs can also be modified in the same way, by **intensifiers** such as *very* and *really*.

(64) a. That book was {very/really} nice
      b. That book was written {very/really} nicely

Where such intensifiers have *-ly* they may also be 'flattened', especially when modifying another non-*ly* element.

(65) a. %Martha ate it up real quick
      b. %That was a real delicious dinner

Considering the variety of derivational morphemes that change between any two lexical categories,[5] it would also be surprising that there is only a single affix available to convert adverbs to adjectives. Such restricted inventory is much more expected in instances of inflection. For instance, English has only one morpheme indicating singular third person present marking on verbs -*s*, and, apart from a handful of irregular forms, only one morpheme indicating past tense, -*ed*. The affix -*ly* also appears to be inflectional inasmuch as it is highly productive but applies to only one lexical category: adjectives. We do not get deverbal or denominal adverbs.

The counterclaim to these arguments is that there are many frequently-used adverbs that do not have -*ly* endings. For adverbs such as *fast* and *tight* the lack of -*ly* is unproblematic in that it correlates with their being obligatorily post-verbal. Non-*ly* adverbs which are not derived from adjectives, such as *soon*, *still* and *just* are trickier to account for. The closest possible analogous examples would be instances in which inflection is always required, as in terms such as *spectacles* and *trousers*, which are always used in the plural, although with an identifiable plural morpheme. We might also consider *data*, which has no (English) plural morpheme, and may be treated as plural by speakers who do not have the singular *datum* in their lexicons.

Another possibility is that some of these forms are not true adverbs. Words such as *yesterday* or *there* sometimes fulfil adverbial functions, but in other respects show atypical behaviour for adverbs. Both are much more limited in distribution than typical adverbs.

(66) a. Billy (*yesterday) had (*yesterday) read the book yesterday
      b. Martha will (*there) sit (there)

In some contexts they can also behave like NPs or PPs, respectively.

(67) a. Billy read yesterday's paper
      b. {There/On the mat} sat Martha

It may well be that many adverbs not derived from adjectives have other characteristics that separate them from typical adverbs.

---

[5] For example, English can form denominal adjectives using -*ful*, -*less*, -*ish*, -*al* and -*y*, to name just a few:

- help, hope, cheer → helpful, hopeful, cheerful
- love, need, joy → loveless, needless, joyless
- child, book, kitten → childish, bookish, kittenish
- emotion, intention, confession → emotional, confessional, intentional
- wool, wood, juice → woolly, woody, juicy

There is also an argument that adverbs cannot be inflected forms of adjectives because the addition of *-ly* is not semantically transparent: it may lead to adverbs with a range of interpretations, from epistemic to subject-oriented. Here we might argue that the interpretation of adverbs is dependent on the root adjective, and that *-ly* does make a consistent contribution in terms of licensing adverbial behaviour. True examples of *-ly* creating a lexical item with a different meaning, such as *gingerly* and *swimmingly*, are rare, and again may compare to examples such as *spectacles* and *trousers*, where there is a mismatch between the grammatical contribution of the affix and the actual meaning of the word. We will therefore conclude that adjectives and adverbs constitute a single lexical category, with differences in their distribution typically conditioned by a *-ly* inflection.

In some instances an adjective/adverb also acts as an extension of the VP, allowing for modification by an adverb that would not typically be permitted. In several places in the text we have used agent-oriented adverbs such as *intentionally* to test for causativity, noting that these are incompatible with Raising verbs and unaccusatives, both of which lack *v*P projections.

(68)   *Alastair intentionally arrived.

Intentionally may, though, modify any number of adjectives.

(69)   a.   His intentionally {late/stupid/slow} response annoyed me
       b.   His response was intentionally {late/stupid/slow}

It also becomes compatible with non-agentive verbs in the presence of such adjectives/adverbs.

(70)   a.   *He intentionally arrived
       b.   He intentionally arrived {late/stupidly/slowly}

This appears to be another instance of Adverb Climbing, where the adverb is able to Move from its base position to a higher position preceding the main verb.

Returning to the *Think different* slogan at the beginning of the chapter, it becomes apparent that this catchphrase plays on the ambiguity between adverb and adjective for post-verbal *different*. *Different* could also be replaced by an unambiguous adjective that takes no *-ly* such as *big*. Conversely, the adjective/adverb ambiguity and proscriptions against flat adverbs have led to a common hypercorrection, typically with the linking verb *feel*.

(71)   %I feel {badly/terribly} (that I didn't know)

Here the verb *feel* actually selects for an adjectival complement, particularly as evidenced by the unacceptability of (72)b.

(72) a.   I feel {happy/sad/ridiculous}
       b.   *I feel {happily/sadly/ridiculously}

As with the *and I* examples in Chapter 8 we see layering of a prescriptive requirement over what is generated by the syntax to produce a form that would not normally be predicted from that speaker's grammar.

9.7 Summing up adverb placement and order

The proposal we have made here rejects the idea that adverbs are in unique positions in the syntax, suggesting that while they may select for specific projections, variation in their distribution is down to the possibility for adverbs to (Re)Merge in higher positions, rather than, for the most part, Movement of other elements. In this analysis there are relatively few projections that may be selected by adverbs – we have mentioned VP, *v*P, TP and possibly CP – which means that it must be possible for multiple adverbs to adjoin to the same projection, as well as adjoining to projections with other constituents Merged in them. In this respect, therefore, the approach here requires that it be possible for a projection to have more than one specifier/adjunct.

We therefore conclude that c-command, determined by Merge, is still a relevant syntactic configuration. This is not to say that m-command does not play a role in e.g. Agree operations, but it is not enough to determine the relationship among elements within a projection. We have also rejected the LCA in allowing right-adjunction of post-verbal adverbs. As such, we return to the idea that linearisation is a post-syntactic operation that relies on particular PF specifications, rather than mapping directly from hierarchical structure.

One consequence of our analysis is that in allowing for relatively free adverb placement we lose any apparent correlation with adverb order. As we have already suggested for adjectives within the nominal domain, we must therefore conclude that the order of adverbs is semantically rather than syntactically restricted. That said, where an adverb Moves from its original position for reasons of focus, it will typically not cross over another adverb present in the syntax, as the Minimal Link Condition would demand that the closest adverb Move to check a focus feature. 'Lower' adverbs will therefore remain below 'higher' ones for syntactic as well as semantic reasons

9.8 Conclusion

In this chapter we have examined the distribution of adverbs and adjectives. We revisited the concepts of specifier/adjunct/complement, and introduced the Linear Correspondence Axiom. Ultimately our proposals required abandonment of this hypothesis, in favour of a model in which adverbs may be adjoined to the right, and may have a certain amount of leeway in terms of Merge and Remerge within a phase. We can extrapolate this conclusion to apply to adjectives as well, arguing that adjective order is determined semantically. In the last part of the chapter we argued that adjectives and adverbs constitute a single category, related by an inflectional affix -*ly*.

9.9 Further reading

Kayne (1994) proposed the Linear Correspondence Axiom. For extensive discussion of the functional specifier approach to adverb distribution see Cinque (1999). For extensive arguments in favour of a semantic approach to adverb distribution see Ernst (2002).

For a discussion of how the functional structure of the DP might be expanded, see Svenonius (2008). Truswell (2009) gives an account of the order of attributive adjectives. Edelstein (2013) offers a more extensive discussion of Adverb Climbing.

For arguments that adverbs and adjectives belong to the same category see Giegerich (2012); for arguments that they do not see Payne et al. (2010).

9.10 Exercise

1. Further analysis
   There are a handful of attributive adjectives in English that can be postnominal. How can these be accounted for in the structure we have proposed? How would they be accounted for in a structure that corresponds to the LCA?
   a. secretary general
   b. the man full of pride
   c. syntax proper

For Answers see edinburghuniversitypress.com/englishsyntax.

10 Minimalism and microvariation

This book has introduced aspects of the Minimalist Programme of syntax through the medium of English. In doing so we have drawn on evidence from a number of different English varieties. In places this has meant that we have justified particular structures or analyses on the basis of a construction idiosyncratic to a single Non-Standard form that deviates from most varieties of English. In this final chapter we will consider the implications and limitations of our one-language approach in terms of a larger theoretical framework.

10.1 Sources of data

In the introductory chapter of this text we discussed the idea of grammaticality, and briefly considered how this may be assessed through analysis of real-world data, either encountered by happenstance or found systematically in a corpus, and by collection of native speaker judgements, from linguists themselves or non-linguist informants. One question that arose was whether we should take very small amounts of data (a handful of examples from a corpus, or a confirmation from a single person) as sufficient evidence that a particular construction is grammatical. In these circumstances we ideally must seek out further evidence to rule out the influence of performance factors.

This issue applies as well on a broader linguistic scale. Where we have evidence of a particular linguistic construction for a relatively small subset of speakers of a language, in our case English, how generalisable can our analysis of that construction be to the rest of the language, and Language more universally? If we find a particular type of syntactic construction in only one variety of a language, is it generalisable at all?

The short answer is that it must be. For us to maintain a conception of UG as a set of overarching Principles rather than a hodgepodge collection of disparate grammars of individual languages or varieties, we can have no analyses that are so individualised as to be inapplicable elsewhere. Thus, if we encounter a form that appears to necessitate its own unique analysis, we have to either amend our approach or look outside of that particular language or variety for confirmatory evidence. As an example, recall the observation, given in Chapter 7, that in Belfast English Control verbs may have overt complementisers, but Raising verbs do not.

(1) a. %He {tried/wanted} for to leave
    b. *He {seemed/happened} for to leave

The presence of *for* here must be accounted for, but considering the ungrammaticality of sentences such as (1)a in most varieties of English, it is relatively slim evidence on which to base the conclusion that English Control verbs select for CPs.

In Chapter 9 we had further confirmation of the structural size difference between non-finite Control and Raising complements from Adverb Climbing, with the unavailability of AC interpretations for Control verbs indicating that these were constrained by the intervention of a CP phase boundary.

(2) a. He intentionally tried to insult her
    ≠He tried to intentionally insult her
    b. He intentionally seemed to insult her
    =He seemed to intentionally insult her

An even more convincing argument, however, comes from looking crosslinguistically. French, Italian, Dutch, Swedish, Icelandic, Hebrew and Welsh, among others, are all reported to have overt complementisers with Control constructions and disallow them in Raising constructions.

(3) a. French (Adapted from Kayne 1981: 351)
       Jean a essayé **de** partir
       John has tried COMP to-leave
    b. Hebrew (Landau 2003: 488)
       Rina xadla (**me-**)le'acben et Gil
       Rina stopped (from-)to-irritate acc Gil
    c. Dutch (Koster and May 1982: 134)
       John heeft geprobeerd **om** het boek **te** lezen
       John has tried COMP the book to read

This instance demonstrates that we get more information by looking at a set of languages, but also reinforces the importance of looking at variation within a language. By doing both of these we see here that the use of overt complementisers in Control constructions is not some oddity of Belfast English, but consistent with a larger picture of syntax outside of English. It also indicates that we should not take the lack of overt complementisers in Standard English as evidence that the CP structure is not present. Looking at variation within languages therefore can be just as illuminating in terms of our understanding of syntactic structure as making comparisons between them.

The discussion here speaks to the bigger issue of how we define Universal Grammar from a Minimalist perspective. Perhaps the most Minimalist approach possible is one where the only component of UG is Merge, with differences derived from variation in the features of lexical items that drive this operation. As we have noted throughout the text, many other notions relevant to syntactic derivations, such as c-command and locality, can be reduced to Merge. Movement is also just a manifestation of this operation. A model in which there are as few independent syntactic operations as possible is at the heart of what the Minimalist Programme aims for.

10.2 Sources of variation

The use of data from different varieties of English throughout this text has highlighted the differences between speakers who may otherwise speak the same language in a general sense. According to the view of syntax we have taken here, **interspeaker variation** of the grammar within a language is no different from variation of the grammar between languages. All forms of linguistic variation come down to parameters within the confines of UG, or to divergences within the lexicon.

We might, though, want to more precisely pinpoint sources of variation. In our discussion we have seen essentially three kinds of variation between grammars: differences in phonological representation, differences in position, and differences in selection. Each of these can be reduced to how features are input into syntactic derivations from the lexicon.

Differences in phonological realisation depend on how a feature or bundle of features is interpreted at PF. This type of variation is therefore essentially determined at the point of Spell Out, although it will be tied to information from the lexicon. Whether a speaker uses *aren't* or *amn't* to express first person singular *be* is thus relevant to the syntax, but only inasmuch as it reflects a set of syntactic features that are assembled at some point during a syntactic derivation. Similarly, the realisation of an overt complementiser with a Control construction in Belfast English comes down to the particular C selected by a Control verb having its pronunciation specified as *for* rather than Ø: the syntactic features are the same, but the phonological ones are not.

Differences in position arise from feature-checking. This can manifest in three ways. One possibility is that one variety possesses a feature in a particular part of the syntax that another does not, prompting Movement in the first variety but not the second. There may also be contrasts in feature strength, with one variety having a strong feature where another has a weak one, again prompting a Movement not seen elsewhere, as we encountered for lexical *have*, which for some speakers undergoes Head Movement to T and for others does not. We have also suggested that feature-checking may be ordered for a particular phrase, prompting Merge of one element before another, as we saw for the order of direct and indirect objects in ditransitive constructions, resulting in the difference between, for example, *give it me* and *give me it*.

Differences in selection depend on what features may be chosen by a particular lexical item at the point of Merge. Thus in many varieties of English a verb such as *need* selects for a non-finite TP complement, but in others it selects for a VP passive or progressive participle, giving us the *needs to be washed/needs washed/needs washing* alternation. This selectional difference again arises from the lexicon.

10.3 Intraspeaker variation

While many varieties within a language may have a set of distinct Parameters or sets of features, the speakers who use these varieties or grammatical constructions do not necessarily fall into discrete groups. We must therefore consider not only what variation means for the grammar of a language as a whole, and the entirety of Universal Grammar, but how this plays out for individual speakers.

There are really two types of **intraspeaker variation**. The first is **optionality**, where all speakers of a particular language or variety have multiple options for a particular structure. This choice may be a relatively free one, affected by language-external factors, such as the alternation between *that* and Ø complementisers, which appears to be a decision made at Spell Out according to level of formality. It could also be tied to factors relating to information structure, such as the active/ passive alternation or the placement of adverbs, where it may be mediated by topic or focus features within the syntax.

The second type of intraspeaker variation is use of more than one variety by a single speaker. Most of us are to some extent bidialectal, employing both Standard and Non-Standard forms of our native language. For such speakers the question is whether this variation represents two distinct grammars, or is akin to optionality within a single grammar.

Our feature-based account points to the latter analysis. In the same way that different languages do not constitute distinct entities but represent an array of parameter settings within UG, we can assume that for speakers with command of differing grammatical constructions they have multiple possible parameter settings. Within the lexicon a speaker may also have lexical items with distinct formal characteristics, such as English -*n't* and Scottish -*nae*, which are not just superficially different in terms of pronunciation but also do not have the same syntactic properties. Where the difference is selectional, it is not dissimilar from that within a language, where a lexical item may have more than one type of complement.

Intraspeaker variation can therefore also be seen as feature-driven on a fundamental level. For speakers, the choice of which features to instantiate may still be influenced by a number of extra-syntactic or performance-related factors. Nevertheless, the presence of such features is a part of each speaker's lexicon and syntactic repertoire, and where they have multiple overlapping (morpho)syntactic constructions these constitute a single grammatical system.

10.4 Conclusion

This final chapter has presented a brief overview of issues related to the study of Minimalist syntax through the prism of microvariation in English. As a whole this text presents only a small slice of the larger pie that is the Minimalist Programme. In restricting our discussion to English we have been able to explore some particular crossvarietal puzzles, but have also missed out on a number of phenomena in English and beyond. That said, all of the theoretical architecture and concepts introduced in this text are universal in their development and application. In that respect this book should serve as a stepping-stone to students wishing to move on to getting a crosslinguistic grasp of the approach to syntax that we have outlined.

10.5 Further reading

For one discussion of variation in the context of Minimalism see Adger and Smith (2005). For a broader overview of issues related to English dialect syntax see Adger and Trousdale (2007). The chapters in Picallo (2014) give an overview of linguistic variation in Minimalism from a crosslinguistic perspective.

Bibliography

Abney, Steven P. (1987). The English noun phrase in its sentential aspect. PhD thesis. Massachusetts Institute of Technology, Cambridge, MA.

Adger, David (2003). *Core Syntax: A Minimalist Approach.* Oxford: Oxford University Press.

Adger, David (2006). Remarks on minimalist feature theory and Move. *Journal of Linguistics* 42(3): 663–673.

Adger, David and Smith, Jennifer (2005). Variation and the Minimalist Programme. In Leonie M. E. A. Cornips and Karen P. Corrigan (eds), *Syntax & Variation: Reconciling the Biological and the Social.* Amstedam/Philadelphia: John Benjamins, pp. 149–178.

Adger, David and Svenonius, Peter (2011). Features in Minimalist syntax. In Cedric Boeckx (ed.), *The Oxford Handbook of Linguistic Minimalism.* Oxford: Oxford University Press, pp. 27–51.

Adger, David and Trousdale, Graeme (2007). Variation in English syntax: Theoretical implications. *English Language & Linguistics* 11(2): 261–278.

Åfarli, Tor A. and Mæhlum, Brit (2014). Language variation, contact and change in grammar and sociolinguistics. In Tor A. Åfarli and Brit Mæhlum (eds), *The Sociolinguistics of Grammar.* Amsterdam/Philadelphia: John Benjamins, pp. 1–12.

Alexiadou, Artemis (1997). *Adverb Placement: A Case Study in Antisymmetric Syntax.* Amsterdam: John Benjamins.

Alexiadou, Artemis (2006). A note on non-canonical passives: The case of the *get*-passive. In Hans Broekhuis et al. (eds), *Organizing Grammar: Linguistic Studies in Honor of Henk van Riemsdijk.* Berlin: Mouton de Gruyter, pp. 13–21.

Alexiadou, Artemis (2012). Non-canonical passives revisited: Parameters of non-active Voice. *Linguistics* 50: 1079–1110.

Antonenko, Andrei (2012). Feature-based binding and phase theory. PhD thesis. Stony Brook University, Stony Brook, NY.

Baltin, Mark (2003). The interaction of ellipsis and binding: Implications for the sequencing of Principle A. *Natural Language & Linguistic Theory* 21(2): 215–246.

Barrie, Michael (2011). Unifying antisymmetry and Bare Phrase Structure. In *Dynamic Antisymmetry and the Syntax of Noun Incorporation. Studies in Natural Language and Linguistic Theory* 84. Dordrecht: Springer, pp. 53–91.

Barss, Andrew and Lasnik, Howard (1989). A note on anaphora and double objects. In Howard Lasnik (ed.), *Essays on Anaphora*. Dordrecht: Springer, pp. 143–148.

Battistella, Edwin L. (1995). The syntax of the double modal construction. *Linguistica Atlantica* 17: 19–44.

Biberauer, Theresa, Holmberg, Anders, Roberts, Ian and Sheehan, Michelle (2014). Complexity in comparative syntax: The view from modern parametric theory. In Frederick J. Newmeyer and Laurel B. Preston (eds), *Measuring Grammatical Complexity*, Oxford: Oxford Scholarship Online, pp. 103–127.

Blanchette, Frances (2013). Negative concord in English. *Linguistic Variation* 13(1): 1–47.

Blanchette, Frances (2015). English negative concord, negative polarity, and double negation. PhD thesis. CUNY Graduate Center, New York.

Blanchette, Frances, Nadeu, Marianna, Yeaton, Jeremy and Déprez, Viviane (2018). English negative concord and double negation: The division of labor between syntax and pragmatics. *Proceedings of the Linguistic Society of America* 3(53): 1–15.

Bobaljik, Jonathon D. (1995). In terms of Merge: Copy and Head Movement. In *MIT Working Papers in Linguistics 27: Papers on Minimalist Syntax*. MITWPL: Department of Linguistics and Philosophy, pp. 41–64.

Boeckx, Cedric (2006). *Linguistic Minimalism: Origins, Concepts, Methods, and Aims*. Oxford: Oxford University Press.

Boeckx, Cedric and Hornstein, Norbert (2003). Reply to 'Control is not movement'. *Linguistic Inquiry* 34: 269–280.

Boeckx, Cedric and Hornstein, Norbert (2004). Movement under control. *Linguistic Inquiry* 35: 431–452.

Boeckx, Cedric and Hornstein, Norbert (2007). The virtues of control as movement. *Syntax* 9: 118–130.

Boeckx, Cedric, Hornstein, Norbert and Nunes, Jairo (2007). Overt copies in reflexive and control structures: A movement analysis. *University of Maryland Working Papers in Linguistics* 15: 1–46.

Bour, Anthony R. (2015a). Exotic multiple modals: Semantic and morphosyntactic survey. *Scottish Language* 34: 14–42.

Bour, Anthony R. (2015b). Multiple modal constructions in the Western English-speaking world. *Linguistica Atlantica* 34(1): 45–59.

Bour, Anthony R. (2017). Negated and inverted syntax of modal combinations in the Scottish Borders: Traditional double modals, hybrid double modals and exotic triple modals. *Scottish Language* 36: 21–54.

Bour, Anthony R. (2018). Multiple modality in the Lallans Territory: Current vernacular (un)acceptability of the syntax of modal combinations in South-Eastern Scotland. *Colloquium: New Philologies* 3(1): 63–86.

Brinton, Laurel J. (1985). Verb particles in English: Aspect or aktionsart? *Studia Linguistica* 39: 157–168.

Brody, Michael (1993). θ-theory and arguments. *Linguistic Inquiry* 24(1): 1–23.

Bruening, Benjamin (2001). Raising to object and proper movement. Unpublished manuscript, University of Delaware.

Bruening, Benjamin (2009). Selectional asymmetries between CP and DP suggest that the DP hypothesis is wrong. *University of Pennsylvania Working Papers in Linguistics* 15(1): 27–35.

Burton, Strang and Grimshaw, Jane (1992). Coordination and VP-internal subjects. *Linguistic Inquiry* 23(2): 305–313.

Cann, Ronnie, Kaplan, Tami and Kempson, Ruth (2005). Data at the grammar-pragmatics interface: The case of resumptive pronouns in English. *Lingua* 115(11): 1551–1577.

Carnie, Andrew (2010). *Constituent Structure*. Oxford: Oxford University Press.

Chametzky, Robert. A. (2003). Phrase Structure. In Randall Hendrick (ed.), *Minimalist Syntax*. Malden, MA: Blackwell, pp. 192–225.

Cheng, Lisa Lai-Shen (2003). Wh-in-situ. *Glot International* 7(4): 103–109.

Chomsky, Noam (1957/2002). *Syntactic Structures*. Berlin: Walter de Gruyter.

Chomsky, Noam (1965). *Aspects of the Theory of Syntax*. Cambridge, MA: MIT Press.

Chomsky, Noam (1981). *Lectures on Government and Binding*. Dordrecht: Foris.

Chomsky, Noam (1986). *Barriers*. Linguistic Inquiry Monograph 13. Cambridge, MA: MIT Press.

Chomsky, Noam (1986). *Knowledge of Language: Its Nature, Origin, and Use*. Santa Barbara, CA: Greenwood Publishing Group.

Chomsky, Noam (1995). Bare phrase structure. In G. Webelhuth (ed.), *Government and Binding Theory and the Minimalist Program*. Oxford: Blackwell, pp. 385–439.

Chomsky, Noam (1995). *The Minimalist Program*. Cambridge, MA: MIT Press.

Chomsky, Noam (2000). Minimalist inquiries: The framework. In Roger Martin et al. (eds), *Step by Step: Essays on Minimalist Syntax in Honor of Howard Lasnik*. Cambridge, MA: MIT Press, pp. 89–155.

Chomsky, Noam (2001). Beyond explanatory adequacy. *MIT Occasional Papers in Linguistics* 20. Cambridge, MA: MIT Working Papers in Linguistics.

Chomsky, Noam (2001). Derivation by phase. In M. Kenstowicz (ed.), *Ken Hale: A Life in Language*. Cambridge, MA: MIT Press, pp. 1–52.

Cinque, Guglielmo (1995). *Italian Syntax and Universal Grammar*. Cambridge: Cambridge University Press.

Cinque, Guglielmo (1999). *Adverbs and Functional Heads: A Cross-linguistic Perspective*. Oxford: Oxford University Press.

Cinque, Guglielmo (2004). Issues in adverbial syntax. *Lingua* 114: 683–710.

Cinque, Guglielmo (2010). *The Syntax of Adjectives: A Comparative Study*. Cambridge, MA: MIT Press.

Collins, Chris (2001). Eliminating labels. *MIT Occasional Papers in Linguistics* 20. Cambridge, MA: MIT Working Papers in Linguistics.

Collins, Chris and Postal, Paul M. (2014). *Classical NEG raising*. Cambridge, MA: MIT Press.

Collins, Chris and Postal, Paul M. (2017). Interclausal NEG raising and the scope of negation. *Glossa: A Journal of General Linguistics* 2(1): 1–29.

Collins, Chris and Stabler, Edward (2016). A formalization of minimalist syntax. *Syntax* 19(1): 43–78.

Condoravdi, Cleo (1989). The middle: Where semantics and morphology meet. *MIT Working Papers in Linguistics* 11: 16–30.

Cook, Vivian. J. (1991). The poverty-of-the-stimulus argument and multicompetence. *Interlanguage Studies Bulletin (Utrecht)* 7(2): 103–117.

Cormack, Annabel and Smith, Neil (2002). Modals and negation in English. In S. Barbiers, F. Beukema and W. van der Wurff (eds), *Modality and its Interaction with the Verbal System.* Amsterdam/Philadelphia: John Benjamins, pp. 133–164.

Culicover, Peter W. and Jackendoff, Ray (2001). Control is not movement. *Linguistic Inquiry* 32(3): 493–512.

Culicover, Peter W. and Jackendoff, Ray (2006). The simpler syntax hypothesis. *Trends in Cognitive Sciences* 10(9): 413–418.

Culicover, Peter W. and Jackendoff, Ray (2006). Turn control over to the semantics. *Syntax* 9: 131–152.

Dąbrowska, Ewa (2015). What exactly is Universal Grammar, and has anyone seen it? *Frontiers in Psychology* 6: 852.

Davies, Mark (2004–). *BYU-BNC.* (Based on the British National Corpus from Oxford University Press.) https://corpus.byu.edu/bnc/

Davies, Mark (2018–). *The 14 Billion Word iWeb Corpus.* https://corpus.byu.edu/iWeb/

Dehé, Nicole (2015). Particle verbs in Germanic. In Peter O. Müller (ed.), *Word-Formation: An International Handbook of the Languages of Europe Volume 1.* Berlin/Boston: De Gruyter Mouton, pp. 611–626.

Dehé, Nicole, Jackendoff, Ray, McIntyre, Andrew and Urban, Silke (eds) (2002). *Verb-Particle Explorations.* Berlin/New York: Mouton De Gruyter.

Duncan, Daniel (2019). Grammars compete late: Evidence from embedded passives. *University of Pennsylvania Working Papers in Linguistics* 25(1): 89–98. https://repository.upenn.edu/pwpl/vol25/iss1/11

Edelstein, Elspeth (2013). Adverb climbing as evidence for the structure of non-finite complements in English. Unpublished manuscript. https://www.isle-linguistics.org/assets/content/documents/hogg/edelstein2013.pdf

Edelstein, Elspeth (2014). This syntax needs studied. In Raffaella Zanuttini and Laurence Horn (eds), *Micro-Syntactic Variation in North American English.* Oxford: Oxford University Press, pp. 242–268.

Elsman, Minta and Dubinsky, Stanley (2009). Double modal syntactic patterns as single modal interactions. *University of Pennsylvania Working Papers in Linguistics* 15(1): 75–83.

Embick, David (2004). On the structure of resultative participles in English. *Linguistic Inquiry* 35(3): 355–392.

Epstein, Samuel D. and Seely, T. Daniel (2006). *Derivations in Minimalism.* Cambridge: Cambridge University Press.

Ernst, Thomas (1994). M-command and precedence. *Linguistic Inquiry* 25: 327–335.

Ernst, Thomas (1998). The scopal basis of adverb licensing. In *Proceedings of NELS 28*. Amherst: GLSA, University of Massachusetts, pp. 127–142.

Ernst, Thomas (2002). *The Syntax of Adjuncts*. Cambridge: Cambridge University Press.

Ernst, Thomas (2004). Principles of adverbial distribution in the lower clause. *Lingua* 114: 755–777.

Ernst, Thomas (2006). On the role of semantics in a theory of adverb syntax. *Lingua* 117: 1008–1033.

Ernst, Thomas (2009). Speaker-oriented adverbs. *Natural Language and Linguistic Theory* 27: 497–544.

Forsyth, Mark (2013). *The Elements of Eloquence: How to Turn the Perfect English Phrase*. London: Icon Books.

Freeman, Jan (2007, 11 November). Lawn needs cut. *Boston Globe*. http://archive. boston.com/bostonglobe/ideas/articles/2007/11/11/lawn_needs_cut

Fukui, Naoki (2017). Merge and bare phrase structure. In *Merge in the Mind-Brain*. New York/London: Routledge, pp. 17–42.

Gerwin, Johanna (2013). Give it me!: Pronominal ditransitives in English dialects. *English Language & Linguistics* 17(3): 445–463.

Gerwin, Johanna (2014). *Ditransitives in British English Dialects*. Berlin: De Gruyter.

Giegerich, Heinz J. (2012). The morphology of -*ly* and the categorial status of 'adverbs' in English. *English Language & Linguistics* 16(3): 341–359.

Goldberg, Adele E. (2016). Tuning in to the verb-particle construction in English. In Léa Nash and Pollet Samvelian (eds), *Approaches to Complex Predicates*. Leiden and Boston: Brill, pp. 110–141.

Haddican, William (2010). Theme–goal ditransitives and theme passivisation in British English dialects. *Lingua* 120(10): 2424–2443.

Haddican, William and Johnson, Daniel Ezra (2012). Effects on the particle verb alternation across English dialects. *University of Pennsylvania Working Papers in Linguistics* 18(2). https://repository.upenn.edu/pwpl/vol18/iss2/5

Haegeman, Liliane (1994). *Introduction to Government and Binding Theory*. Hoboken, NJ and Boston, MA: Wiley-Blackwell.

Haegeman, Liliane (1995). *The Syntax of Negation*. Cambridge Studies in Linguistics. Cambridge: Cambridge University Press.

Haegeman, Liliane and Zanuttini, Raffaella (1991). Negative heads and the neg criterion. *The Linguistic Review* 8: 233–252.

Haegeman, Liliane, Weir, Andrew, Danckaert, Lieven, D'Hulster, Tijs and Buelens, Liisa (2015). Against the root analysis of subject contact relatives in English. *Lingua* 163: 61–74.

Hale, Kenneth and Keyser, Samuel Jay (1986). Some transitivity alternations in English. *Anuario del Seminario de Filología Vasca Julio de Urquijo* 20(3): 605–638.

Hale, Kenneth and Keyser, Samuel Jay (1993). On argument structure and the syntactic expression of lexical relations. *The View from Building 20: Essays in Honor of Sylvain Bromberger*. Cambridge, MA: MIT Press, pp. 5–109.

Harley, Heidi (2010). Thematic roles. In Patrick Hogan (ed.), *The Cambridge Encyclopedia of the Language Sciences*. Cambridge: Cambridge University Press.

Harley, Heidi and Miyagawa, Shigeru (2018). Syntax of Ditransitives. In *Oxford Research Encyclopedia of Linguistics*. Oxford: Oxford Research Encyclopedias.

Hendrick, Randall (ed.) (2008). *Minimalist Syntax*. Malden, MA: Blackwell.

Henry, Alison (1995). *Belfast English and Standard English: Dialect Variation and Parameter Setting*. Oxford: Oxford University Press.

Henry, Alison (2012). Phase edges, quantifier float and the nature of (micro-) variation. *IBERIA: An International Journal of Theoretical Linguistics* 4(2): 23–39.

Heycock, Caroline and Zamparelli, Roberto (2003). Coordinated bare definites. *Linguistic Inquiry* 34(3): 443–469.

Horn, Laurence R. (1978). Remarks on Neg-Raising. In Peter Cole (ed.), *Syntax and Semantics 9: Pragmatics*. New York: Academic Press, pp. 129–220.

Horn, Laurence R. (1989). *A Natural History of Negation*. Chicago: University of Chicago Press.

Hornstein, Norbert (1999). Movement and control. *Linguistic Inquiry* 30: 69–96.

Hornstein, Norbert (2000). *Move! A Minimalist Theory of Construal*. Oxford: Blackwell.

Hornstein, Norbert (2003). On control. In Randall Hendrick (ed.). *Minimalist Syntax*. Oxford: Blackwell, pp. 6–81.

Hornstein, Norbert (2007). Pronouns in a Minimalist setting. In Norbert Corver and Jairo Nunes (eds), *The Copy Theory of Movement. Linguistics Today* 107. Amsterdam/Philadelphia: John Benjamins, pp. 351–384.

Hornstein, Norbert and Nunes, Jairo (2008). Adjunction, labeling, and Bare Phrase Structure. *Biolinguistics* 2(1): 57–86.

Hornstein, Norbert, Nunes, Jairo and Grohmann, Kleanthes K. (2005). *Understanding Minimalism*. Cambridge: Cambridge University Press.

Huang, Nick (2011). Multiple modals. *Yale Grammatical Diversity Project: English in North America*. http://ygdp.yale.edu/phenomena/multiple-modals. Updated by Tom McCoy (2015) and Katie Martin (2018).

Huddleston, Rodney D. and Pullum, Geoffrey K. (2002). *The Cambridge Grammar of the English Language*. Cambridge: Cambridge University Press.

Huddleston, Rodney D. and Pullum, Geoffrey K. (2005). *A Student's Introduction to English Grammar*. Cambridge: Cambridge University Press.

Hudson, Richard (1992). So-called 'double objects' and grammatical relations. *Language* 68(2): 251–276.

Jackendoff, Ray (1990). On Larson's treatment of the Double Object construction. *Linguistic Inquiry* 21(3): 427–456.

Jackendoff, Ray and Culicover, Peter W. (2003). The semantic basis of control in English. *Language* 79(3): 517–556.

Jansen, Charissa (2016). Adjectival ordering in English and Dutch in the light of recent theories of noun phrases. Master's thesis. Universiteit Leiden, Leiden, Netherlands.

Jung, Yeun-Jin and Miyagawa, Shigeru (2004). Decomposing ditransitive verbs. In *Proceedings of SICGG*, pp. 101–120.

Kayne, Richard (1981). On certain differences between French and English. *Linguistic Inquiry* 12: 349–371.

Kayne, Richard (1994). *The Antisymmetry of Syntax*. Linguistic Inquiry Monographs 25. Cambridge, MA: MIT Press.

Kayne, Richard S. (2016). *Connectedness and Binary Branching*. Berlin: Walter de Gruyter.

Kibort, Anna (2008). On the syntax of ditransitive constructions. In Miriam Butt and Tracy Holloway King (eds), *Proceedings of the LFG08 Conference*. Stanford: CSLI Publications.

Kitazume, Sachiko (1996). Middles in English. *Word* 47(2): 161–183.

Koizumi, Masatoshi (1993). Object agreement phrases and the split VP hypothesis. *MIT Working Papers in Linguistics* 18: 99–148.

Koizumi, Masatoshi (1995). Phrase structure in minimalist syntax. PhD thesis. Massachusetts Institute of Technology, Cambridge, MA.

Kornai, András and Pullum, Geoffrey K. (1990). The X-bar theory of phrase structure. *Language* 66(1): 24–50.

Kortmann, Bernd (2006). Syntactic variation in English: A global perspective. *The Handbook of English Linguistics*. Malden, MA: Blackwell, pp. 603–624.

Koster, Jan and May, Robert (1982). On the constituency of infinitives. *Language* 58: 349–371.

Lakoff, Robin (1969). A syntactic argument for negative transportation. In R. I. Binnick et al. (eds), *Papers from the Fifth Regional Meeting of the Chicago Linguistic Society*. Chicago: University of Chicago.

Landau, Idan (2000). *Elements of Control: Structure and Meaning in Infinitival Constructions*. Dordrecht: Kluwer.

Landau, Idan (2003). Movement out of control. *Linguistic Inquiry* 34(3): 471–498.

Landau, Idan (2006). Severing the distribution of PRO from case. *Syntax* 9: 153–170.

Landau, Idan (2007). Movement resistant aspects of control. In W. Davies and S. Dubinsky (eds), *New Horizons in the Analysis of Control and Raising*. Dordrecht: Springer, pp. 293–325.

Larson, Richard K. (1988). On the double object construction. *Linguistic Inquiry* 19(3): 335–391.

Larson, Richard (2004). Sentence-final adverbs and 'scope'. In K. Moulton and M. Wolf (eds), *Proceedings of NELS 34*. Amherst, MA: GLSA, University of Massachusetts.

Lasnik, Howard (2002). The Minimalist Program in syntax. *Trends in Cognitive Sciences* 6(10): 432–437.

Lasnik, Howard (2003). On the extended projection principle. *Studies in Modern Grammar* 31(31): 1–23.

Levin, Beth and Rappaport Hovav, Malka (1994). A preliminary analysis of causative verbs in English. *Lingua* 92: 35–77.

Lohndal, Terje (2014). *Phrase Structure and Argument Structure: A Case Study of the*

Syntax-Semantics Interface. Oxford Studies in Theoretical Syntax 49. Oxford: Oxford University Press.

Loss, Sarah Schmelzer (2011). Iron range English long-distance reflexives. PhD thesis. University of Minnesota, Minneapolis.

Loss, Sarah Schmelzer (2014). Iron range English reflexive pronouns. In Raffaella Zanuttini and Laurence R. Horn (eds), *Micro-Syntactic Variation in North American English*. Oxford: Oxford University Press, pp. 215–241.

McCloskey, James (2000). Quantifier float and *wh*-movement in an Irish English. *Linguistic Inquiry* 31(1): 57–84.

McCoy, Tom (2016). Subject contact relatives. *Yale Grammatical Diversity Project: English in North America*. http://ygdp.yale.edu/phenomena/subject-contact-relatives. Updated by Katie Martin (2018).

McDaniel, Dana and Cowart, Wayne (1999). Experimental evidence for a minimalist account of English resumptive pronouns. *Cognition* 70(2): B15–B24.

McIntyre, Andrew (2007). Particle verbs and argument structure. *Language and Linguistics Compass* 1(4): 350–367.

McIntyre, Andrew (2013). Adjectival passives and adjectival participles in English. In Artemis Alexiadou and Florian Schaeffer (eds), *Non-Canonical Passives*. Amsterdam/Philadelphia: John Benjamins, pp. 21–42.

McIntyre, Andrew (2013). English particle verbs as complex heads: Evidence from nominalization. In Holden Härtl (ed.), *Interfaces of Morphology*. Berlin: Akademie Verlag, pp. 41–57.

Marantz, Andrew (1988). Clitics, morphological merger, and the mapping to phonological structure. In M. Hammond and M. Noonan (eds), *Theoretical Morphology*. San Diego, CA: Academic Press, pp. 253–270.

Massam, Diane (1990). Cognate objects as thematic objects. *Canadian Journal of Linguistics/Revue canadienne de linguistique* 35(2): 161–190.

Matushansky, Ora (2006). Head Movement in linguistic theory. *Linguistic Inquiry* 37: 69–109.

Miller, Jim (2016). *Introduction to English Syntax*. Edinburgh: Edinburgh University Press.

Milroy, James and Milroy, Lesley (2012). *Authority in Language: Investigating Standard English*. New York/London. Routledge.

Mintz, Toben H. (2010). Language Development. In H. A. Whitaker (ed.), *Concise Encyclopedia of Brain and Language*. Amsterdam: Elsevier, pp. 266–271.

Myler, Neil (2011). Come the pub with me: Silent TO in a dialect of British English. *NYU Working Papers in Linguistics (NYUWPL)* 3: 120–135.

Narita, Hiroki (2014). *Endocentric Structuring of Projection-free Syntax*. Amsterdam/Philadelphia: John Benjamins.

Odijk, Jan (1997). C-selection and s-selection. *Linguistic Inquiry* 28(2): 365–371.

Palmer, Frank (1979). *Modality and the English Modals*. London: Longman.

Palmer, Frank (1995). Negation and the modals of possibility and necessity. In J. Bybee and S. Fleischman (eds), *Modality in Grammar and Discourse*. Amsterdam/Philadelphia: John Benjamins, pp. 453–471.

Payne, John (2011). Genitive coordinations with personal pronouns. *English Language & Linguistics* 15(2): 363–385.

Payne, John, Huddleston, Rodney and Pullum, Geoffrey K. (2010). The distribution and category status of adjectives and adverbs. *Word Structure* 3(1): 31–81.

Pesetsky, David and Torrego, Esther (2001). T-to-C movement: Causes and consequences. *Current Studies in Linguistics Series* 36: 355–426.

Phillips, Collin (2003). Linear order and constituency. *Linguistic Inquiry* 34: 37–90.

Picallo, M. Carme (ed.) (2014). *Linguistic Variation in the Minimalist Framework.* Oxford: Oxford University Press.

Postal, Paul (1974). *On Raising.* Cambridge, MA: MIT Press.

Pullum, Geoffrey K. (2011, 24 January). The passive in English. *Language Log.* https://languagelog.ldc.upenn.edu/nll/?p=2922

Radford, Andrew (1997). *Syntax: A Minimalist Introduction.* Cambridge: Cambridge University Press.

Ramchand, Gillian (2008). *Verb Meaning and the Lexicon.* Cambridge: Cambridge University Press.

Rappaport Hovav, Malka and Levin, Beth (2001). An event structure account of English resultatives. *Language* 77(4): 766–797.

Rappaport Hovav, Malka and Levin, Beth (2008). The English dative alternation: The case for verb sensitivity. *Journal of Linguistics* 44(1): 129–167.

Reed, Lisa A. (2011). *Get*-passives. *The Linguistic Review* 28(1): 41–78.

Reinhart, Tanya (2003). The theta system – an overview. *Theoretical Linguistics* 28(3): 229–290.

Reinhart, Tanya and Reuland, Eric (1993). Reflexivity. *Linguistic Inquiry* 24(4): 657–720.

Reuland, Eric (2001). Primitives of binding. *Linguistic Inquiry* 32(3): 439–492.

van Riemsdijk, Henk (1998). Categorial feature magnetism: The endocentricity and distribution of projections. *The Journal of Comparative Germanic Linguistics* 2(1): 1–48.

Roberts, Ian (2010). *Agreement and Head Movement: Clitics, Incorporation, and Defective Goals.* Linguistic Inquiry Monographs 59. Cambridge, MA: MIT Press.

Rubin, Edward J. (2003). Determining Pair-Merge. *Linguistic Inquiry* 34(4): 660–668.

Runner, Jeffrey T. (2006). Lingering challenges to the raising-to-object and object control constructions. *Syntax* 9: 193–213.

Safir, Ken (2008). Coconstrual and narrow syntax. *Syntax* 11(3): 330–355.

de Saussure, Ferdinand (2011). *Course in General Linguistics.* New York: Columbia University Press.

Schlüter, Julia (2008). Constraints on the attributive use of 'predicative-only' adjectives. In Graeme Trousdale and Nikolas Gisborne (eds), *Constructional Approaches to English Grammar.* Berlin: Mouton de Gruyter.

Schueler, David (2005). Attitude predicates, locality, and NPI licensing. Manuscript. UCLA.

Schütze, Carson T. (2016). *The Empirical Base of Linguistics: Grammaticality Judgments and Linguistic Methodology*. Berlin: Language Science Press.

Seely, T. Daniel (2015). Merge, derivational c-command, and subcategorization in a label-free syntax. In Samuel D. Epstein, Hisatsugu Kitahar and T. Daniel Seely (eds), *Explorations in Maximizing Syntactic Minimization*. New York/London: Routledge, pp. 136–174.

Shlonsky, Ur (1989). A note on Neg Raising. *Linguistic Inquiry* 19: 710–717.

Siewierska, Anna and Hollmann, William (2007). Ditransitive clauses in English with special reference to Lancashire dialect. In M. Hannay and G. J. Steen (eds), *Structural-functional Studies in English Grammar: In Honour of Lachlan Mackenzie*. Amsterdam: John Benjamins pp. 83–102.

Stowell, Timothy A. (1981). Origins of phrase structure. PhD thesis. Massachusetts Institute of Technology, Cambridge, MA.

Stowell, T. (1982). The tense of infinitives. *Linguistic Inquiry* 13: 213–276.

Strazny, Philipp (2013). *Encyclopedia of Linguistics*. New York: Fitzroy Dearborn.

Svenonius, Peter (1994). C-selection as feature-checking. *Studia Linguistica* 48(2): 133–155.

Svenonius, Peter (1996). The verb-particle alternation in the Scandinavian languages. Manuscript. University of Tromsø.

Svenonius, Peter (2008). The position of adjectives and other phrasal modifiers in the decomposition of DP. In Louise McNally and Chris Kennedy (eds), *Adjectives and Adverbs: Syntax, Semantics, and Discourse*. Oxford: Oxford University Press, pp. 16–42.

syntax, n. (2019, March). *OED Online*.www.oed.com/view/Entry/196559

Tenny, Carol (1998). Psych verbs and verbal passives in Pittsburghese. *Linguistics* 36: 591–598.

Travis, Lisa (1988). The syntax of adverbs. In D. Fekete and Z. Laubitz (eds), *McGill Working Papers in Linguistics: Special issue on Comparative Germanic Syntax*. Department of Linguistics, McGill University, pp. 280–310.

Truswell, Robert (2009). Attributive adjectives and nominal templates. *Linguistic Inquiry* 40(3): 525–533.

Tyler, Matthew (2016). Bare *got*. *Yale Grammatical Diversity Project: English in North America*. http://ygdp.yale.edu/phenomena/bare-got. Updated by Katie Martin (2018).

Watanabe, Akira (2001). *Wh*-in-situ languages. In Mark Baltin and Chris Collins (eds), *The Handbook of Contemporary Syntactic Theory*. Malden, MA: Blackwell, pp. 203–225.

Wechsler, Stephen (2005). Resultatives under the 'Event-Argument Homomorphism' model of telicity. In Nomi Erteschik-Shir and Tova Rapoport (eds), *The Syntax of Aspect*. Oxford Studies in Theoretical Linguistics 10. Oxford: Oxford University Press, pp. 255–273.

Weir, Andrew (2013). The syntax of imperatives in Scots. In Janet Cruickshank and Robert McColl Millar (eds), *Before the Storm: Papers from the Forum for Research on the Languages of Scotland and Ulster Triennial Meeting*. Aberdeen: Publications of the Forum for Research on the Languages of Scotland and Ulster.

Wurmbrand, Susanne (1999). Modal verbs must be raising verbs. In S. Bird et al. (eds), *Proceedings of the 18th West Coast Conference on Formal Linguistics (WCCFL 18)*. Somerville, MA: Cascadilla Press, pp. 599–612.

Zanuttini, Raffaella (2001). Sentential negation. In M. Baltin and C. Collins (eds), *The Handbook of Contemporary Syntactic Theory*. Oxford: Blackwell, pp. 511–535.

Zeller, Jochen (2002). Particle verbs are heads and phrases. In Nicole Dehé et al. (eds), *Verb-Particle Explorations*. Berlin/New York: Mouton de Gruyter, pp. 233–267.

Zribi-Hertz, Anne (1989). Anaphor binding and narrative point of view: English reflexive pronouns in sentence and discourse. *Language* 65(4): 695–727.

Zwicky, Arnold M. and Pullum, Geoffrey K. (1983). Cliticization vs. inflection: English N'T. *Language* 59(3): 502–513.

Index